ATTRACTING
BIRDS
to your
GARDEN
IN AUSTRALIA

ATTRACTING
BIRDS *to your* GARDEN
IN AUSTRALIA

John Dengate

PHOTOGRAPHIC CREDITS

ABPL/C Haagner: p 61 (top left); **S Brandt:** pp 49 (centre right), 92 (bottom left), 158 (right); **Norman Chaffer/Nature Focus:** pp 33 (top), 147 (left); **Graeme Chapman:** front cover (top left, bottom left, top right, centre right), spine, back cover (bottom left, second from top left, top right, second from top right, bottom right), front flap, back flap, half title, title page, pp 4, 5, 6-7, 9 (top right), 10-11, 13 (top), 14 (top), 16, 17 (top), 21 (top), 23, 24 (bottom), 25, 28-29, 39 (right), 40-41, 47, 48, 50-51, 52 (top), 54, 62, 63, 66 (top), 74-75, 78 (top), 84-85, 86 (top), 88 (top, bottom left), 90 (left), 91 (right) 94 (top), 96, 97, 98, 99, 100 (top right, bottom left), 101 (left), 102, 103, 104, 105, 106, 107 (left), 108 (top), 109, 110 (top right, bottom left), 111, 112 (left), 114 (top), 115, 116, 117, 118, 119, 120 (left), 121, 122 (left, top right), 123 (left), 124, 125 (left), 126, 127, 128 (left), 129, 130 (bottom left, bottom right), 132 (left, centre), 133 (left), 134, 135, 136 (bottom left), 137, 138 (top left), 140, 141 (left, top right), 142 (left), 143, 144 (left, top right), 145, 146, 147 (right), 148, 149 (right), 150 (left), 152, 153, 154, 155, 156 (top right, bottom), 157 (left), 158 (left), 159, 160, 162 (left, top right), 163, 164, 165, 166, 167, 168, 169, 170, 171 (left), 172, 173 (right, bottom left), 174, 175 (right), 176, 177, 178, 179 (right), 180, 181 (left, top right), 182, 183, 184 (left, bottom right), 185 (left, top right), 186 (left), 187, 188, 189 (left, top right), 190 (right), 191 (left, bottom right), 192 (top, bottom), 193, 194 (bottom right), 195, 196, 197, 198, 199, 200, 201 (left), 203 (right); **Mike Coupar/Nature Focus** p 139 (top left); **Nigel Dennis/ABPL:** back cover (second from bottom right), p 91 (left); **Ecopix/Wayne Lawler:** pp 76 (right), 101 (right), 128 (right), 150 (right), 157 (bottom right), 175 (left), 179 (left), 181 (bottom right), 185 (bottom right), 186 (right); **Percy Fitzpatrick Institute of African Ornithology:** p 202 (top right, bottom left); **Alan T Foster/Nature Focus:** p 131 (right); **Jim Frazier/Mantis Films:** pp 192 (left), 203 (left); **Denise Grieg:** pp 13 (bottom), 15, 17 (bottom), 20, 26 (top), 46, 49 (top right, bottom right), 53, 66 (bottom), 67 (top left), 68 (bottom), 73 (bottom), 81 (top, centre), 82 (top), 83 (top), 87 (top), 89 (top), 90 (right), 92 (top left, centre left), 114 (bottom), 122 (bottom right), 138 (right), 156 (left); **Lex Hes:** front cover (centre left), back cover (second from bottom left), pp 14 (bottom), 21 (bottom), 26 (bottom), 30, 32, 35, 36, 37, 38, 39 (left), 44 (bottom), 45 (bottom), 55, 56, 57, 58 (top left), 61 (bottom left, bottom centre, bottom right, centre right), 67 (bottom), 77 (bottom), 88 (bottom right), 89 (bottom), 110 (bottom right), 123 (right), 125 (top right), 132 (right), 136 (centre), 141 (bottom right), 144 (bottom right), 157 (top right), 184 (top right), 189 (bottom right), 191 (top); **N Larson:** p 80 (top right); **Stirling Macoboy:** pp 33 (bottom), 73 (top), 82 (centre), 100 (bottom right), 108 (bottom); **Walter Mangold/World of Birds:** p 87 (bottom); **K McLeod:** pp 68 (top), 69, 70 (bottom), 71, 72; **MR & IM Morecombe:** p 125 (bottom right); **NHIL:** p 194 (top right); **NHIL/Shaen Adey:** pp 24 (top), 92 (right), 162 (bottom right); **NHIL/Denise Grieg:** pp 8 (top, bottom), 10/11 (ghost image), 28/29 (ghost image), 40/41 (ghost image), 42, 43, 45 (top), 50/51 (ghost image), 64/65 (ghost image), 67 (top right), 74/75 (ghost image), 78 (bottom), 84/85 (ghost image), 107 (right), 112 (right), 120 (bottom), 161 (bottom right), 201 (right); **NHIL/Anthony Johnson:** pp 9 (bottom left), 161 (bottom left); **NHIL/Nick Rains:** pp 12, 27 (bottom), 76 (top); **RG Palmer/Nature Focus:** p 151 (right); **Bronwyn Rennex:** p 34; **HG Robertson/South African Museum:** pp 77 (top), 79 (top); **Lorna Rose:** p 70 (top); **LF & OG Schick/Nature Focus:** p 139 (right); **Maryann Shaw:** pp 31, 94 (bottom); **SIL/Leonard Hoffmann:** pp 27 (top), 49 (left), 79 (bottom), 80 (top left), 138 (bottom left), 139 (bottom left), 173 (top left); **SIL/Peter Pickford:** pp 58 (bottom left), 80 (top centre); **P Steyn:** pp 190 (left), 202 (bottom right); **J Szymanowski:** pp 44 (top), 149 (left); **Glen Threlfo:** back cover (top left), pp 64-65, 113, 130 (top), 151 (left), 171 (right); **AD Trounson/Nature Focus:** p 161 (top right); **Murray Upton CSIRO:** p 83 (bottom); **Hein von Horsten:** front cover (bottom right), pp 52 (bottom), 86 (bottom), 93, 95; **L von Horsten:** p 133 (bottom); **Z Wahl:** pp 60, 142 (right), 136 (top right); **Dave Watts:** front cover (main picture), p 194 (left); **C Webster/Nature Focus:** p 131 (left); **P Zborowski CSIRO:** p 81 (bottom).

First published in 1997 by
New Holland Publishers Pty Ltd
London • Cape Town • Sydney • Singapore

Produced in Australia by
New Holland Publishers Pty Ltd

3/2 Aquatic Drive
Frenchs Forest NSW 2086
Australia

80 McKenzie Street
Cape Town 8001
South Africa

24 Nutford Place
London W1H 6DQ
United Kingdom

Copyright © 1997 New Holland Publishers Pty Ltd
Copyright © 1997 in text: John Dengate
Copyright © 1997 in photographs (see left)
Copyright © 1997 in illustrations: Lesley Elkan, Clarence Clark
Copyright © 1997 in maps: New Holland Publishers Pty Ltd

Publishing Manager: Mariëlle Renssen
Commissioning Managers: Averill Chase, Sally Bird
Editors: Jacquie Brown, Anouska Good
Senior Designer: Lyndall Hamilton
Cartographer: Lyndall Hamilton
Picture Researcher: Bronwyn Rennex
Illustrators: Lesley Elkan, Clarence Clarke
Reproduction: cmyk prepress
Printing and binding: Tien Wah Press (Pte) Ltd, Singapore

All rights reserved. No part of this publication may be reproduced, stored in a retrieval system or transmitted in any form or by any means, electronic, mechanical, photocopying, recording or otherwise, without the prior written permission of the copyright owners.

ISBN 1 86436 223 5

Top: *Crested Pigeon*
Opposite: *Male King Parrot*
Half-title page: *Lewin's Honeyeater*
Title page: *(left) Crimson Rosella; (right) Spotted Pardalote*
Contents page: *Zebra Finches*

Acknowledgements

I would like to thank my long-suffering family who have put up with endless so-called 'holidays' checking out birds and plants. They've also endured having their husband and father slumped over the computer each evening mumbling incoherently about structural and floristic diversity, while being less than communicative on life matters.

John Dengate

CONTENTS

Introduction 8

1
Planning
the Garden 10

2
Feeding your
Feathered Friends 28

3
Water in
the Garden 40

4
Providing a
Nesting Garden 50

5
Maintaining an
Indigenous Garden 64

6
Controlling Pests 74

7
Birds on Small Farms 84

8
Directory of
Garden Birds 94

Useful Addresses 204

Further Reading 205

Index 206

If you thought gardening was for the birds, you're right! With a bit of thought and care, you need only sit on your favourite chair on the verandah to hone your birdwatching skills rather than push your way through spiky shrubs trying to see if a little brown bird is a thornbill or a warbler.

INTRODUCTION

Watching birds' antics in your garden can be a great way to spend your time. So is planning and nurturing the plants and features that make it more enticing to people and wildlife. With bushland being encroached upon more and more, suburban gardens may become one of the most vital domains in which some wildlife can survive. In developing your garden you can consider what birds like to eat, where they can nest, how best to provide water, and the plants most likely to help fulfil these functions.

For Australia's original inhabitants, the land, its plants, birds and wildlife were crucial to survival in both a practical and spiritual way. When Captain James Cook arrived, the botanists accompanying him were so amazed by the continent's flora that the harbour in which his ship, the *Endeavour*, anchored in this strange land was given the name Botany Bay. And later, the headlands of Botany Bay were called Cape Banks and Cape Solander – after the *Endeavour*'s two botanists.

Above: *Strelitzia species are introduced, but can still be a good source of nectar – particularly the larger ones.*

The English upper classes were enchanted by the exotic plants collected on that voyage, and in the late 1700s and early 1800s rare specimens were traded at extraordinary prices. Australian botanist Angus Stewart noted that one obscure but aromatic daisy, *Calomeria amaranthoides*, was grown as a large potted plant in well-to-do houses where its supposed aphrodisiac qualities were thought to liven up parties!

But while the English gentry used glasshouses and horticultural equipment to learn more about Australian plants, the early settlers used axes. Battling against the alien bush with the single aim of subduing it became something of a national obsession. Even some botanists shared this view. Prominent botanist Robert Brown wrote in the early 1800s, 'there is an endless variety of genera and species of shrub but the general impression is dismal.' It took a long while for this society to realise that its indigenous plants were unique and spectacular with an attraction all their own. It also took a long time to realise the flora's important role in creating an environment in which the country's wildlife is able to survive.

Landscape fashions come and go but native plants have been a prominent feature of Australian gardens since Europeans first arrived. Whether people prefer the formal English cottage garden look or strive for more casual arrangements, indigenous plants are a popular and complementary choice, not only for their authentic look, but because of the many qualities they have which attract wildlife. Australian plants have a vital role to play in today's gardens. They have had millions of years to evolve naturally, and some have been carefully selected by horticulturists over the last hundred years or so. Many of our best cultivars have somehow turned up in gardens, and proved to be more hardy than the plants from which they derived. For instance, the first Robyn Gordon grevillea – named after a little girl smitten by the plant in her father's garden – was an accidental hybrid between *Grevillea banksii* and *G. bipinatifida*.

A garden can be a peaceful, private retreat of plants and flowers but it can also be a shared environment. Just as we share the rest of our country with an incredible range of wildlife, so we share our gardens with many other fellow travellers on earth. Plants can surprise us with their flowers or unannounced shoots, but the real garden surprises come from animal visitors. A garden is so much more interesting when you know you might spy a blue-tongue lizard sunning itself in spring, hear mysterious Flying Foxes feeding on fruit, or watch the twisting, fluttering flight of a spinebill feasting on your callistemons.

Attracting Birds to Your Garden is aimed at keeping that sense of anticipation and wonder that comes from both the animals and the plants that share our gardens. It's also about helping our precious wildlife to flourish. The more natural a habitat our gardens and backyards provide, the more our native birds and other wild creatures can find shelter and protection from the relentless clearing that comes with urban sprawl and agricultural development.

Contained in this book are discussions on feeding birds, providing nesting sites and creating water features, all of which are aimed at capturing the interest of birds and ensuring they become regular visitors – or perhaps even residents – to your garden. There are guidelines to maintaining and caring for plants and lists of indigenous plants that birds love. A directory of birds at the back of the book includes informative profiles of over 100 bird species. These profiles contain information on the habitat preferences of each species, as well as its preferred choice of food and its nesting requirements.

Planning and nurturing a garden in order to make it a place birds will want to visit adds new purpose to gardening and will certainly bring many rewards. Whether you decide to create a garden waterway boasting numerous bird species or whether you merely choose to erect a platform on a windowsill from which to feed transient visitors, one thing is sure: you will enjoy waking each morning to the sound of birds feeding, bathing, singing and generally welcoming in the new day.

Top: *Male Flame Robins are a garden favourite.*
Above: *A wide range of indigenous plants is a great way to attract insects, and therefore birds.*

CHAPTER 1

PLANNING THE GARDEN

A bird-friendly garden is all the more enjoyable when it is also people-friendly. The way you design the garden and the plants you choose to realise that design will play a crucial role in satisfying the needs of both birds and people. Another benefit of creating a bird-friendly oasis is that by providing good habitats in cities and towns, we contribute to the continual survival of our wildlife.

Like most birds, Silvereyes enjoy a simple birdbath.

Great gardens take time to mature. Very few other pastimes or occupations need as long a time for the results of a person's work to be fully realised. This means it is vital to take the time at the beginning to get the planning right – especially with new gardens where the temptation to simply plant a few shrubs to get started can be overwhelming.

PLANNING THE GARDEN

Every autumn, hundreds of young birds set out from their parents' territories, looking for a new home. Imagine you are one of these flying over the suburbs. Where will you land? It's a fair bet it won't be near manicured lawns, introduced cypress trees and carefully arranged annuals. Much more to your liking would be the friendly backyard, where layers of Australian trees and shrubs complement the pond and provide the perfect balance for the lawns and other features that inscrutable humans seem to like.

LOCATION

They say the three most important aspects in the property market are location, location and location. It's the same in the bird world. Studies in several parts of Australia have shown that being close to large chunks of natural bushland is one of the most important factors in determining the number of birds visiting a garden. For instance, shrike-thrushes and White-throated Treecreepers will visit only those gardens that are close to natural areas.

Living near the bush, though, means there are some fairly serious compromises to be made. Having a home on the edge of a national park or State forest will be great for birds, but not good if it means you need to travel long distances to your place of work. Living near the bush also means you have to take into consideration the possibility of bushfires. It's especially important to avoid living on bush slopes that face west and, to a lesser extent, north. These slopes dry out in spring and summer and as a result will burn with frightening intensity. Don't buy a block at the top of such a slope, or even halfway up, if there is only bush below you.

Most of us, however, inherit an established garden that is the product of previous owners' ideas, bank balances and past garden trends. It can be a daunting task to re-do such a garden from scratch, but even small changes can bring large benefits. For instance, a few large hybrid grevilleas and a pond or birdbath can have a dramatic effect on the number of birds that will be attracted to your garden.

This bird's-eye view of certain suburbs doesn't look too inviting to feathered creatures – so many roofs and not many plants!

PLANNING THE GARDEN

MAKE A LIST

Having resolved the location dilemma, the next step in planning a new garden or revitalising an old one is to list the things you want the garden to do. Attracting birds and other wildlife is a major consideration, but there will be competing needs as the space has to be used efficiently for all the roles a backyard needs to perform. For instance, the garden may have to provide a play area for kids (for at least 10 to 15 years), entertainment areas, privacy and a serene setting in which to forget the cares of the world.

You also need to list the positive and negative features of the site. The negatives may include some plane trees or other introduced plants that don't do anything for wildlife. On the positive side there may be aspects that no amount of money can buy, such as mistletoe, large established indigenous trees or bird-friendly plants like *Leucopogon* and geebungs (*Persoonia* sp.) that are difficult to grow.

Recognising and saving the site's good points can be very valuable. If you end up owning one of the tallest eucalypts in the neighbourhood you can be assured of a passing parade of ravens, magpies and currawongs as well as unusual visitors like Spangled Drongos, wood-swallows and bee-eaters. This means being very firm with the bulldozer driver if you are preparing a block of land for a new house.

DRAW A PLAN

Having listed the site's good and bad points and what you want to achieve with the garden, the next step is to start drawing and photographing to visualise how you want the garden to eventually look. Scale plans are a great idea and a very useful part of this process, but one of the best approaches is to photograph the existing garden from several different angles and then roughly draw onto these images how you would like the plants to look. You will then be able to see how the garden will appear from various angles, and how one area will look when viewed from another.

It's also important to consider the neighbours. As you will most likely be striving for privacy, you might wish to incorporate a screen of fast-growing wattles (*Acacia* sp.) or she-oaks (*Casuarina* sp.) as part of your garden plan.

Another factor to bear in mind is that matching the colours of your plants and your house to those of the environment around the garden can create a very pleasing effect. This isn't always possible as most nectar-producing flowers are red, yellow or cream, but there are many subtle variations in the colours of foliage and bark, and spending some time thinking about colours can be very rewarding.

Albany Bottlebrush (Callistemon phoenicius).

GARDEN HABITATS

Birds may visit your garden from two sources: there are those birds that live locally, either in the suburbs or nearby bushland, and those that migrate through. Of these, the locals will be the major garden visitors. The habitat needs of passing birds will vary widely and are best served by a garden that has a variety of indigenous plants in a range of levels.

Local birds will be most at home in a garden that matches the surrounding vegetation, whether it is a dense rainforest, bush woodland where the treetops are separate from each other, or an area dominated by shrubs. This means the secret of attracting birds to

These dense shrubs in Perth's Kings Park are ideal sites for wrens and other small birds to hide away from predators.

PLANNING THE GARDEN

your garden is to reproduce the local ecosystem, and especially to incorporate local ecological features that birds find attractive, such as tall trees, dense gullies, fruiting figs or patches of flowering grevilleas and banksias.

There isn't much point in creating an extensive grassland habitat if you live in the middle of a rainforest as the local birds won't like it. But keeping things entirely natural isn't the best bet either. The objective is to improve on what nature has provided. This may sound presumptuous, but it is fairly easy to do by adding extra nutrients and water to your soil. By producing a richer environment many birds will find your garden more attractive than surrounding vegetation.

Another point worth considering is ecotones. These are areas where one habitat, like forest, gives way to another, like grassland. In these circumstances birds from both habitats will keep an eye on the edge of their particular area and do a bit of foraging into the neighbour's territory. This means the best gardens for attracting birds are based on local plant types (but not necessarily the exact local species), and also have a variety of vegetation levels.

Top: *A Red Wattlebird on a* Banksia ashbyi.
Above: *Different levels of vegetation are good for different groups of bird species, with each level supporting a different group.*

Generally, the best flowers to attract birds are red or yellow and either tubular, shaped like a grevillea or like a bottlebrush. The bigger the flower, the better it will be for wildlife. These rules also apply to exotic flowers. For instance, red-hot pokers (*Kniphofia* sp.) and hibiscuses are red or yellow, tubular and great for native birds.

There are four general habitats that help create a bird-friendly garden:

- OPEN AREAS
- SHRUB ZONES
- TREE CANOPIES
- WETLANDS

The lists of plants provided for these habitats include some of Australia's best bird-attracting species, but they are by no means exhaustive. They don't include those that are not widely available, like Dryandras, which can be great in the west but are not as reliable in eastern States. For the best advice on plants for your garden, shop around the local nurseries specialising in Australian species. If they don't have the individual species on the plant lists, they should be able to advise on and supply plants that will serve the same purpose in your local area.

OPEN AREAS

There isn't usually any shortage of open areas in standard suburban gardens. Wide grass lawns are the most common type of open area, but any section free of trees and shrubs provides a habitat for birds that need plenty of space to search for sustenance or to see predators coming. Open areas attract swallows that like to swoop low over the lawn and birds like Willie Wagtails, Magpie-larks and magpies that hunt by walking through the grass.

The edge, or ecotone, between the open areas and the shrub zones can be a great place for birds like Red-browed Firetails and Yellow-rumped Thornbills. These types of bird feed in the open but need shrubs for a rapid retreat when goshawks or currawongs arrive. However, open and shrub areas side by side can appear unnatural if not carefully planned. One of the best ways to avoid this is to plant strips of tufty indigenous grass to soften the edge of the lawn and to provide the transition to the shrub zone.

PLANNING THE GARDEN

Native grass can be difficult to grow from seed so the best approach is to buy it from plant nurseries or to dig up suitable specimens from areas where there is a plentiful supply (after you have obtained the owner's permission!). Most native grasses grow in tufts and don't necessarily create a terrific lawn. However, if you don't require that smooth green look, an open area of indigenous grass can be a great way to tempt even more birdlife. Finches and some of the ground-feeding parrots such as rosellas and Galahs enjoy these environments.

Ground cover plants, such as the prostrate grevilleas like Bronze Rambler or Royal Mantle, Kidney Weed (*Dichondra repens*) and Running Postman (*Kennedia prostrata*), can be used to create an open area but they do not provide as much for wildlife as the seeding grasses or the larger, nectar-producing shrubs. While some ground covers are excellent nectar producers, you should be aware that they can attract honeyeaters down onto the ground where they can fall prey to prowling cats.

SUGGESTED GRASSES FOR OPEN AREAS

Botanical name	Common name
Chloris truncata	Windmill Grass
Danthonia pallida	Red Anther Wallaby Grass
Dichanthium sericeum	Queensland Blue Grass
Pennisetum alopecuroides	Swamp Foxtail Grass
Poa larbillardieri	Snow Grass
Poa australis	Poa Grass
Stipa elegantissima	Feather Spear Grass
Themeda triandra (australis)	Kangaroo Grass

SHRUB ZONES

Shrub zones are the most important parts of the garden, providing food and shelter for a wide variety of species. Satin Bowerbirds, Eastern Spinebills, Lewin's Honeyeaters and New Holland Honeyeaters are among the many birds that feel most at home in this environment.

In designing the shrub zone, aim to provide birds with food and shelter, as well as making a pleasant garden for human visitors.

In most backyards the basic approach is to have a generous bed of shrubs along the boundaries of the yard to screen the fence and provide habitat, especially in the corners where there is more space for plants. Taller plants like Honey Gem or Misty Pink grevilleas make a great backdrop, but they can become very open around the base and often need groups of smaller plants like Captain Cook bottlebrushes and Robyn Gordon grevilleas to provide habitats at the lower levels.

It can also be especially valuable if some of the garden is treated as a 'wild' area, where dense plantings and garden rules make access difficult for children and pets. Corners of the yard are often difficult to get at, which makes them ideal for wild areas.

Seeds from Poa Grass (Poa australis) *and other native grasses can attract beautiful birds like Double-barred Finches and Red-rumped Parrots.*

PLANNING THE GARDEN

Many birds, like these New Holland Honeyeaters, will happily take handouts – but you need to make sure you offer the right food!

Shrubs can also be useful if planted as one or more 'islands' in the open area, if this approach fits in with the rest of the garden design. If you have enough space, a design worth thinking about is to separate one or more open areas into garden 'rooms' by growing groups of taller shrubs into one or more rows, from one side of the garden across towards the other side. Such areas add a lot of variety to a garden, revealing new vistas as you walk through it.

This approach also increases the amount of edge or ecotone where the shrubs join the open area which is an especially rich area for birds. Anything that increases the extent of this habitat in the backyard will be good for birds.

When planting shrub areas, it's important to provide for a wild section of the garden. Here, it's time to dispense with the garden manuals that talk about spacing shrubs so many metres apart so they don't become too crowded. Plant as many shrubs as closely together as your bank balance will allow. Some plants will thrive, some won't, but the end result will be a nice tangled mass of bird-friendly plants, creating a safe haven for them to enjoy a tasty treat of nectar, insects and berries in that section of the garden. Birds such as thornbills, fairy-wrens and scrubwrens, which are often too shy to visit your feeding table, will happily live in these wilder sections of a garden. If you live near the bush in eastern Australia, lyrebirds and brush-turkeys are content to scratch through the litter in this part of the garden.

For the rest of your garden, a good rule is to avoid choosing too many different types of plants. Most natural areas are dominated by only a few plant species and gardens that look attractive re-create this natural feeling. The way to do this is to put in rafts of each species, so that each type makes a substantial contribution to the overall impression. You also need to resist the temptation to pick plants that you like without thinking about how they will relate to each other and to your house.

A great way to finally check how your purchases will look is simply to put the plants in the positions you have chosen and then stand back and take a look. Imagine the scene in five years, once the plants have grown. If you don't like it, move them around until you do!

Providing Food

Most shrub-dwelling birds eat insects, berries, seeds or nectar, and nest in dense, often prickly bushes. So the more of these resources you can supply, the more birds will feel at home in the garden. Providing insects is pretty easy. In fact, the general problem in most gardens is too many insects, rather than not enough. Australia's indigenous plants and insects have evolved together for many

Right: *A Rainbow Lorikeet feeding on a* Banksia serrata.

millions of years. Simply planting native species and avoiding the use of pesticides can ensure a healthy insect population. Plants that produce good nectar supplies also attract insects. Thornbills and many of the honeyeaters enjoy keeping insect numbers under control.

Berries aren't as easy to provide. Few Australian plants have them, and those that do are often difficult to propagate, like the parasitic geebungs (*Persoonia* sp.), Bush Cherries (*Exocarpos cupressiformis*) or specialised alpine plants like the *Coprosma* group of species. This is why it's a great idea to incorporate into your garden plan any existing berry-producing plants. In most parts of Australia, however, there are some berry plants that can be grown in the garden. These include the various *Cyathodes* species, saltbush (*Atriplex* sp.) and domestic fruits such as mulberries or raspberries. Silvereyes, currawongs and many of the honeyeaters will happily help themselves to fruits in the shrub layer.

Seed-eating birds don't spend much of their time in the shrub layer. They feed either on the ground, like most finches and ground parrots, or by nibbling seeds in the canopy of trees as rosellas or cockatoos do. These seed plants are discussed further in the Tree Canopies section.

Providing nectar is the best way to attract birds to Australian gardens. Most of the popular garden birds, such as lorikeets and honeyeaters, love nectar and even seed-eating birds, such as rosellas, relish this sweet treat. Because these parrots lack the lorikeets' specialised feeder, they chew up the blossoms to extract the sweetness. To attract nectar-loving birds you need to grow lots of flowers that depend on bird pollination. The larger the flower, the more the birds like it. The big hybrid grevilleas like Honey Gem, Superb and Robyn Gordon are especially good as they flower for most of the year and the flowers have large amounts of nectar.

Australia's birds have been sharing the landscape with the native plants ever since the Australian landmass split off from Antarctica around 55 million years ago. This unique background has produced a very close symbiotic relationship between them: the plants that produce nectar to feed the birds are, in return, pollinated by the birds' feeding habits. Some plants have developed clever tricks to ensure they get what they need out of this relationship. For example, grevilleas hang their pollen on the end of a stalk which daubs pollen on the forehead of any honeyeater that dips its beak into the nectar at the flower's base; bottlebrushes carry their pollen on dozens of stalks through which a lorikeet has to push its bill to get at the nectar; while plants like Correas have tubular flowers lined with little anthers of pollen. When a bird pokes its beak into the tube, it is covered in the fine grains; the next time the bird feeds on another flower, it fertilises that flower with the pollen on its beak or face. Bird-pollinated flowers are easily distinguishable because of their tubular shape or their myriad little stalks holding pollen.

Top: *A Brown Honeyeater keeps a sharp lookout.*
Above: *Both native and exotic plants can be used effectively to provide shelter near a pool or pond.*

PLANNING THE GARDEN

THE BIRD-UNFRIENDLY GARDEN

A typical urban property, its garden planned without regard for birdlife, offers little encouragement and no incentive for birds to visit.

A Expansive lawn with token birdbath in exposed position.

B Entertainment area with pergola and shade tree.

C Driveway bordered by neatly manicured beds of annuals and flanked by islands of exotic plants.

D Neat garden bed planted with a variety of annuals.

E Boundary beds planted with various low-growing exotic plants (eg. azaleas, camellias, agapanthus, strelitzias/birds of paradise, spruce).

The elements of this garden make for a barren environment from a bird's perspective and, aside from a single shade tree, offer few opportunities for feeding, roosting or breeding. Indigenous plant material is lacking and there is a marked absence of any significant protection or cover for birds. As such, the garden fails to offer any viable bird habitats.

PLANNING THE GARDEN

THE BIRD-FRIENDLY GARDEN

Planned with the needs of birds in mind, the same urban property is transformed into a haven for birds.

A The lawn area is encroached on to a greater extent by garden beds.

B Entertainment area incorporates indigenous leafy creeper over the pergola, which will attract nesting birds.

C Driveway is bordered by the same neatly manicured beds, but flanked by beds of indigenous plants which flow into corridors of native vegetation around the house.

D A continuous green corridor of indigenous shrubs and tall trees (canopy habitat) replaces the garden bed.

E A wild area has been created by extending a boundary bed.

F A small wetland area has been created in front of the wild area, including a shallow, natural-looking pond. The wetland is planted with indigenous reeds and grasses.

G Birdbath moved to more protected area near trees.

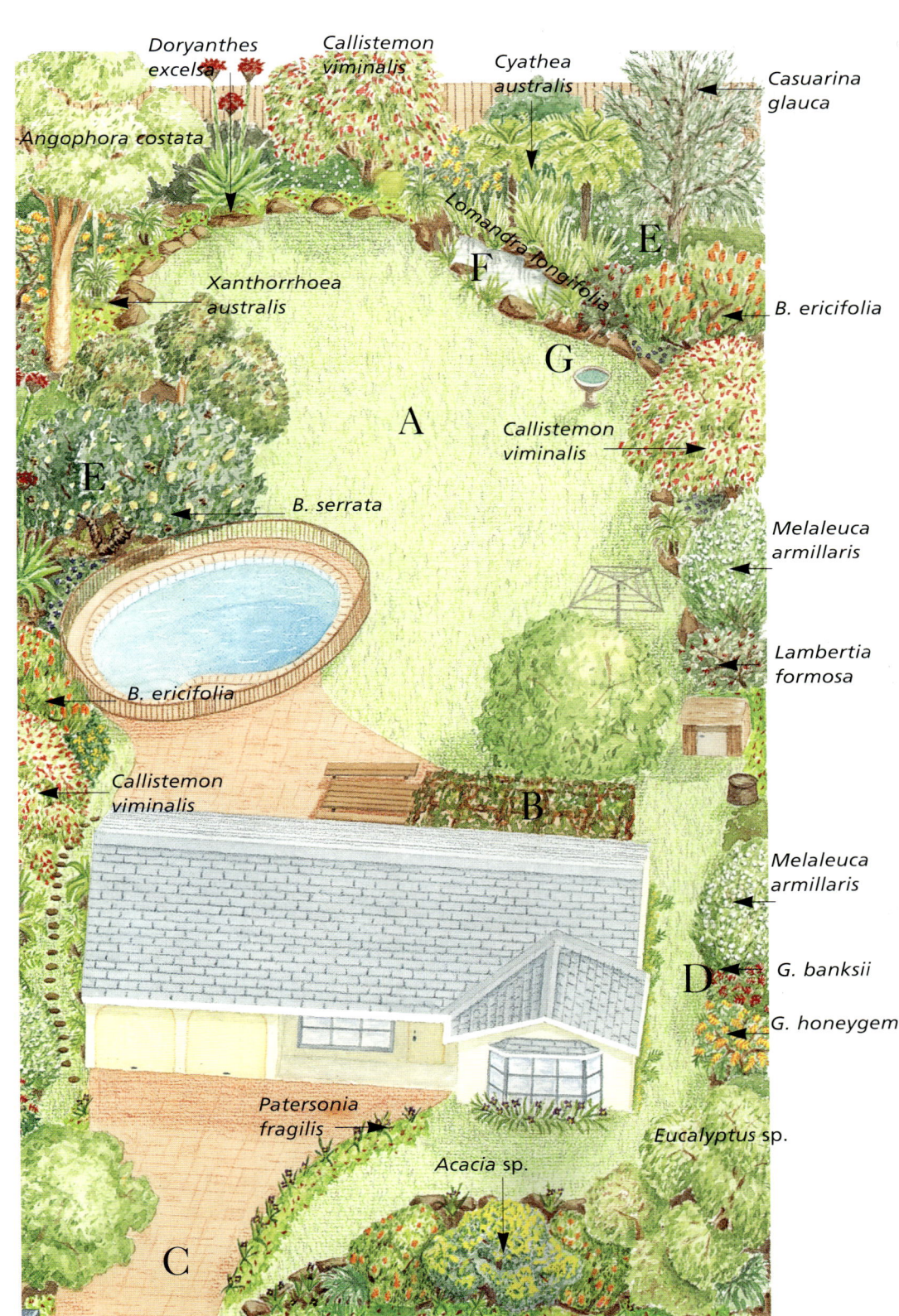

PLANNING THE GARDEN

SUGGESTED SHRUBS TO ATTRACT BIRDS

Botanical name	Common name	Height / Spread
Acacia oxycedrus Sh Se	Prickly Wattle	2m x 2m
A. paradoxa Sh Se	Kangaroo Thorn	2m x 3m
A. verticillata Sh Se	Prickly Moses	2m x 2m
Acmena smithii Hedgemaster B	Dwarf Lilly Pilly	1m x 50cm
Anigozanthos Bob and Blanche's wedding N	Boofy Kangaroo Paw	70cm x 40cm
Anigozanthos Bush Gold N	Bush Gold Kangaroo Paw	1m x 50cm
Anigozanthos Bush Sunset N	Bush Sunset Kangaroo Paw	2m x 1m
Atriplex sp. B	saltbush	50cm–2m x 1–4m
Banksia Giant Candles N	Giant Candles Banksia	4m x 4m
Banksia ericifolia N	Heath-Leaved Banksia	5m x 4m
Banksia robur N	Swamp Banksia	2m x 2m
Bursaria spinosa Sh	Blackthorn	3m x 1m
Calamus sp. Sh	Lawyer Vine	climber
Callistemon citrinus N	Crimson Bottlebrush	4m x 2m
Callistemon King's Park Special N	King's Park Bottlebrush	3m x 3m
Callistemon phoeniceus N	bottlebrush	2m x 1.5m
Callistemon subulatus N	bottlebrush	1m x 1m
Callistemon viminalis Captain Cook N	Captain Cook bottlebrush	2m x 2m
Callistemon viminalis Hannah Ray N	Hannah Ray Bottlebrush	5m x 2m
Calothamnus quadrifidus N	one-sided bottlebrush	2m x 2m
Correa reflexa N	Indigenous Fuchsia	1m x 1m
Cotoneaster sp. Se	Cotoneaster *	4m x 6m
Crataegus sp. Se	Hawthorn *	4m x 6m
Cyathodes glauca B		2m x 1m
Darwinia fascicularis N	Darwinia	1m x 1m
Dianella caerulea B	Flax Lily	1m x 1m
Doryanthes excelsa N	Gymea Lily	2m x 2m with 5m flower spike
Epacris impressa N	Common Heath	1m x 1m
Eremophila latrobei N	Emu Bush	2m x 2m
Eucalyptus lehmanii N Se	Bushy Yate	4m x 5m
Grevillea Bronze Rambler N	Bronze Rambler Grevillea	50cm ground cover
Grevillea Honey Gem N	Honey Gem Grevillea	4m x 2.5m
Grevillea Misty Pink N	Misty Pink Grevillea	3m x 2m
Grevillea Robyn Gordon N	Robyn Gordon Grevillea	2m x 3m
Grevillea rosmarinifolia N	Grevillea	1.5m x 2m
Hakea gibbosa Sh Se	Needlebush	3m x 1.5m
Hakea sericea Sh Se	Needlebush	4m x 3m
Hakea laurina Sh N	Pin Cushion Hakea	4m x 3m
Lambertia formosa N Sh	Mountain Devil	2m x 1.5m
Leucopogon lanceolatus B	Leucopogon	2m x 1.5m
Melaleuca hypericifolia N	Melaleuca	3m x 2.5m
Melaleuca nesophila N	Melaleuca	4m x 1.5m
Melaleuca pulchella N	Melaleuca	1m x 1m
Melaleuca steedmanii N	Melaleuca	1.5m x 1m
Pyracantha sp. Se Sh	Firethorn *	4m x 6m
Solanum aviculare B		4m x 5m
Telopea speciosissima N	Waratah	3m x 1.5m
Xanthorrhoea australis N	Grass Tree	3m x 1.5m with 3m flower

Se seeds • N nectar • B berries • Sh shelter • * introduced

Mountain devil.

Melaleuca nesophila.

Pincushion hakeas produce amazing flowers, supply honeyeaters with nectar, and provide shelter for smaller birds.

Shelter

Most shrubs provide shelter to some extent, and many birds, such as fairy-wrens, use the densest bushes for their nests. At other times birds use shrubs of all types to hide from passing predators. There are some wonderfully spiky indigenous plants, like the needlebush hakeas and the 'prickly moses' wattles, that provide excellent shelter. These plants work best when grown in groups. They can also have some unexpected benefits: a clump of *Hakea gibbosa* under the bedroom window not only offers close-up viewing of nesting honeyeaters, it also means a burglar who manages to push through it won't be in any condition to bother anyone.

An excellent addition to the shrub area is a strategic sprinkling of logs and rocks, which can also provide vital wildlife habitat. Logs and rocks shelter creatures such as insects, spiders and lizards, which birds love to feast on. They are also interesting in their own right; you just have to make sure the rocks look natural when positioned. You can do this by selecting only one type of rock and taking note of its natural structure, for instance, make sure the strata in sandstone rocks run parallel to each other. Keep moving the rocks and logs around until you like the effect – or until your back or your labourer gives up!

TREE CANOPIES

While many birds like to live in the shrub layer, a number also inhabit the canopies of forests or woodlands. Trees act as a beacon to attract birds and having the tallest tree in the area ensures a fascinating passing parade of wildlife. The birds who frequent treetops include the larger denizens of the forest like rosellas, ravens and currawongs, and smaller birds like Yellow-faced Honeyeaters, kingfishers and such wonderful creatures as Mistletoebirds and Rainbow Bee-eaters.

Trees can give a pleasing sense of scale to buildings that would otherwise dominate a block of land. They also provide nesting hollows. These are an essential resource for parrots, lorikeets, kingfishers and some of the thornbills – as well as a fascinating array of tiny bats and possums. A River Red Gum (*Eucalyptus camaldulensis*) will need a couple of centuries to produce the kind of hollows Superb Parrots need, but many trees will produce some hollows much earlier than this. Large trees do take forever to grow to maturity so it's an excellent idea to incorporate any existing large trees in your garden plan if you are buying a block of land. Caring for existing trees is the only way you're going to have a really great nesting tree on your property.

Of course, trees need to be pruned carefully to avoid old branches dropping and causing damage, and problems may be created by the shade they provide. Shade can reduce the flowering of many of the best bird-attracting plants as the lack of sunlight can stunt their growth. Vegetables can also grow poorly when there is not sufficient direct sunlight.

Canopies can be especially valuable for birds when similar tree species are grouped together to create different levels of vegetation.

SUGGESTED TREES FOR THE CANOPY AREA

Botanical name	Common name	Height / Spread
Acacia baileyana Se Sh	Cootamundra Wattle	10m x 6m
A. elata Se	Cedar Wattle	25m x 8m
A. longifolia Se	Sydney Golden Wattle	6m x 3m
A. melanoxylon Se Sh	Blackwood	15m x 10m
A. podalyriifolia Se	Queensland Silver Wattle	6m x 5m
A. pycnantha Se	Australian Golden Wattle	10m x 4m
Acmena smithii B N Sh	Lilly Pilly	20m x 10m
Acronychia oblongifolia B Sh	Acronychia	14m x 8m
Amyema sp. B N Sh	Mistletoe	3m x 1m
Angophora floribunda N Se Sh	Rough-barked Apple	20m x 15m
Archontophoenix cunninghamiana B	Bangalow Palm	13m x 2m
Banksia integrifolia N	Coast Banksia	15m x 5m
B. serrata N	Old Man Banksia	10m x 8m
Bridelia exaltata B	Bridelia	30m x 15m
Callitris sp. Se Sh	Native Cypress	10–15m x 4–6m
Elaeocarpus obovatus B	Ash Quandong	30m x 12m
Elaeocarpus reticulatus B	Blueberry Ash	15m x 5m
Erythrina vespertilio N	Bat's Wing Coral Tree	25m x 20m
Eucalyptus calophylla N Se	Marri	20m x 10m
E. caesia N Se	Gungurru	8m x 3m
E. cladocalyx N Se	Sugar Gum	12m x 6m
E. ficifolia N Se	Red-flowering Gum	9m x 5m
E. gummifera N Se	Red Bloodwood	25m x 10m
E. melliodora N Se	Yellow Box	30m x 20m
E. microcorys N Se	Tallow Wood	40m x 25m
E. robusta N Se	Swamp Mahogany	15m x 12m
E. sideroxylon N Se	Mugga Ironbark	15m x 8m
E. sieberi N Se	Black Ash	12m x 6m
E. torquata N Se	Coral Gum	8m x 9m
Exocarpos cupressiformis B S	Bush Cherry	8m x 5m
Ficus macrophylla B Sh	Moreton Bay Fig	40m x 60m
F. rubiginosa B Sh	Port Jackson Fig	12m x 18m
F. watkinsiana B Sh	Fig	40m x 60m
Geijera parviflora B Sh	Wilga	12m x 18m
Glochidion ferdinandi B Sh	Cheese Tree	25m x 15m
Grevillea robusta N	Silky Oak	25m x 12m
Livistona australis B	Cabbage Tree Palm	25m x 5m
Lophostemon confertus N Se	Brush Box	30m x 15m
Lysiphyllum caronii	Bauhinia	5m x 3m
Melaleuca quinquinervia N Sh	Paperbark	25m x 10m
Melia azedarach B	White Cedar	15m x 10m
Morus B	Mulberry *	8m x 12m
Pittosporum undulatum B	Pittosporum	10m x 6m
Schinus molle B	Pepper Tree *	8m x 12m
Syzygium australe B N Sh	Lilly Pilly	15m x 10m

Se seeds • N nectar • B berries • Sh good shelter • * introduced

The way to get around this dilemma is to plant most trees on the southern side of the block as the sun casts its shadow from the north.

The best place for trees is in the corners of the yard where they will make perfect focal points for any wild area. Many garden birds don't like crossing open areas, so a continuous layer of foliage and branches provides an ideal foraging and sheltering zone. The tops of the taller bottlebrushes, banksias and grevilleas should reach almost to the bottom of the tree canopy. Such areas can also be very useful for the people living on the property, as having a green belt of trees around the edge can reduce traffic noise, wind and air pollution.

One special aspect of the canopy is mistletoe. Most gardeners see this as a pest to be cut out, but it is actually a valuable resource. Like many other parasites, it produces berries – a rare treat in most types of bushland. It also provides nectar as well as having the extraordinary ability to sprout from bird droppings on the barest, dry bark in full sun. Wildlife surveys in the coastal forests of the Victoria–New South Wales border show that mistletoe is a particularly valuable part of the forest ecosystem. Mistletoebirds and some honeyeaters love the berries and the nectar is attractive for a wide variety of other birds. So, if you have any, look after it!

Trees can provide insects, seeds, nectar and berries. Nectar is usually the best way to attract most birds. Eucalypts can be especially valuable as they provide seeds for rosellas and cockatoos, and nectar for honeyeaters and lorikeets. On the coast, Swamp Mahoganies (*Eucalyptus robusta*) and bloodwoods (such as *E. gummifera*) are some of the best, while inland, Yellow Box (*E. meliodora*) is hard to beat. Some of the Western Australian eucalypts like the Gungurru (*E. caesia*) are spectacular but do not do so well in the eastern States where they need excellent drainage. However, they can be grafted onto local species if you are into experimental horticulture.

Banksias also provide both nectar and seeds. The nectar supplies are excellent, but the seeds are contained in the plant's large, woody cones where few birds can get at them. In fact, it's only the largest cockatoos, such as the yellow-tailed blacks, that have enough strength in their beaks to crack them. The world's largest grevillea, the Silky Oak (*Grevillea robusta*), is another great tree which literally drips golden nectar (so don't put the clothes line underneath this plant!).

Apart from eucalypts, most wattles including the Sydney Golden Wattle (*Acacia longifolia*) and Cootamundra Wattle (*A. baileyana*) are an excellent source of seeds and they also have beautiful golden flowers and attractive foliage. Shade and shelter are provided by blackwoods (*A. melanoxylon*). There are lots of good berry trees including Blueberry Ash (*Elaeocarpus reticulatus*), White Cedar (*Melia azedarach*) and, if you have space, indigenous figs (*Ficus* sp.) or Bridelia (*Bridelia exaltata*). These trees can be great for migrating rainforest pigeons, currawongs and tiny Silvereyes, who fly each year from Tasmania to northern New South Wales.

From a bird's point of view, shelter is an important aspect of any canopy. All but the largest birds need a place to hide from predators, as well as an area for hunting tasty insects. For these purposes, it's hard to go past the rough-barked angophoras such as *Angophora floribunda*, the rainforest figs or Lilly Pillies like *Acmena smithii*.

Cootamundra Wattle.

A bit of mistletoe proves to be harmless to a large tree but useful to wildlife as it supplies them with both nectar and tasty berries.

PLANNING THE GARDEN

Waterlilies look attractive and reduce the amount of light reaching the water where it can cause excessive algal growth.

WETLANDS

A water feature in a garden can add considerable appeal for birds, and also attract frogs, lizards and other fascinating creatures. Details on how to build a water feature are supplied in Chapter Three, but before you rip into the ground with a mattock, make sure the idea fits your garden plan. If you haven't done a garden plan, stop reading now and go and do one immediately!

A wetland can be a swampy or boggy area, but it is much more interesting if it includes open water. This can be as elaborate or as simple as you want to make it, but simple is often the best approach. Unless the pond is to be a major water attraction for aquatic birds, it need only be 10–15cm deep. This is quite adequate for most garden birds to bathe and drink.

The wetland needs to combine elements of both the open and shrub areas. Shy birds like White-browed Scrubwrens will skulk around in the plants on the edge of the pond, whereas bolder types like honeyeaters will perch on the edge and then splash around in the shallow water. The open area is very important for birds who need to take off suddenly. It's also the best way for you and your visitors to enjoy fascinating glimpses of any visiting birds. No-one knows how Spangled Drongos got their name, but the fact that they like to plunge in from a great height may well have something to do with it.

Water features are more attractive if the water is moving. This can be as elaborate as a fountain or as simple as a hose draped over a tree so it drips slowly into the pond. For such an arid country, Australia has a wealth of water plants, which you will discover as you create your water tract. Some plants, such as

SUGGESTED PLANTS FOR THE WETLAND AREA

Botanical name	Common name	Height / Spread
Adiantum hispidum	Rough Maidenhair Fern	30cm x 60cm
Anigozanthos Pink joey	Pink Joey Kangaroo Paw	50cm x 30cm
Banksia robur	Swamp Banksia	2m x 2m
Blandfordia grandiflora	Christmas Bells	45cm x 20cm
Brachycome graminea	Indigenous Daisy	20cm high ground cover
Callistemon speciosus	Bottlebrush	2m x 1m
Carex fascicularis	Tassel Sedge	1m x 30cm
Chorizandra enodis	Black Bristle Rush	40cm x 15cm
Cyperus lucidus	Sedge	1.3m x 50cm
Eleocharis sphacelata	Rush	1.5m single stems
Ghania melanocarpa	saw sedge	1m x 1m
Ghania microstachya	saw sedge	80cm x 80cm
Ghania sieberana	saw sedge	1.5m x 1m
Lemna minor	Duckweed	tiny floating leaves
Marsilea drummondi	Nardoo	10cm x 10cm
Nymphaea gigantea	Water Lily	30cm flowers on stalks
Nymphoides crenata	Nymphoides	floating 3cm flowers
Todea barbara	King Fern	1.5m x 3m

Silver Gull.

the Cyperus and Chorizandra reeds and the saw sedges like *Ghania microstachya*, are excellent for the soggy ground at the edge of water. The saw sedges are particularly valuable for their tiny red seeds which Red-browed Finches like to eat. Other plants such as Nardoo (*Marsilea* sp.) and Nymphoides waterlilies live in the water, sheltering fish, snails, dragonfly larvae, tadpoles, water fleas and an endless variety of other creatures.

WITH NEIGHBOURLY HELP

The number of birds and other wildlife attracted to an area depends on the quality and quantity of the habitats provided. By planning your own garden with wildlife in mind you can do a lot for the quality, but the best way to increase the quantity of habitats is to enlist the help of your neighbours. In these times of increasing community awareness, encouraging your neighbours to be active in the wildlife gardening business is easier than it used to be. Demonstrating by example is a great start, as is giving presents of appropriate, not-too-large plants.

Many people interested in indigenous plants end up propagating their own, and this gives them a lot more seedlings than they can possibly use. Giving these to neighbours, or organising with them and the council to plant them along nature strips can greatly increase the habitat value of your suburb. One of the most valuable approaches is to create corridors of trees and shrubs that link existing natural areas. The best routes for such corridors are along the sides of roads, and along back fences where the wilder sections of backyards can be linked up.

Many councils run plant nurseries and you can lobby them to grow more bird-friendly plants in your street. Local conservation groups can be a powerful force to promote habitat regeneration schemes in their local areas. Streets, like the bush, look better when there are plenty of only a few species of trees, rather than lots of different species with only a few of each.

There is a range of State and Federal grant schemes that will provide funds to community groups for tree and shrub planting. Just remember that getting the plants in the ground is only the start. Most planting schemes fail because plants aren't watered or weeded well enough.

Brilliantly coloured Rainbow Lorikeets, among the world's most striking parrots, are common in many Australian gardens.

ATTRACTING BIRDS TO SMALLER GARDENS

While smaller gardens don't always have the same potential to attract wildlife as larger ones do, a bit of careful planning and co-operation with the neighbours can achieve surprising results. For instance, it's possible to see Brown Goshawks swooping around the streets of Coburg, and New Holland Honeyeaters in many inner-city parts of south-east Australia. Even Rufous Whistlers have been seen in the concrete canyons of Sydney's Clarence Street.

One of the best ways to overcome limited garden size is to involve the neighbours in a plan to make the area more attractive to birds. Birds don't bother about property boundaries and several adjoining small gardens can be as good or better than one large one, if they are well planned. Planting modest-sized trees or larger shrubs along the fences can be a great start, providing corridors of green as 'roadways' for birds – larger grevilleas and smaller eucalypts are an excellent choice for planting along fences. Denser plants like Honey Gem grevilleas are probably the best as they provide privacy for human occupants as well as shelter and nectar for honeyeaters and lorikeets.

If the same group of plant species can be used through a group of gardens it not only provides better wildlife habitat, it also gives a unifying landscape theme to the area, which creates a much more pleasant place in which to live. This is why streets of

PLANNING THE GARDEN

CHOOSING PLANTS

Eucalypts are an excellent source of nectar, seeds and shelter for a range of species.

With less space to play with, careful planning is especially important. To get the most out of a small area, it's useful to focus on plants that are the very best nectar producers, or those that will provide several purposes at once. For instance, dense grevilleas like Honey Gem, Superb or Ned Kelly provide nectar and shelter. If you have the space, lilly pillies such as *Syzygium leuhmannii* provide great berries, some nectar and quite good shelter. Smaller eucalypts such as the Red-Flowering Gum (*E. ficifolia*) or the Bushy Yate (*E. lehmannii*) can be good for seeds as well as nectar – just remember that the gum will become a tree with a very open base and will look better filled in with grevilleas or bottlebrushes such as Captain Cook. Banksias are a magnificent source of nectar – Giant Candles is one of the best for smaller areas. Some of the kangaroo paws (*Anigozanthos* sp.) are outstanding plants for smaller gardens – the smaller ones like Bush Gold and the larger Bush Sunset are excellent additions to any garden.

the one tree species often look much better than those where many different types are planted haphazardly. It may also be possible to have larger trees in the corners where four properties meet. This can provide shade for people as well as resources for birds. Silky Oaks (*Grevillea robusta*) have a slim, upright shape and can be elegant in a corner position. Their flowers replete with golden nectar are an excellent resource for lorikeets and honeyeaters.

If a group of people is serious about improving an area's value for birds, it's worth considering making each garden a specialist area. For instance, one garden could be, primarily, a water feature, one a shrub area and one dominated by trees. This takes a great deal of co-ordination and is unlikely to work in every area, but it is always worth a try.

WATER FEATURES

Although a full-scale wetland is an unlikely addition to a small garden, a feature is quite possible – even the smallest pond can become a great attraction for birds. A pond can be easily fitted next to a fence, in a corner or adjacent to a wall (provided the pond is totally leak-proof!). Fibreglass ponds are available in most garden centres and are easy to install. You can also build your own water feature (*see* Chapter Three).

If a pond isn't your forte, you can always use the hose. As long as there are no water restrictions, regularly putting the sprinkler on each summer afternoon provides birds with a pleasant shower while you water the garden. This approach works especially well if the sprinkler is regularly used in the shrub area where birds can enjoy the water without exposing themselves to predators.

Birdbaths are a favourite haunt for a range of garden birds like this Silvereye.

PLANNING THE GARDEN

Baby birds are one of the rewards of a well-planned garden where different levels of vegetation support different groups of species.

NESTING

Nest boxes come into their own in smaller gardens. With natural nesting sites in short supply, artificial ones add to the habitat value of the garden. Nest boxes can be useful for parrots like rosellas and lorikeets, as well as for pardalotes. *See* Chapter Four for details on how to build your own nest box.

If there are no suitable trees, nest boxes can be attached to the eaves or wall of the house. The local climate will determine where the best spot is. It's important to make sure the box doesn't get too hot from hours of direct sun or too cold from constant, deep shade. Dense plants or creepers can also provide natural nest sites to complement the artificial ones. Spiky plants outside bedroom windows can offer extra security, as well as closer encounters for you with nesting birds.

FEEDING

While natural food from Australian plants is the best source for birds, it is sometimes in short supply at different times of the year. For instance, insect numbers dwindle in winter, while in many areas nectar is easy to get in winter and hard to find in summer. Offering extra food at any time of the year can be an important part of attracting birds to smaller gardens. A feeding table takes up little room, and is great for birds, especially if healthy food is offered regularly, but make sure you put out small quantities that won't make the birds dependent.

With smaller gardens, minimising harmful influences is especially important. This means banning pesticides if possible and keeping cats away. Rowdy children and dogs aren't terrific for birds either but, of course, they're nice to have around. First-time bird visitors are often quite shy and may not take food unless it is offered in the branches or shrubs. Once the birds are obviously more comfortable, you can gradually move the food to more convenient locations. *See* Chapter Two for details.

HIGH-RISE BIRD GARDENS

You can still attract birds to your garden if you live in a block of flats. It might sound silly to consider attracting birds to a balcony or rooftop garden, but in many parts of Australia, that's exactly what people are doing. In such areas extra food for the birds is much more important than it is in larger gardens, but it is still useful to have a few potted grevilleas like Robyn Gordon, Ned Kelly or Superb. It's possible to attract a range of fascinating birds, like gaudy raucous Rainbow Lorikeets, which are one of the world's more extraordinary bird species. They readily visit balcony gardens for a handout of nectar mix or to feed from a grevillea or two.

A window box with a good potting mix can make an area more attractive to people and wildlife.

CHAPTER 2

FEEDING YOUR FEATHERED FRIENDS

Feeding birds can be a wonderful pastime. Responsible feeding offers the chance to observe birds at close quarters, to study their behaviour and to understand them more fully. Although behaviour at feeding tables isn't always the same as in the wild, it can still give you an insight as to how birds relate to each other. You can, for instance, decide if all parrots really are left-footed!

Rainbow Lorikeets are always quick to find a new feeding table.

Putting out food for birds can be a great complement to the natural diet provided by indigenous plants. It is also just about the only way to get numbers of birds to visit high-rise balconies. Feeding birds is a heavy responsibility, with both positive and negative aspects. The trick is to profit from the positive and eliminate the negative.

FEEDING YOUR FEATHERED FRIENDS

The number of species and individual birds that visit your feeding table depends on how much food is available, how regularly it is offered and how varied the menu is. Too little food won't do much to attract the birds. Too much will attract plenty of birds – and plenty of problems. It's important to put out food that is nutritious for birds in quantities that still encourage them to find their natural food. Overfeeding makes them dependent on you, and sooner or later you will go on holiday or move house and the birds will starve.

Another reason not to overfeed is that the food you put out may not be exactly right for the birds' health, and with too much free food they won't forage for their natural diet. Eating only what you supply can cause health problems for birds. For example, some baby lorikeets that are fed low-protein 'fast food' never grow their feathers properly. Too much of the wrong food can also cause the birds to become egg-bound. This is a nasty condition where the bird can't lay its eggs.

Extra food can benefit some species to the detriment of others. For instance, intelligent, adaptable birds like currawongs can do very well from feeding tables, quite possibly raising more young than if they had to find their own food. This could mean more currawongs in the neighbourhood – and when currawongs aren't snaffling leftovers, they are robbing the nests of smaller birds. Feeding birds can also spread disease if large numbers of them congregate together. They can become more vulnerable to predators, too, because they are less wary when squabbling for food.

By this time you might be thinking anyone who feeds birds is some kind of environmental vandal, but there are ways of providing food that can go a long way towards eliminating the problems and providing real benefits for the birds and their human benefactors.

WHAT TO FEED

The first step is to put out the right food. This varies according to the local species you would like to attract. Seeds are one of the easiest foods to provide and are very attractive to finches, many pigeons and most parrots. An easy way to provide seeds which are the right size for the birds in question is to buy a bag of mixed seed for the appropriate species from the local supermarket or pet shop. If you're not sure what combinations and amounts you need, buy both small and large mixes and see who comes to dinner.

Make sure you don't offer too much sunflower seed, which is very high in oil. Birds love these seeds and will choose them before anything else – a bit like people who go for chocolate cake rather than vegetables. There is some evidence that birds who concentrate on such a rich food source tend to suffer health problems, so it's best to play it safe and offer a mixture of seeds.

When seeds sprout, all sorts of amazing biochemical things happen which increase their food value. If you are so inclined, sprouting the seed can provide a special treat for your garden visitors.

To do this, put the seed in a container, fill it with water and then drain it, putting a damp cloth over the top to keep in the moisture. Rinse the seeds a few times a day to prevent mould from forming and they will be ready to serve after a few days.

Grain that isn't yet ripe can also be very attractive. Many birds love getting into seed heads when the grain is still milky. Of course, the easiest way to provide this is by growing seeding grasses on the edge of the open parts of the garden. Greens like cabbage, broccoli or spinach can also be quite popular with seed-eaters.

Lorikeets and honeyeaters need a nectar mix. Each group has a 'sweet tooth' but their needs are different. When lorikeets feed, they push their faces into the flower, using the dozens of tiny short bristles on their tongues to collect nectar and pollen. They can digest both of these, taking carbohydrates from the nectar and protein from the pollen. This means a nectar mix for lorikeets needs to contain both protein and carbohydrates if it is to be healthy for them and provide the protein they need to grow feathers and properly develop muscles.

Honeyeaters also like nectar but get some of their nutrients from a different source. They don't seem to be able to digest pollen, so they need to eat insects in order to obtain protein. The energy expended in catching insects in some heathland areas is replenished by the copious supplies of local nectar. Because honeyeaters obtain their protein from this source it isn't so important to include protein in their mix – but it won't do any harm either. In general, honeyeaters will enjoy the lorikeet nectar mix (with or without the protein), along with fruit.

Both insect- and meat-eating birds will enjoy a range of food from cooked chop bones to wriggling mealworms and pet food. These types of birds include magpies, currawongs, butcherbirds and kookaburras as well as smaller species like Noisy Miners, and tiny blue fairy-wrens. Some people are lucky enough to have falcons like Australian Kestrels visiting their balconies to procure a piece of meat. The important point for such birds is to make sure they are getting a reasonable balance of calcium, phosphorus and vitamin D.

A useful source of protein is baby cereal, and a good nectar mix is:

- one part sugar (it doesn't seem to matter what sort, but don't use honey, it can spread bee diseases);
- three parts baby cereal (high protein if possible);
- pet vitamins according to directions;
- ten parts of water (to make it nice and porridge-like).

This nectar mix has to be made freshly each day because it goes off within a few hours.

Lorikeets will also need:
- mixed seeds (as for other parrots);
- greens (like cabbage, broccoli or spinach);
- fruit or fruit peels (but not citrus or banana peel).

To avoid the birds becoming dependent, give only a teaspoon of the mix for each bird per day. For the rest of the lorikeet food, put out only as much as the birds will eat each day in a feeding session of about half an hour. If you don't have the time to prepare the nectar mix, a reasonable compromise is to put one teaspoon of sugar and three of baby cereal on a slice of wholemeal bread and offer the food dry.

A Meal of Worms

Mealworms are the caterpillar-shaped larvae of black *Tenebrio* beetles and insect-eating birds will do anything to get them. You can buy them at many pet stores, but a more economical approach is to farm your own in a plastic bucket with a close-fitting lid.

Cut a 10cm hole in the lid to allow air to circulate and cover it with fine gauze to keep out competitors, who can overrun the colony. Put 10cm of bran in the bucket and a thin layer of sliced potatoes or apple for the worms to eat. Every few days, remove the old vegetable matter and give the farm a day's rest before you put the next layer in. This helps prevent the bran becoming too moist and turning into an unpleasant composting mixture. Always make sure you keep some beetles in the mix so that new generations will be in constant supply.

The largest worms will hide in the surface layers, so you don't have to dig deep to find them. Mealworms are best offered in a bowl or dish so they can't wriggle away before the birds spy them. If the mealworms are offered regularly, the local birds will soon get the idea. Mealworms have a larger fat:protein ratio than adult insects and if a bird eats too many of them, it may suffer dietary problems. Feed as many as the birds can eat in one feeding session of five minutes or so.

Meat contains plenty of phosphorus, but not much calcium, so if you want to give the butcherbirds some meat, it should be sprinkled with calcium carbonate (from the chemist). If this sounds complicated, a much easier approach is to simply use pet food, which has been nutritionally balanced in the factory. (There are many currawongs around the country who have studied a family cat's routine so they can sneak in and help themselves to leftovers while the cat's away.) You can use either the canned or dried food. If you use the dried product, it's best to rehydrate it for five minutes or so before giving it to birds.

Cheese can also be a reasonable food for insect and meat eaters. It is especially popular with Superb Fairy-wrens and magpies. And all birds like cuttlebone which provides extra calcium and on which they sharpen their beaks. Make it more attractive by cracking it into smaller pieces or by crushing it.

Whatever food you are offering, cleanliness is essential to avoid disease outbreaks. The feeding table needs to be hosed down once a day or so and any old food disposed of. Seeds can be left out for longer periods, as long as they are in some sort of container with raised edges so the supply can't be fouled by the birds.

Some of the best food mixtures for garden birds are those designed for raising orphaned native animals. These imitate the birds' natural diet as closely as possible and come in a powder form. You can get them through your local wildlife rescue group.

Finally, dried fruit, particularly raisins or currants, can be very attractive to birds. As a general rule, putting out a mix of different types of foods will attract a good variety of local birds.

Worker termites desperately repair a feeding tunnel after it has been destroyed by a marauding brush-turkey.

WHERE TO FEED

Birds feed and live at each level of the garden's vegetation. Where you choose to offer food depends on how much energy you want to devote to this aspect of bird gardening. You can simply sprinkle some breadcrumbs or birdseed on a windowsill for passing sparrows, or you can go all the way with feeders in many different parts of the garden.

It takes animals a while to work out that free food is on offer and patience may be needed at first. There are two important aspects: making sure food is available at the same time each day and, at first, putting the food where it is easy for the birds to reach. Initially this may mean wasting some food and putting it where you won't be able to watch the birds as closely. But once they are in the habit of visiting the garden, there is less wastage and you can gradually move the feeder to a spot more convenient for you.

Brown Gerygones are also called Brown Warblers.

Seeds will attract many species, including doves like these Spotted Turtle-doves, pigeons and a range of parrots. Make sure you go easy on the fatty sunflower seeds.

When setting up a bird feeder, try to put it in a quiet part of the garden, but make sure you still have a good view of the birds. Putting the feeder outside a window can be a great idea if there is a dense garden so the birds aren't disturbed. It's especially good when the light is coming from outside the window because birds looking in will see only their reflections, while people looking out have an intimate view of the unsuspecting visitors.

For many birds, flicking small pieces of cheese or pet food near them can be a good way to start. This can work well with a range of birds, from tiny ones like Superb Fairy-wrens to large ones like magpies or butcherbirds. The trick is to flick the food like you might shoot a marble (you remember!). If you throw it, the rapid movement of your arm will frighten the birds and completely spoil their appetites.

With honeyeaters, put a feeding bottle in or near some flowering plants to allow them to become accustomed to feeding from it. It may even help to mount a glitzy red plastic tubular flower on the end of the feeding nozzle as the birds may identify it as a food source. Once they realise the food comes from the bottle, the plastic flower can be removed.

Even the traditional feeding table will work best if it is initially placed near shrubs and gradually moved closer to the house once the birds are visiting regularly. However, cats, and even rats, will need to be managed around bird feeders. If possible, discourage cats from the yard. (They hate water – especially at high pressure!) If your household includes a cat, feed the birds only when you're around. That way you can make sure it's only the birds who are dining.

Make sure any cats in your house are well fed and have bells on their collars. Some cats are models of virtue and never catch anything. Others are incorrigible and the only hope for birds around such killing machines is if the cat wears a really big bell – one that slows it down a bit! If your cat is in the latter category you have to be especially vigilant if you want to attract birds. In such circumstances, putting the feeder beyond the cat's jumping height in the middle of an open area may be the best idea. It won't be so popular with birds, but it will still attract them – and the cat won't be able to sneak up on them as he/she would if the feeder was nicely nestled in the shrubbier parts of the garden.

Rats are intelligent, and they will quickly work out that there is a free meal going at the local feeding table. They are best dealt with by minimising the amount of food spilt, stopping them climbing up to the feeder and using a few carefully placed rat traps. You can minimise spillage by putting seed supplies in a container that has sides a few centimetres high. This allows the birds access to the food but keeps the seeds in place. Feeding tables can also be rat-proofed by nailing 15cm of tin around the top of each leg. Hanging feeders can be protected by running the string through the centre of a plastic plate, which is held in place over the feeder by a knot or two.

Rat traps are the most satisfying way of dealing with these interlopers. To minimise the chance of whacking a visiting possum, put the traps inside boxes with rat-sized holes in them. Curiosity will eventually get the rats, although this curiosity is tempered by caution, and if a trap doesn't catch them the first time it goes off, they will be difficult to snare for weeks. The way around this is to put the traps out with bait on them, but not to set them for a few nights. Once the rats are used to a free feed, set all the traps one night and your problems should disappear!

A mesh bag is an easy way to offer birds fruit pieces.

FEEDER SHAPES AND SIZES

There are many elaborate commercial bird feeders on the market, all designed, packaged and labelled for the job. They are easy to use, and from the birds' point of view: if it holds food, they'll be there! Remember that all containers need drainage holes to make cleaning easier. There are many types of feeders, so you should be able to find one that's exactly right for your garden.

COMMERCIAL FEEDERS

The gravity-fed plastic seed holders are one of the most convenient types of bird feeders. They hang out of reach of cats and rats, they are mostly easy to fill, weather-resistant and they minimise spillage. However, they concentrate birds in a small area, so the most aggressive ones tend to grab all the food.

Mesh Bags

A plastic mesh bag, fine enough to hold nuts or small pieces of fruit, can be a useful hanging bird feeder. It is easy to clean by spraying with the hose, and when the cockatoos tear holes in it, you can easily obtain another one the next time you buy oranges. You can also use wire mesh. It's more durable but not nearly as easy to work with. This type of feeder has limitations in that some species, such as doves, don't like to hang onto the side of things when they feed.

Feeding platforms

Some kind of platform, which stands on one or more legs or is suspended from a branch, is the most convenient way of providing food for birds. You can buy a variety of ready-made models or make your own simple or elaborate construction (*see* pp. 38–39).

The important aspects to remember with this type of feeder are that it:

- is easy to clean with the hose and occasionally with a laundry brush;
- minimises spillage of seeds or nectar mix by keeping food in a container with low sides, which still allows easy access for birds;
- has wooden dowel spikes or nails (not galvanised) to hold fruit pieces;

FEEDING YOUR FEATHERED FRIENDS

Fruit is a great source of food for birds and can simply be impaled on wooden spikes or nails. The roof helps to keep the rain off.

- has a fresh water supply, like a drinking bottle from a parrot cage or just a water bowl, that is cleaned daily;
- keeps rain off the food (otherwise it will rot);
- is built from materials that will survive all weather conditions.

Terracotta, marine ply, hardwood and, to a lesser extent, plastic are quite suitable construction materials. Pine will last if well painted with marine varnish or similar finish, or if it is factory-treated to resist decay. The chemicals in treated timber aren't supposed to pose any threat to people or animals using the timber, but there are several non-chemical alternatives that work just as well, so to be safe you're better off avoiding chemically-treated timber.

While high-protein nectar mixes for lorikeets can be offered in a bowl or dish, honeyeaters need a more specialised dining arrangement. A guinea-pig feeding bottle is a good option, as are water dispensers used in bird cages. The position of the platform depends on your garden plan, but remember that the kitchen or other windowsill can be a great place to attach a bird feeder.

NATURAL FEEDERS

By using your imagination you can make feeders that are rather more decorative than the traditional bird table, and which blend more naturally with the rest of the garden. Pieces of driftwood can make excellent bird feeders, or parts of a feeder. For a natural look, they can be suspended with manila rope or leather thongs (oiled regularly).

Mixed seeds can be put into natural or artificial holes in the wood, and fruit pieces can be impaled on the ends of nails (not galvanised) driven halfway into the wood. Feeding logs can be made easily by sawing off a 30cm length of a log (not too thick) and drilling fat holes into it, to a depth of 3cm or so. You can then put bird puddings or a mixture of seeds and peanut butter into the holes for the birds to peck out. Dowels drilled into the log next to the holes allow birds to perch easily while they work away at extracting the food. To hang the log up, screw a heavy cup hook into the end of the log or drill a hole right through it, and insert a loop of rope to serve as an attachment point.

Pine cones that are fully open can also make great bird feeders, especially the monster ones from a Coulter's Pine (*Pinus coulteri*). Kids love plastering the cones with various bird mixtures and hanging them up to watch the birds work away at them. These feeders need to be cleaned regularly – a thorough blasting with the hose will usually suffice. You will need to be more careful if you have been feeding sticky mixtures to the birds. If you use peanut butter, try to mix seed or rolled oats with it so that it's fairly dry – and don't squeeze it too far into the pine cone.

Right: *Working the food out of the holes in this log can keep birds busy in your garden for hours.*

BIRDS AND YOUR FRUIT AND VEGETABLE GARDEN

Having a prolific fruit and vegetable garden is not always easy to reconcile with attracting birds to the garden. But with careful planning, a few precautions and a positive attitude, you can have your birds and eat your produce as well. One of the best approaches

OTHER BITS AND PIECES

Foods such as cheese, meat scraps and bacon rinds can be useful for garden birds but you need to be very careful with them as they aren't all that good for birds if eaten in large quantities.

A left-over cooked potato is a reasonable addition to the feeding table, especially with currawongs and bowerbirds about.

Bacon scraps are very popular with birds but all that salt and fat has to be offered in moderation – especially as young birds can choke on the rinds.

Bread, both white and wholemeal, is popular with a range of seed-eating birds.

Cheese in small pieces or grated is great for a range of birds from magpies to fairy-wrens.

Suet is pure fat with a very high energy value. It can be useful during times when other food supplies are low.

FRUIT FEASTS

Fruit is a great temptation for a range of birds, from currawongs to bowerbirds and honeyeaters to Silvereyes. Fresh or overripe fruit placed regularly in the same spots in the garden can be a great supplement to natural food.

Sticky pear juice makes this fruit particularly attractive to a range of birds.

Bananas are ideal for squashing into cracks – as long as they are cleaned out if not eaten in a day or so.

Juicy orange halves or slices can be attractive to honeyeaters.

to sharing your produce with birds is to simply plant a bit more than you need. That way both you and the birds get what they need, without a lot of effort.

Fruit trees are very attractive to birds and not always easy to share with them. Covering parts of the tree with netting is the best way to ensure that both you and the birds get a fair share. You can buy bird netting from most hardware stores. If possible, make sure the netting is taut so birds or flying foxes don't get tangled in it. If the netting doesn't go all the way to the ground, it may function as a bird trap, which won't endear you to the local wildlife authority! Paper bags can also be used to protect individual fruits – although the lack of sunlight can be a problem for ripening.

Vegetables are usually less attractive to birds, although bowerbirds can shred a lot of green vegetables in a fairly short time. The simplest way around this problem is to put small, triangular-prism-shaped covers over garden beds, especially when seedlings are little. An easy way to make the covers is to nail together three pieces of wood to make a triangle about 50cm high. Then make another one. These are the ends of the prism. Nail five or so lengths of wood between the triangles to make the prism and put bird netting over it.

Apples that are a bit too ripe are often better than crispy ones that dry out more rapidly in the sun.

Dried fruit is a longer-lasting alternative to the fresh variety.

FEEDING THE SEED EATERS

A commercial seed mix, available from pet shops for cage-birds, is readily consumed by wild seed eaters too.

Popcorn will be enjoyed by larger seed-eating birds such as doves and parrots.

A finer seed mix harvested from wild grasses is a favourite food of finches.

Mixed poultry grain can also be fed to garden birds, the doves and parrots in particular.

FEEDING YOUR FEATHERED FRIENDS

Bird Puddings

This English treat is a food mixture held together with fatty suet, available from a butcher. It is acceptable to feed this to birds in Australia, so long as it is not supplied too often.

To make the pudding, you melt the suet carefully on the stove, pour it into a container and stir in as much of the bird food as you can. Ingredients can include seeds, nuts and dried items like peas, lentils and fruit. Don't use vegetables as they will decompose. Store the puddings in the freezer and take out a little each time you want to give the birds something extra. This approach doesn't work all that well on hot days when the fat can melt, and it is a bit high in calories for regular use.

Seed bells are a popular and weatherproof variation on this theme, except the binding ingredient isn't suet, it's glue – PVA-type glue, in fact. While this glue is non-toxic, it isn't part of a bird's natural diet and is probably best avoided.

A somewhat better approach is to use a sugar toffee mix to hold the seeds together. This isn't so weatherproof, and sugar isn't the greatest food for birds, but at least it's a more natural ingredient than glue!

HOW TO BUILD A SIMPLE FEEDING PLATFORM

The simplest feeding platform takes the form of a pole sunk into the ground with a flat piece of wood secured to it.

Materials:
1 x 1736mm x 36mm x 36mm length of pine
1 x 1500mm x 70mm x 46mm length of treated pine
1 x 305mm x 460mm x 18mm pine plank
18 x 40mm nails
4 x 60mm brass screws
marine varnish

Cut the 1736mm length of pine into eight pieces (B–I) as illustrated.

Nail the platform (A) to the four lengths of skirting (B–E).

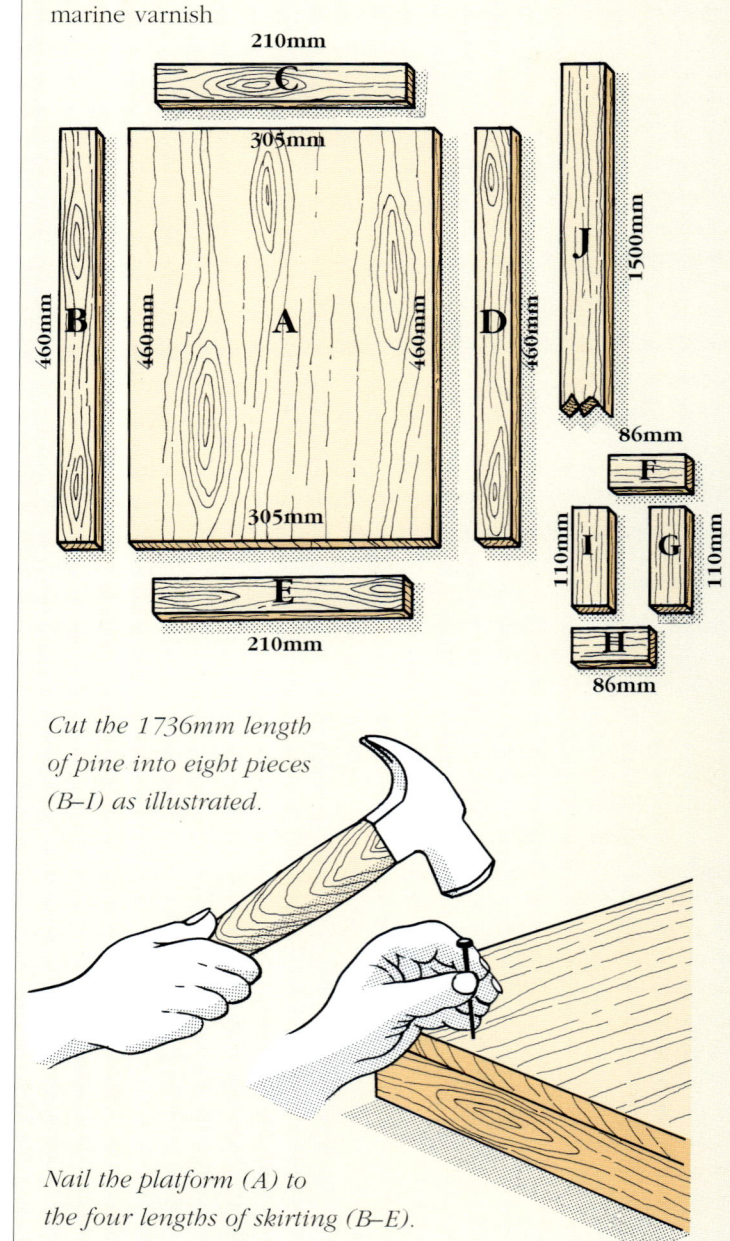

FEEDING YOUR FEATHERED FRIENDS

Using a set square, mark out the position underneath the platform for the four pole supports (F–I).

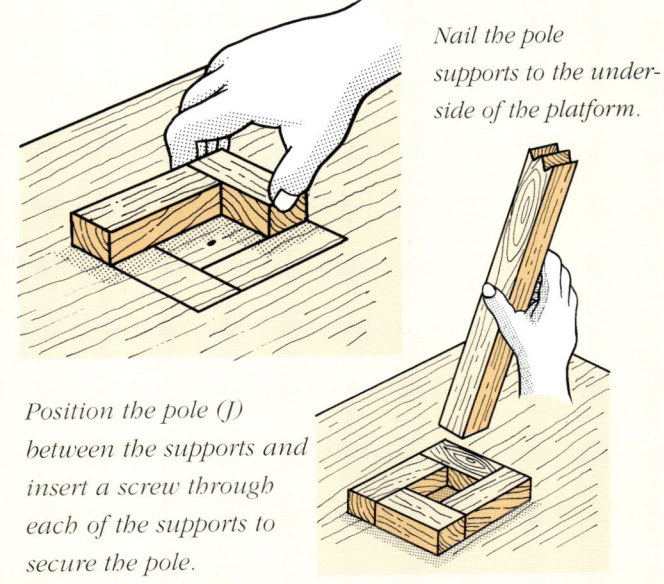

Nail the pole supports to the underside of the platform.

Position the pole (J) between the supports and insert a screw through each of the supports to secure the pole. Apply three coats of varnish, sanding lightly between each coat.

The finished product. An inverted plastic bowl is secured to the pole to discourage rodents.

To create a hanging feeder, use the platform section only and suspend it from each corner using cup hooks and four even lengths of rope.

NIGHTWATCHING

Installing almost any sort of lighting system in the garden can add a fairyland feeling to the most mundane area, as well as attracting insects that provide food for a range of nocturnal birds and other creatures. A light that is at least 1.5m off the ground can act as a beacon for tiny insect-eating bats, and birds such as frogmouths and Boobook Owls. On steamy summer nights frogs will congregate on the ground under a light, and in tropical areas geckos will adorn any nearby walls.

Using a strong torch or spotlight to spy animals at night can be a memorable experience, especially for younger folk. Spotlights are a useful tool in finding nocturnal visitors because of the way their eyes shine. Some people run a spotlight off a rechargeable motorcycle battery, but for backyard use, any of the larger torches will do.

Listening in the garden for night sounds is also a great idea. It is often the 'mo-poke' call of a Boobook or the low, repetitive 'oom oom oom' of a frogmouth that tells you there is a very special visitor in the garden. If you're really into seeing rare nocturnal creatures like owls, a devilish trick is to play tapes of their territorial calls. This approach can be effective but can work too well – constantly hearing an invisible rival in its territory is enough to send any owl cuckoo!

Tawny Frogmouths nest in the larger suburban trees with rough bark.

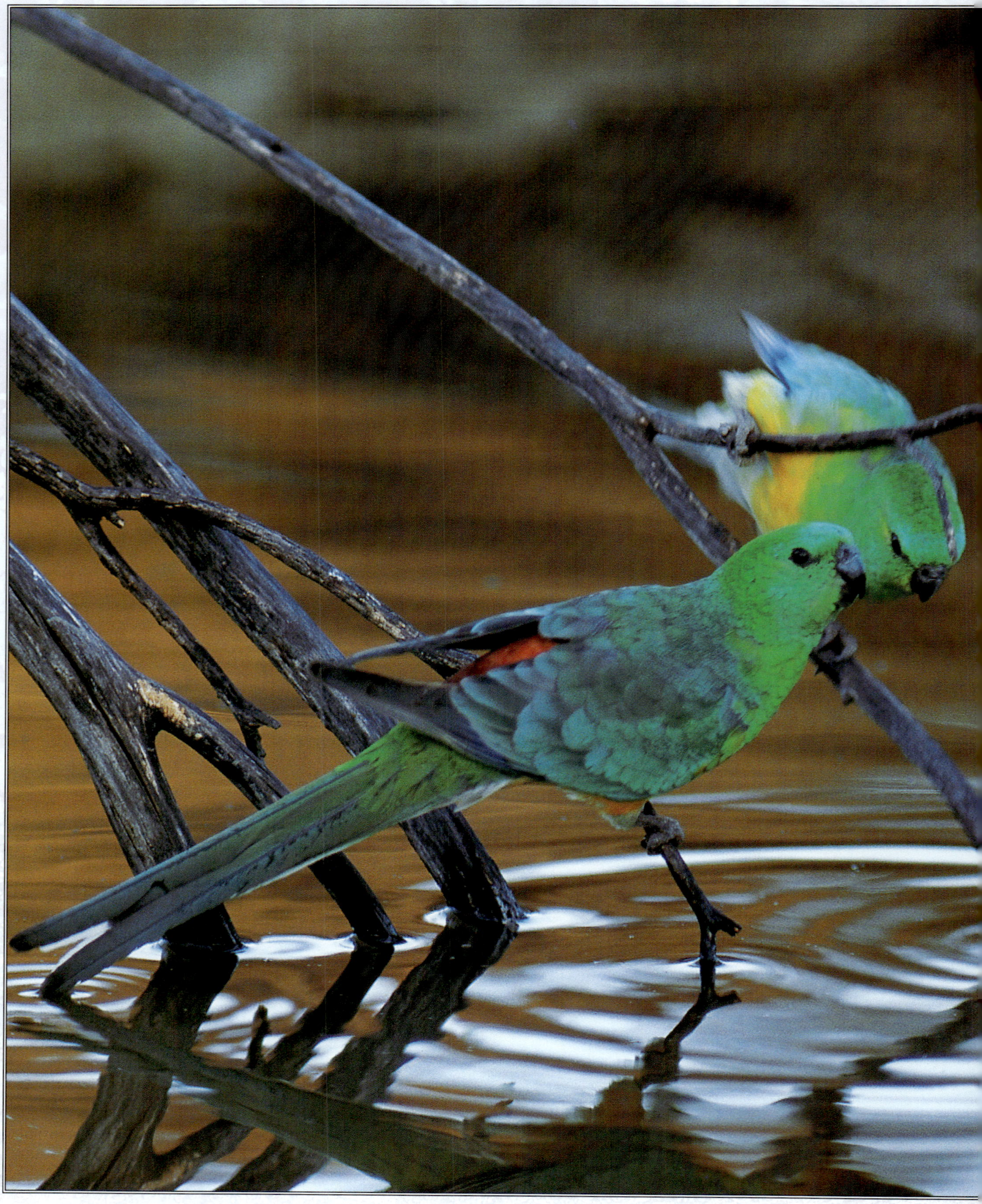

CHAPTER 3

WATER IN THE GARDEN

Water, one of nature's most valuable commodities, has a place in every garden – especially one designed to attract birds and other wildlife. Aside from the many birds that like to bathe in the water, all except the insect eaters will need to drink each day. Even the most modest water feature will attract a surprising range of aquatic creatures that can be as interesting as the birds.

Red-rumped Parrots are commonly found near water.

Nearly all birds appreciate a water supply in the garden. It can be an elaborate water feature that makes a grand impact on the backyard or a very simple terracotta dish, upturned garbage bin lid or even an old hub cap!

WATER IN THE GARDEN

A water feature provides an opportunity for gardeners to express their creativity. There are many effective ways to provide water in the garden, each with its own advantages. Whatever method you choose, it's sure to be great for both birds and people.

When planning to create a water feature for your garden, a good idea is to visit a natural bush setting to see how water naturally blends into the landscape. Observing how birds use such an area is also really valuable. You may notice that some like to splash about or simply drink at the edge, while others will plunge into the deeper areas, or, like swallows, drink by swooping low over the surface. Some will even take the trouble to land on a log or rock in the middle of the water so they can drink without being ambushed.

CHOOSING A SITE

A traditional birdbath on a pedestal allows you a good view of the birds enjoying themselves. Another advantage is that it's easy to move to suit your garden design. Marauding cats will also have nowhere to lie in wait for unwary bathing birds. But such a set-up will attract only the boldest birds who don't mind being exposed to aerial predators like goshawks. A birdbath can be moved into the shrubbier parts of the garden to provide for the shyer species, but water at ground level gives a more natural and pleasing appearance and also fits in more easily with the birds' natural instincts.

Water is found only at the lowest levels of the landscape. This might sound obvious, but it's surprising how often you see water features built up in the higher parts of gardens so they look a bit like a

Tree ferns can be an excellent setting for a pond – but if you have attracting birds in mind, ferns don't do a lot for them.

kind of silly hanging pond – or built exactly at ground level so that when rocks are put around them to make the edge more natural-looking, they sit up above ground level, instead of being flush with it.

You can also note how the rocks and vegetation appear around natural ponds. Your choice of rocks will have an impact on how they are placed around it. For instance, sandstone rocks always have their strata parallel, while granite rocks are often rounder and slope into the water in a curved line, not a straight or jagged one like sandstone.

However you design your pond or water feature, try to create some cosy nooks and crannies where ferns and similar plants can thrive and where lizards and other creatures can find shelter. It's also a good idea to aim for an ecological balance with fish, plants and microbes. This will produce a self-sustaining water feature and provide shelter for a much more interesting range of wildlife. Try to position the pond where it will receive only dappled sunlight. Full sun all day can overheat the water and cause excess algal growth.

An ideal approach is to channel water from an open area through the shrub area to the water feature. If your block of land has any slope at all, it can be very effective to plan a series of ponds with waterfalls or streamlets between them. One point to remember is that all areas of flowing water need to run across rock, concrete, fibreglass or plastic to avoid erosion. This is especially important with the lip of a waterfall. A dished rock can protect against erosion and also channel the falling water away from the 'cliff face' so it tumbles down in a pleasing manner, rather than just a dribble.

Water features can be excellent places for plants such as the Common Heath (*Epacris impressa*) and the Native Fuchsia (*E. longiflora*). These shrubs are very good for birds, but they thrive only where their sandy soil is continually moist and where the water can seep away to avoid a build-up of fungi. The plants grow naturally in cracks where water seeps slowly out of the rocks, and if the conditions are right, it may be possible to create a similar spot in your water feature.

HOW TO MODIFY AN EXISTING WATER FEATURE

There are some simple ways to improve the wildlife value of an existing water feature. Think about incorporating a range of rocks and logs around your pond which, besides looking great, provides habitat for creatures like frogs and insects, and camouflages the edge of the pond.

Different birds prefer different water depths so ponds with both deep and shallow areas are best. Older style ponds with steep sides and no shallow areas look fine, but don't offer much for birds – unless you have a healthy local population of flamingos! Having shallow water on the sides of the pond next to the shrubs provides areas for small birds like thornbills as well as larger wading types such as herons.

If your pond has no shallow areas, you can build them by filling part of the pond with rocks or gravel topped off with a beautiful, gnarled old log. Aim to have some sections that are only a few centimetres deep, as well as much deeper areas if possible. The shallow areas are best if they are lined with sand or if the concrete is nice and rough, so birds don't have to practise their fancy footwork to balance while they're having a drink.

For the especially adventurous, structural modifications are possible if the pond is made of brickwork rendered with cement – and if you are ready for a tough job. The idea here is to drain the pond, break out one side of the brickwork and dig out the area behind so the pond now slopes away gradually on that side. You can then rebuild the brickwork, using a concrete bonding agent to help the new mortar get a grip on the old. This can be a difficult job and you need to ensure the pond will again hold water. You can waterproof it by rendering it with one of the commercial waterproofing mixtures or by lining it with fibreglass.

Waterlilies like this Nymphaea caerulea *are an attractive feature in any pond.*

WATER IN THE GARDEN

BUILDING A WATER FEATURE

Although ponds are an excellent addition to any garden, few suburban backyards have them, and it's often because people think they are expensive to install. Don't be discouraged. An attractive, bird-friendly pond can be created at a modest cost. You can buy a fibreglass one that only needs setting into the ground, you can use a pond liner or, if you have the energy, build a concrete one. Whichever option you choose, plan how you want the pond to look and how it will fit into the garden design before digging a hole.

READY-MADE PONDS

Fibreglass ponds can be bought at larger garden centres. They are not the cheapest option, but they very rarely leak and are the easiest to install.

You will need to dig a hole about 10cm deeper and wider than the pond. Use a levelling device, such as a spirit level or a plastic water-filled tube, to make sure the pond will sit evenly in the hole. If you are building a wetland area next to the pond, you could tilt the pond slightly in that direction. Line the hole with sand (the type that goes under brick pavers is best) to make sure the pond is well supported. Trial fittings may be needed before the base and sides are sitting evenly on the sand. Doing this carefully pays dividends later when little unforeseen accidents occur – like when the kids throw each other into it!

Fibreglass ponds can be a simple way to provide water in the garden. A natural look will be achieved once the plants become established.

Pond liners have to be installed carefully for long-term results but they allow more creativity than other methods.

POND LINERS

Pond liners allow a little more creativity than commercial fibreglass ponds as you can create your own shape, with deep and shallow areas, and islands and streams for a variety of birds. You should also allow for the water to be at least 30cm deep as it helps to keep an even temperature, so fish find the pond more attractive. You will need to check with your local council first, though, as you may be required to erect a pool fence if the pond reaches a certain depth.

A pond lining can consist of a membrane like butyl rubber or PVC (available from garden centres or specialist outlets), polyethylene, or a compound like bentonite clay. They can be custom-made but it's cheaper to use standard sizes. Butyl rubber is much better than PVC and if there's a choice of grades, get the thickest one (7mm for butyl rubber and at least 550 microns for PVC). Polyethylene sheeting, which needs to be at least 250 microns thick, will have a much shorter life than the 40 years you can expect from butyl rubber or the 20 years from PVC. Bentonite clay will also keep a pond fairly waterproof. It is derived from volcanic ash and swells when it gets wet, blocking the tiny spaces in the soil that usually allow water to pass through. Bentonite only works in still water and only when applied according to the manufacturer's directions; you need to be very careful to get it right.

When you start digging, make sure that lumpy stones or any roots protruding through the area are removed and the soil is stamped down by foot or by using a commercial device. Line the hole with a few centimetres of damp sand (larger hardware or landscaping supplies centres can advise on the best local type to use), or with glass fibre bats, polyester matting or synthetic carpet underlay. Once you've placed the liner, cover any exposed edges with sand or rocks so the sun's UV rays don't damage it. Repair kits are available, although finding a puncture in a pond lining is a rotten job. It is advisable to use the best liner you can and to ensure that the hole preparation is as thorough as it can be.

Small areas of water are very attractive with the right plants.

CONCRETE

This option will require strenuous building activity, and the soil and concrete need to be carefully prepared. However, of all the options available, this method can result in a pond that is enduring and shaped to fit your garden design more precisely.

Plan the pond as you would if using a pond liner. Dig the hole and check the levels, then compact the soil with a commercial compacting device or at least with the back of a shovel. Line the hole with a couple of thicknesses of galvanised chicken wire. For larger ponds it's best to use commercial reinforcing rather than chicken wire. To do its job, the reinforcing has to be encased in the concrete and small mesh wire will give a better result than large mesh.

Cement mixes vary from state to state, and your local supplier of ready-mixed or bagged products can advise on the best mix for the job. For waterproof applications, a rich mix of 1 part cement, 2 parts sand and 3 parts gravel is generally about right. Add as little water as you can – the drier the mix, the more it will hold water. All the concrete needs to be poured on the same day to make sure there are no joins, which could leak later on. Getting the concrete to cover both sides of the mesh can be difficult if you simply pour the concrete straight onto the mesh. For larger ponds, prop the reinforcing up with rocks so the concrete can set all around it. For smaller ponds using chicken wire, a better approach is to put the reinforcing in, stomp it into shape with your boots, take the reinforcing out, spread half the concrete onto the sides of the hole, put the reinforcing on top of the poured concrete and tip the rest of the concrete on top of the reinforcing, working it back and forth to make sure it settles nicely into the mesh. If the pond sprouts a leak, you can render it with one of the commercial waterproofing mixtures – or you can line the inside with fibreglass matting and resin.

For larger ponds, you need to ensure that the concrete is at least 15cm thick; 10cm thick for smaller ponds that are 1–2m across. You can also make a concrete pond with vertical sides by using formwork – make sure the concrete is at least 10cm thick and reinforced with wire mesh.

Concrete takes a while to cure, and during this process it keeps sucking up water. If there isn't any water, it won't be as strong, so you have to keep it wet by covering it for at least three days with wet hessian material, old towels or a sheet of plastic. Wetting the soil before you lay the concrete aids this curing process.

Rushes and reeds grow happily in the soggy wetland soil next to the pond – giving it a more natural appearance and providing shade and cover for visiting birds.

Cement releases all sorts of unpleasant salts for the first few weeks, so after curing for a week, fill the pond with water and let it stand for three weeks. Then drain and refill, and let it stand for a few days to get any chlorine out of the water. It should then be ready for fish, plants and other life forms.

BREATHING LIFE INTO THE POND

Plenty of creatures will be attracted to the pond by themselves. These include flying insects like dragonflies and mayflies that have aquatic larval stages, as well as frogs like the Striped Marsh Frog (*Lymnodynastes peronii*) that live in damp places in many parts of Australia, always on the lookout for a new area to colonise. One of the most useful ways you can introduce extra life into your pond is to add some mud and plants from a nearby wetland. It's amazing what you can acquire this way – for instance, water fleas, ostracods (pinhead-sized crustaceans) and snails.

Fish are a fascinating addition to any pond, but you will need to introduce them carefully. New fish should be put into the pond by floating their container in the water for half an hour (this way the temperature of the container will adjust to the pond's temperature) before mixing some pond water into their container and then releasing them.

In selecting the type of fish you want, you can take the easy way out and add a few goldfish (*Carassius auratus*) to smaller ponds or koi carp to larger ones, or you can do something adventurous and obtain some indigenous fish. Suitable species are Empire Fish (*Hypseleotris compressa*) or rainbow fish of the genus *Melanotaenia*, such as the Eastern (*M. splendida splendida*) or the Crimson-spotted (*M. splendida fluviatilis*). Indigenous fish aren't all that easy to obtain, but you may be able to get in touch with a local supply through aquarium shops, State fisheries departments or the fish department of your State museum. You can also catch your own if fisheries regulations permit, but you never know what you're getting that way and a lot of trial and error may be needed before you get the sort of fish you like. Many foraging expeditions to local streams will net only Mosquito Fish (*Gambusia affinis*), a ravenous environmental disaster that your pond doesn't need.

Lots of birds like kookaburras, kingfishers and White-faced Herons love to eat fish and you may need to organise a bit of a compromise on this point. The more cover the pond offers the fish, the better they will be able to avoid predators. So plenty of rocks, logs and water plants will help the fish survive as well as improving the pond's appearance. Indigenous fish tend to be faster and more wary than goldfish so if the birds are too good at catching the goldfish, replacing them with indigenous species might be the best idea. If you have a series of ponds linked together, you can provide separate habitats for creatures that normally eat each other.

For instance, fish will often make quick work of frog spawn or baby tadpoles, but with separate ponds, you can have your fish in one and frogs in the other. If your ponds are attached in some way, make sure you put the fish in the bottom pond. That way a few taddies might get eaten if they get washed over the edge, but if the tadpoles are in the bottom pond, it only takes one fish to get washed into it for most of the tadpoles to be eaten in a few days.

Nardoo (Marsilea drummondii) *shelters fish, and also produces edible spore caps – if you're prepared to go to the effort of grinding them up.*

Achieving an Ecological Balance

The best ponds have an ecological balance, where nutrients are recycled through the various animals and plants and the whole ecosystem is self-sustaining. Some basic rules for achieving such a balance are:

An Australian Wood Duck with her brood of 12 chicks.

- At least half the surface of the pond should be shielded from direct sunlight with overhanging plants, waterlilies or floating plants. Sunlight is great for plants, but too much can cause algae to grow in the pond, killing off the other plants and making life difficult for the fish.
- The pond needs an open approach on one side to allow an escape route for bathing birds.
- Another side needs to provide dense habitat, either from adjoining shrubs or reeds and rushes which grow in soggy soil next to the pond. A swampy section adjoining the pond can extend the habitat and improve its value.
- By keeping suitable species of fish in the pond, you can eliminate mosquito wrigglers which would otherwise breed in it.
- At least one section of the pond should slope gently down from the edge to provide shallow areas for baby fish to hide and birds to bathe in.
- The pond will be better for fish if it has an area deeper than 30cm (preferably a lot deeper) – but make sure you abide by your State's pool fencing regulations.
- Ponds are better for wildlife if they have a deep layer of sand on the bottom and the odd leaf is allowed to decompose in the pond.

CREATING A GARDEN WETLAND

In nature, swampy or boggy areas act as biological filters and often improve the quality of adjoining areas of open water by removing sediment and excess nutrients. A boggy area can have the same function in the garden, as well as providing habitat for a unique range of plants, birds and other animals.

Choose a site for the mini swamp and dig out the soil to at least 75cm over an area of at least $2m^2$. Like the adjoining pond, the size of the wetland will depend on your energy levels and bank balance. Once you have dug the hole, line it with plastic sheeting. Glue or at least fold the joints several times to reduce leakage and then tip all the soil back in again. Once the plastic is in position and the soil has been returned to its rightful place, it's time to turn on the waterworks.

A hose dripping into the wetland will do the trick, but a better option is to leave it dripping into the pond and have the pond overflow into the wetland. That way the pond has a continuing supply of fresh water. You can also do this the other way around, with the wetland flowing into the pond. This is a more natural option, but it needs careful planning if the wetland plants are not to obscure your views of the pond. Make sure the hose isn't dripping too much or you will make a wetland out of your whole garden and the foundations of your house! If in doubt, it might be better to give the area a good soaking once a week or so rather than use a dripping hose.

If you have a series of ponds, creating water movement can be achieved by putting a small pump in the lowest pond to recycle the water back to the highest one. Movement of the water seems to make the pond especially attractive to birds.

You could also shape your lawn so it directs any rainwater into the wetland and from there into the pond. This approach would replicate the way nature works, but a problem could arise when thunderstorms charge through. A sudden gush of water could send your prized fish and half the water plants across the garden to be sieved out against the back fence. So be careful in your planning and try and allow for these acts of nature.

WATER IN THE GARDEN

WETLANDS, THE BOGGY BIRD PARADISE

Despite its erratic climate, Australia has many wetland areas that are renowned for their rich variety of wildlife. Sadly, you seldom see water features in suburban gardens and even less often do you come across boggy areas that have been created intentionally. But just as wetlands can be vital for birds in the wild, so garden wetlands can be excellent for suburban birds and other creatures. The combination of water and dense vegetation produces a great habitat for a range of birds and for the insects they feed on.

Start by converting a small part of your garden, but be warned, once you start to develop a taste for it, building wetlands can develop into a passion. You may be in danger of joining the ranks of the more fanatical 'wetlanders', some of whom have converted their gardens into a series of ponds and boggy areas.

Sacred Kingfishers are a common site around larger water features, especially when nearby trees offer Indian Myna-free hollows for nesting.

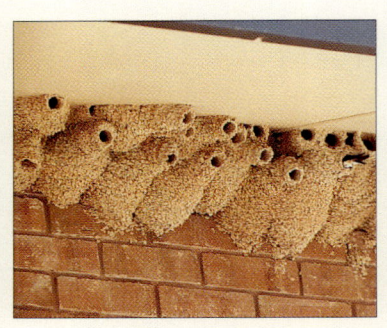

Fairy Martins love wet areas and the myriad flying insects they attract. Their half-bottle-shaped nests can be an extra attraction.

Red-browed Finches enjoy the dense vegetation that occurs in wetlands and feast on the seeds of grasses or saw sedges (Ghania sp.).

CLEANING THE POND

Some people are concerned that building a garden pond will result in endless hours of cleaning, but this isn't necessary. In fact, when it comes to cleaning, the best advice is – don't bother! Too much cleaning will only disturb the natural balance of the pond. The only ponds that ever need cleaning are shallow ones that are beginning to fill up with fallen leaves or silt that has washed in from ungrassed areas of the garden.

Keeping leaves out of the pond can be a difficult compromise. Making sure that no plants grow above the pond removes the leaf problem, but allows full sunlight which causes algae to grow. Algae is alright but all the algal cells can die at once so the decaying material sucks the oxygen out of the water, suffocating the fish and other wildlife. The best solution is to put all the plants on the northern and western sides of the pond, which will shelter them from the worst of the sunlight.

In the unlikely event that the pond needs cleaning, it's important to do it with minimal disturbance. The lower layers of that black stuff on the bottom can contain rotten egg gas produced by the bacteria that live happily there without any oxygen. If you stir up enough of this stuff it can cause all sorts of problems for the fish.

The best way to clean the pond is to use the garden hose as a siphon. Get it started by sucking, but be careful you don't get a mouthful of pondwater.

DRAGONFLIES

These high-velocity aerial predators are often seen darting around ponds, hunting for food or laying eggs in the water. Their larvae are dark-coloured camouflaged creatures that prowl the bottoms of ponds hunting for tadpoles and other little animals. They can shoot out their bottom 'lip', complete with raptorial jaws, to grab any passing creatures of prey.

Dragonfly larvae are able to shoot themselves along by squirting water out of the end of their abdomen.

SELECTING PLANTS FOR YOUR WETLAND

Most nurseries have at least a few plants that thrive in boggy areas. If your local nursery doesn't stock them, it's always possible to get some stock from a local farm dam or wetland. Generally only a few plants are sufficient to start your wetland and most farmers don't mind if you take a few plants from their dams.

Many of the plants that are happy in a water feature also do well in the adjoining boggy area. These include the Tassel Sedge (*Carex fascicularis*), Black Bristle Rush (*Chorizandra enodis*), the saw sedges (*Ghania sp.*) and even Nardoo (*Marsilea drummondi*), which mostly looks better when growing in the water.

The Swamp Banksia (Banksia robur) *is one of the few banksias that does well in damp soil. It grows and flowers best in full sun on the edge of the wetland.*

Bulrushes (Typha *sp.*) *grow only in water or very soggy soil. The fluff from the flower is valuable nesting material and the long stems are great places for Reed Warblers to nest.*

King ferns (Todea barbara) *provide shelter for scrubwrens and other small birds such as Brown Thornbills. They give a lush feel but don't produce flowers or much nesting material.*

If you'd rather not, just fill the hose with water, put one end into the pond and get someone to take the other end downhill with their finger over the end to keep the water in. When you're ready, tell them to take their finger off and you direct your end of the hose to where you want to siphon. Make sure you don't suck up the fish – but if you do, they are usually okay, as long as they are returned to the pond immediately. Just in case this happens, it can be good to run the hose out into a sieve so it's easy to retrieve the fish or tadpoles.

Leave at least a few centimetres of detritus on the bottom of the pond for the tadpoles and other creatures that live on it – a totally clean pond is less productive than one with a nice mucky bottom. Don't scrub the pond or use cleaning agents like chlorine, which, of course, will be especially bad for the fish and plants.

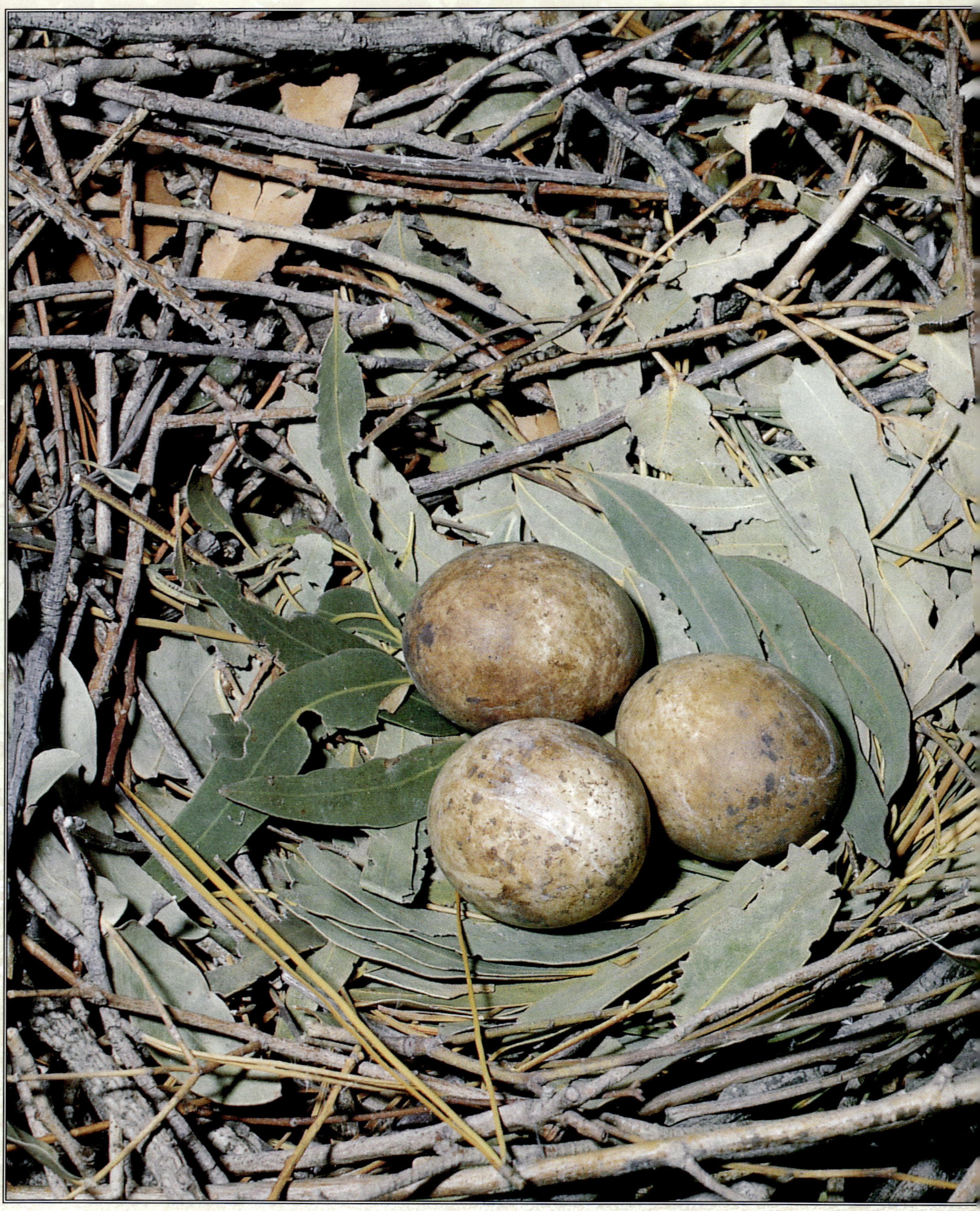

CHAPTER 4

PROVIDING A NESTING GARDEN

Depending on where you live in Australia, winter, spring or summer brings a surge of life to every garden. Insects scurry through, making the most of their short lives, plants flower abundantly and birds fight for nesting territory. A garden with several levels of vegetation, plenty of dense bushes and hollow trees makes an attractive nest site, but if you supply a range of artificial nesting boxes, even more birds will visit your garden.

Black-shouldered Kites sometimes line their nests with gumleaves.

Birds are especially fascinating when they are breeding. They exhibit all sorts of behaviours that you can't see at any other time of the year. Having birds nesting in your garden is the only way to see Superb Fairy-wrens doing their imitation of an escaping mouse or little lorikeets smacking into a tree hollow at an extraordinary speed.

PROVIDING A NESTING GARDEN

While it is fairly simple to attract birds to your garden, enticing them to set up a nesting site is more of a challenge. Most birds and other animals won't breed unless conditions are just right, as there's no point investing a lot of resources into breeding unless you have a good chance of success. Common urban birds like Spotted Turtle-doves aren't too fussy about their nest sites and a few Australian birds like magpies and wattlebirds are quite adaptable, but the ultimate challenge is succeeding in convincing shy birds like honeyeaters or Silvereyes that your garden is the best place in which to build their nest and raise their offspring.

Virtually all birds need to claim and set up a territory before they can successfully raise a family. Watching territorial disputes between the birds can be particularly entertaining, such as a high-altitude tussle between rival gangs of magpies or a more civilised laughing battle between kookaburra families. Some particularly aggressive birds like Common (Indian) Mynas can exclude others from the garden, but the more native plants you grow, the less the mynas will like the area. Native plants will also attract more indigenous birds such as magpies, who will also discourage the Common Mynas.

NATURAL NEST SITES

In most gardens there are some areas that birds can use for nesting. However, if you have planned the garden with birds in mind, the possibilities will be much wider. Many suitable sites can be provided by a healthy garden which includes areas of dense shrubs, a substantial tree canopy, a wetland and open areas – giving birds a 'room with a view'.

HOME AMONG THE TREETOPS

Most bird species feel safest above the ground, so a tree canopy is one of the most important nesting areas in the garden. If you're lucky enough to own the tallest tree in the neighbourhood, it will be especially attractive to larger birds – species such as magpies, currawongs and ravens – which are quite

Like most doves and pigeons, Laughing Doves build a scrappy nest. They mostly build it within a few metres of the ground.

PROVIDING A NESTING GARDEN

Melaleuca quinquinervia *provides nectar for birds and bats; it also has interesting paperbark and affords good shade.*

Pincushion hakeas (Hakea laurina *and* H. petiolaris) *grow rapidly and supply good nectar in the cooler part of the year.*

happy to nest in such trees, even if they are very open and provide little cover. Tall dense trees like figs (*Ficus* sp.), paperbarks (such as *Melaleuca quinquinervia*) and Silky Oaks (*Grevillea robusta*) are attractive to birds like Magpie-larks, wattlebirds, figbirds and orioles.

Old trees with a few dead branches can also attract a wide range of fascinating birds to your garden. Many of our parrots, kingfishers and smaller birds nest in hollows – plus the odd owl or sugar glider. As old trees in the suburbs become unstable and are removed, nesting hollows are becoming increasingly rare. Retaining hollow trees is an excellent idea as long as they are no risk to anybody's house or personal safety.

THE SHRUB LAYER

A dense bank of shrubs in the wild area of your garden can provide nesting habitats for a wide range of species. By planting groups of shrubs close together, you can achieve a really cosy tangle of growth, with weaker plants tending to fill in the area under the stronger ones. Shrubs that are especially suitable are the prickly sort which will provide protection against cats, currawongs and misguided egg collectors. The prickly moses wattles (such as *Acacia paradoxa*), the Kangaroo Thorn (*A. verticillata*), the spiky hakeas (like *H. sericea*) and blackthorn (*Bursaria spinosa*) are all excellent nesting shrubs. *Grevillea rosmarinifolia* and some of its cultivars give reasonable shelter – with the bonus of nectar.

Many banksias have the habit of sprouting several shoots from one point once they have flowered – producing a shape like the ribs of an upside-down umbrella. This means each well-grown plant will have dozens of possible nest sites as well as a profusion of nectar supplies. Particularly suitable banksia species are *B. integrifolia*, *B. ericifolia* and *B. serrata*.

GROUND FLOOR APARTMENTS

Although most birds prefer to nest well off the ground, some species can happily build their nests at ground level. The best way to provide for such species is to grow tussock-forming grasses such as the Red Anther Wallaby Grass (*Danthonia pallida*), Snow Grass (*Poa larbillardieri*) and Kangaroo Grass (*Themeda triandra* [*australis*]) and to ensure that the shrub layer is dense all the way to ground level. White-browed Scrubwrens and Superb Fairy-wrens will use the lowest layers of the shrub area, with the scrubwrens also occupying tussocks near the shrub layer. Richard's Pipits love to nest in tussocks –

PROVIDING A NESTING GARDEN

Little Wattlebirds like to nest in a low dense bush that helps hide their chicks.

although finding their invisible nests with their precious cargo of greenish speckled eggs is a real feat.

It can also be useful to have areas of short grass or gravel for plovers to use, but these areas need to be quite large (tens of metres wide) before they are suitable. If you have enough habitat area to attract plovers they can make fascinating house guests. Watching them dive-bomb other creatures who intrude too close to their chicks can be quite a spectacle.

Plovers' nests are reasonably easy to find because you can see one of the birds sitting on the same spot each day, but their chicks are another matter. The baby birds leave the nest very soon after hatching and are led by their parents to a grass or gravel area where the chicks can catch their own food. They look a lot like furry golf balls on legs, but as soon as they stop moving, their camouflage is so good they just seem to disappear. The best way to see them is to sit quietly at least 50m away from the parents and just watch. After a while the parents will relax and the chicks, who earlier froze when you approached, will start moving around. You might be able to walk up to one and have a close look, but bear in mind that the parents will start diving within inches of your head as soon as you are too close – and they don't call these birds spur-winged for nothing!

OTHER NESTING SITES

A well-trained creeper can be an excellent nesting site for a range of birds, like Silvereyes and Double-barred Finches, which prefer the shrubbier areas of a garden. Creepers are especially attractive to birds if they can be grown in a quiet corner. Birds tend to nest between the creeper and the fence, so it's a good idea to train the vine on battens nailed to the fence to increase the nesting area behind the vine. One of the best vines is Traveller's Joy (*Clematis aristata*), so named because the aroma from the crushed leaves is supposed to ease headaches. The Wonga-wonga Vine (*Pandorea pandorana*) and its relative *P. jasminoides* are showy climbers which provide some nectar as well as good nesting sites. The *Tecomanthe hillii*, a vigorous Queensland climber with impressive orange trumpet flowers, is also great.

Termite nests in trees can make excellent nest sites for kookaburras and kingfishers (and the odd goanna!). While it might be a frightening thought to tolerate these potential home-wreckers in your backyard, tree-dwelling termites rarely attack houses. It's the ones that live on the ground that you need to worry about.

ARTIFICIAL NESTING SITES

If you wait long enough, your trees will mature into majestic specimens with lots of nice hollows. The problem with this is that a decent eucalypt will take about three times more than your lifetime to mature. While you're waiting, artificial sites can be an excellent way to attract passing birds.

Nest boxes are also great if you prefer not to have dead branches decorating your garden trees but would still like to provide hollows for the birds. They can also be an excellent educational source for children and it's an exciting time when the first birds take up residence in one of these nesting boxes.

Australia has more hollow-nesting birds than most other countries. Nearly one in five of our birds

Magpie-larks have adapted so well to life in the suburbs that you will even find them nesting on electrical installations. Here the male is feeding one of the chicks.

PROVIDING A NESTING GARDEN

uses hollows compared to about one in ten in South Africa and North America, so nest boxes can be a particularly useful garden attribute here. Boxes can be built and sited to suit the individual tastes of the various birds that like to visit gardens. They are particularly useful in smaller gardens where there isn't space for hollow trees, but can also be valuable in larger or established gardens – because hollows are always in short supply.

NESTING LOGS

No Australian birds are capable of hollowing out anything harder than a termite mound, so all nesting logs need to be hollow to start with. From time to time hollow logs are available from garden centres, but the supply isn't always reliable so it may be better to make your own. Of course, the best place to find natural hollow logs is in the bush but in that environment, they are valuable to the local wildlife. If the hollows are to be destroyed by clearing or by firewood collection, then rescuing them for the garden is a good idea.

Most parrots like a vertical hollow with a hole at the top of one side, while kingfishers and kookaburras like a horizontal one with the hole at the end. Striated Pardalotes and some of the thornbills don't mind which way the log is oriented. Generally, the higher the location of the nesting log the better; few logs lower than head height will be used by birds.

Attach the log to a tree by wrapping galvanised wire firmly around each end of the log. It's a worthwhile exercise to protect the tree by padding the wire with hessian. As breeding is less likely between January and March, this is the best time to adjust the wire to allow for the tree's growth. You can also use galvanised chains, tensioned with a substantial galvanised spring at least 2cm in diameter. To shelter the nesting log, attach it to the tree trunk so it is under a branch or fix it to the underside of the branch itself. For better weather protection, nail a flat marine ply roof onto the log or attach it to the wall of your house under the eaves.

MAKING YOUR OWN NESTING LOGS

A nesting log is easier to make with softwood, like pine or white cedar, but the logs will last longer if they are made from hardwood.

To make an average-sized hollow log, select a branch at least 20cm wide and cut off a length at least 50cm long. Cut off a 3cm slice from one end and hollow out a cavity in the log, leaving the bottom intact. This can be done with a combination of power drill, hammer and chisel. If you're a good shot with a chain saw, the sky's the limit. Once the centre is hollowed out, use waterproof glue and galvanised nails to re-attach the end you sawed off. Drill out an entrance hole at the top of one of the sides.

The size of entrance hole depends on the species you want to house. If you're not sure, somewhere between 7cm and 10cm in diameter is a good compromise. Smaller birds like Scaly-breasted Lorikeets need a smaller hole, about 6cm, while birds the size of kookaburras like an entrance of about 15cm in diameter.

Ducks prefer much larger hollow logs with an entrance of about 17cm and an internal diameter of at least 35cm – quite a carpentry job! Duck nesting logs need to be placed vertically near wetland areas. Make sure the log is attached to a solid post or tree, with the ends firmly secured.

Nesting logs in various shapes and sizes are made to suit different birds.

NEST BOXES

Nest boxes might not look as natural as hollow logs, but they are a whole lot easier to make and seem to be just as attractive to birds, bats and other wildlife. Traditional budgie or Cockatiel (quarrion) nest boxes from the pet shop are quite suitable for similar-sized wild birds as long as the boxes are painted well to protect them from the weather. Building your own boxes is very satisfying, and they can be tailored to the needs of particular species.

The important points about nest boxes are that:
• the entrance hole is the right size for the species in question;
• the internal size will accommodate a nest full of chicks and the shape is right for the species;
• they are well insulated, especially against overheating, and don't allow rain or light in;
• you can check them and evict pest species;
• they will last in all types of weather;
• they are securely attached to their supports in a way that leaves trees unrestricted;
• the hollow is either vertical or horizontal, depending on the needs of local bird species.

A more open nest box will appeal to shrike-thrushes, doves and the odd possum! Follow the instructions overleaf but use a shorter front panel (about 120mm) without an entrance hole.

Sparrows can make an absolute mess of finch nest boxes. It is best to evict them before things develop to this stage!

It's important to get the size right for the bird you have in mind, especially the entrance hole. Birds like an entrance they can just fit through so unwelcome visitors like goannas can't get at their eggs or chicks. A good trick with parrots is to make the hole a bit bigger than the birds need, and then cover it with a piece of thin plywood, with a hole that's too small in the middle. The birds will invariably use their powerful beaks to enlarge the hole to their exact needs – so ensuring a perfect fit. Of course, this won't work with birds like thornbills, ducks or kingfishers, which don't share parrots' impressive beak power.

Generally, the box should be several times higher or longer than it is wide. For birds such as parrots, who like a vertical nest box, they can hop in the entrance and then climb down inside, onto the bottom where they feel safe. For birds that prefer a horizontal box, like kookaburras, the hole should be at the end so the bird goes through the hole and then walks along the floor to the end of the box.

The inside of the box needs to provide enough footholds so the birds can climb up and down easily. You can make sure of this by nailing fine wire mesh or pencil-thickness wooden slats to the inside of the box. Naturally hollow trees are sufficiently rough for the bird to get an easy grip for perching, but dressed timber is too smooth. Most birds need a perch attached to the outside of the box, just below the entrance.

The table opposite gives some suggestions for nest box dimensions, but they are only approximate as some birds nest in any place that takes their fancy.

Nest boxes are best when made out of wood, but you can use other material like ferro-cement, pottery or even fibreglass or plastic. Whatever you choose, the important aspects are that the box is as well-insulated as possible, especially from overheating, and that the materials will last through all types of weather. Don't use metal boxes – if birds lay their eggs in spring, the metal can cause chicks to become heat-exhausted in summer.

PROVIDING A NESTING GARDEN

Suggested Nest Box Sizes

Species	Entrance diameter (cm)	Inside diameter (cm)	Orientation + horizontal/ vertical	Preferred* location
Pardalotes	4	13	H**	L–M
Thornbills				
Buff-rumped	4	13	V	L
Chestnut-rumped	4	13	V	L–M
SMALL PARROTS				
Red-rumped Parrot	6	14	either	M
Scaly-breasted Lorikeet	6	14	V	H
Cockatiel	7	15	V	L–M
Rainbow Lorikeet	7	15	either	M–H
Sacred Kingfisher	7	15	H	M
Dollarbird	7	15	V	H
MEDIUM PARROTS				
Rosellas	8	20	V	H
King Parrot	9	24	V	H
Superb Parrot	8	25	V	H
Ringneck Parrot	8	24	either	M–H
Boobook Owl	12	40	V	M–H
Barn Owl	12	45	either	M–H
LARGE PARROTS				
Sulphur-crested Cockatoo	15	30	V	M–H
Little Corella	14	25	V	M
Galah	12	22	V	M–H
Gang-gang Cockatoo	12	22	V	H
Laughing Kookaburra	14	30	H	M–H
Ducks	16	35	V	L–H

* Preferred locations. These figures are approximate only.
  For instance, Sulphur-crested Cockatoos will nest from 2m to 18m off the ground!

+ Vertical nest boxes have a hole at the top of one of the sides.
  Horizontal ones have the hole at the end.

** Need a 30cm entrance with a 4cm-wide tunnel.

H   high (10m or more)
M   medium (3–10m)
L   low (1–3m)

PROVIDING A NESTING GARDEN

As the name suggests, Barn Owls are often attracted to buildings, where they like to nest in the roof spaces.

BARN OWLS

Barn Owls enjoy nesting in shed roofs and garages, as well as in natural tree hollows. These birds are deadly to rats and have the uncanny ability to swoop accurately on a rodent being guided only by the faint sounds of the animal scuttling through leaves.

Having a hungry family of up to seven Barn Owls in the garage means you get excellent pest control as well as the fascination of an unusual creature nesting on your property. In the roof of the house it is not so good! This is very unlikely, but if it happens where you live try to put up with the birds until they have left the nest. It only takes about two months and then you can block up the access to the roof and build a Barn Owl nest box in the garage for the next year.

A clutch of hungry Barn Owl chicks may number up to seven – news that's bound to make local rats nervous!

HOW TO BUILD A STANDARD NEST BOX

This box can be used by a variety of wonderful birds, including rosellas, lorikeets and Red-rumped Parrots.

Materials
20mm-thick treated pine or other outdoor timber
waterproof wood glue
30mm brass wood screws
outdoor timber finish – clear or coloured
hole sawing device (such as brace and bit or hole saw)
try square.

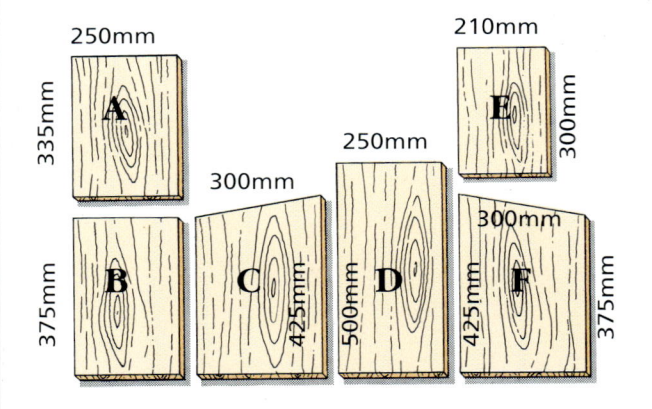

A: 250mm × 335mm
B: 300mm × 375mm
C: 300mm × 425mm
D: 250mm × 500mm
E: 210mm × 300mm
F: 300mm × 425mm / 375mm

Cut the timber into six pieces A–F as shown above

On the back panel (D) mark the positions of the side panels (C and F), using the try square (above).

Glue side panels (C and F) to back (D) and screw together while the glue is wet (right). Attach base (E) to sides and back using glue and screws.

PROVIDING A NESTING GARDEN

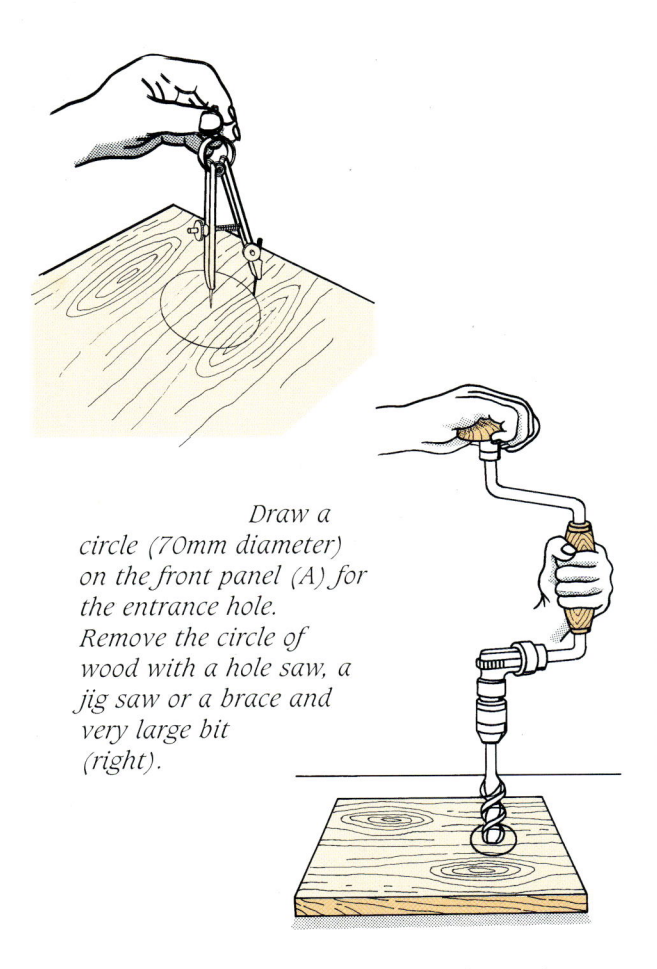

Draw a circle (70mm diameter) on the front panel (A) for the entrance hole. Remove the circle of wood with a hole saw, a jig saw or a brace and very large bit (right).

Glue and screw the front panel (A), then the roof (B). Seal any cracks with a gap-filling glue and give three coats of the surface finish, lightly sanding with fine paper between coats.

If you want to keep an eye on the breeding cycle, you can hinge the lid with a piece of brass piano hinge or even a strip of rubber. Lift the lid only when the parents are away, or you risk them deserting the nest.

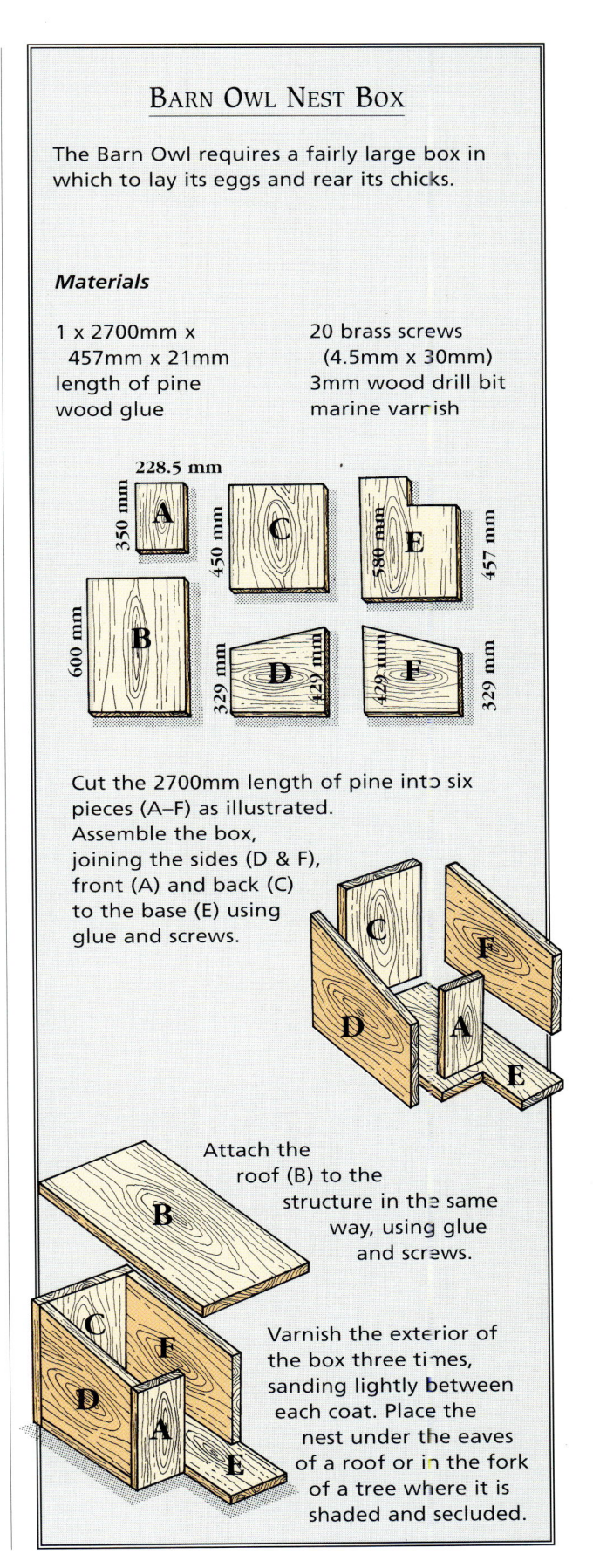

BARN OWL NEST BOX

The Barn Owl requires a fairly large box in which to lay its eggs and rear its chicks.

Materials

1 x 2700mm x 457mm x 21mm length of pine
wood glue

20 brass screws (4.5mm x 30mm)
3mm wood drill bit
marine varnish

Cut the 2700mm length of pine into six pieces (A–F) as illustrated. Assemble the box, joining the sides (D & F), front (A) and back (C) to the base (E) using glue and screws.

Attach the roof (B) to the structure in the same way, using glue and screws.

Varnish the exterior of the box three times, sanding lightly between each coat. Place the nest under the eaves of a roof or in the fork of a tree where it is shaded and secluded.

59

Exterior ply is fine and marine ply is very strong, but expensive. Many types of plywood have toxic glues, so it's advisable to leave the box in the hot sun for a few weeks so that the harmful chemicals evaporate. Most types of particle board are best kept indoors. In the rain, they will turn soggy – no matter what you paint them with. Sawmill face cuts with the bark still attached look great and the bark provides insulation, even if the unequal dimensions tax your woodworking skills. Because they are sapwood you need to choose particularly long-lasting timbers, like red gum, tallowwood, jarrah or cypress pine. Ideally, the wood should be at least 20mm thick for insulation, although this isn't always possible.

To hold the box together use waterproof glue and galvanised nails (cement-coated are the best), and metal strips to reinforce the joints if you're not so confident with your carpentry skills. Screws are okay but they don't hold as well as nails in the end grain. Then give the box several coats of exterior water-based paint in natural colours. Don't paint the entrance as many birds will idly chew on this and paint is not good for their digestion!

Putting some old termite mound (without the former occupants) or old sawdust in the bottom of the box can make it more natural and attractive to birds, and a few drainage holes in the bottom will let out any water that gets in. If possible, include a hinged lid or small inspection hatch so you can evict pests like sparrows, starlings, Common Mynas or feral bees. Inspection hatches will also allow you to take a peep at the baby birds but, as has been mentioned previously, make sure you do this only when the parents are away, and even then, don't do it more than once a week or so to minimise the chances of scaring the parents into deserting the nest. The lids need to be set up so that they are kept closed by gravity and a catch, or by a spring system to deal with windy days.

Unless you live on a very cold, south-facing slope, the box needs to be somewhere shady to avoid overheating. January to March is not usually breeding time so this is the best period during which to clean the inside of the box. This will ensure you get rid of any bird-biting mites and will make the box more attractive the following season.

If bees take up residence, you can get rid of them by putting a pest strip in through the entrance hole. This is best done very late at night with a pole or fishing rod at least 3m long and a torch with a red filter (bees don't see red very well). After a week or so, the bees will be gone. If that sounds too much like a *Fawlty Towers* script, contact a beekeeper through your State agriculture department. The bees can be zapped or even taken away for productive use. Once the bees have gone, clean the inside of the box with methylated spirits to get rid of bee smells which will attract bees in the swarming season next spring.

Finally, it's okay if your offer of accommodation hasn't received any takers in the first few months. Many birds start looking for nest sites as early as late autumn and winter, so it might take until next season or even the one after for the box to be occupied.

EXTRAORDINARY NESTS

Some birds choose amazing nest sites and even use a range of artificial objects. There are records of a White-throated Treecreeper using an old kettle as a nest site and swallows nesting in fireplaces and traffic lights and even on a boat in the Hawkesbury River in New South Wales. You can hear Wood Ducks doing their low cackling 'come-and-see-my-nest-hollow' call from suburban chimney pots and starlings have been known to nest on a sheep's back! If birds use even the silliest objects for nests, they are certainly likely to avail themselves of your well-thought-out nest boxes.

Birds don't always nest in trees or shrubs – spots like this time-worn niche with its tangled vines have great potential.

PROVIDING A NESTING GARDEN

NESTING MATERIAL

Birds use their excellent vision to find nesting material, even in the suburbs. Some, like magpies, can adapt to human landscapes by building nests entirely out of wire, and many urban birds such as currawongs and wattlebirds seem to find it easy to gather sufficient nest material in the average backyard. You can still make it easier for our feathered friends by ensuring a good supply of nesting material, which a well-designed garden certainly will provide. Bark from stringybarks and tallowwoods (*Eucalyptus microcorys*) is great for nest linings or, in the case of pardalotes, for whole nests. Twigs from many native shrubs such as tea-trees (*Leptospermum* sp.) form the foundation of many nests. Try to leave dead branches and twigs in place. You can even gather up dead branches and stand them up at the back of the shrub area where they are out of sight

Doves are especially adaptable where nesting sites are concerned. Even an old headlight makes a cosy home.

FEATHERING THE NEST

You can give birds a helping hand during the breeding season by offering a range of natural and artificial nesting materials. Piles of suitable material should be left at various spots in the garden where they are out of reach of cats but easily accessible to the birds.

Each species needs its own nesting materials, so whatever you provide, there is likely to be a local bird that will use it. Keep trying different items until you find the most popular ones.

Below: Body feathers are used to line many nests. They are soft and provide essential insulation to help keep the eggs warm.
Below centre: Twigs and sticks are the foundation of most nests and are popular with a wide range of birds.
Right, top and bottom: Nesting birds love pulling threads from scraps of fabric. Don't use polyester, nylon or any thread that is not easily broken as it may end up wrapped around a chick's legs and cause some very unpleasant problems. A loosely woven bag of goodies hung in a tree makes the birds' task much easier.

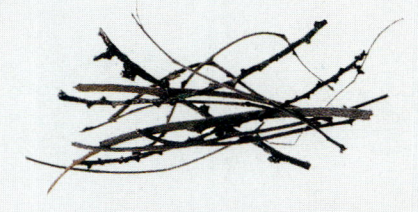

PROVIDING A NESTING GARDEN

Yellow Robins often use sticky strands from spider webs to attach pieces of bark and other camouflage to their nests.

but still available for birds. Long grasses and pieces of palm frond are popular with many birds including fairy-wrens and finches.

Spider webs are an indispensable glueing agent for the nests of many species including cuckoo-shrikes, fantails, Willie Wagtails and honeyeaters. This means it's a good idea to be nice to web-building garden spiders – all of which are pretty harmless.

Mud-nesting birds such as peewits and Fairy Martins will enjoy gathering mud on the edge of the wetland area.

Even if your garden already offers a range of nesting materials, you can often improve on nature by hanging up a small plastic or string bag with some extra nesting goodies. Feathers, grass, fur or scraps of material can be very attractive to nesting birds, and watching them extracting their various treasures can be fascinating. Just make sure any material is cut into lengths of only a few centimetres so there are no threads that can get caught around the baby birds' legs.

Don't be tempted to stuff nesting material into a nesting log or nest box. Like people, birds enjoy designing their own accommodation, and many birds such as parrots, kingfishers and kookaburras like a fairly bare hollow without any extra material at all.

BABY BIRDS IN THE GARDEN

Having a new addition to the garden bird population and watching a fledgling's first fluttering flights can be quite exciting. You might have an irresistible desire to help, but don't – especially if it looks like a chick has been deserted. Once the fledglings are flapping about the garden, parent birds often leave them for up to an hour at a time. Well-meaning people sometimes try to interfere at this point, but it is seldom necessary. Trying to pick up baby birds will only make the parents crazy and frighten the baby – just let nature take its course.

If you are really concerned that a chick may have been abandoned, you need to watch it for at least an hour from as far away as possible so you don't scare the parents away from it. If no parent comes in that time, the bird may well be abandoned. Watch it for another half-hour or so and if it's still alone, it probably needs looking after. You'll need to get some expert help from a wildlife rescue group like WIRES, which you can contact through your local national parks or wildlife authority office.

Until help arrives keep the bird in a warm, dark, quiet place – a cardboard box lined with newspaper makes a reasonable temporary home. Good sources of warmth include the radiating surface at the back of the refrigerator (prop the box on top, between the

Nankeen Kestrels will create a breeding spot in abandoned nests, in tree or cliff hollows and even on city building ledges.

PROVIDING A NESTING GARDEN

refrigerator and the wall), electric blankets or a carefully monitored lamp shone on the outside of the box from close range. It's best not to try feeding the bird but you can offer it some rehydration fluid using a teaspoon. Make the fluid by mixing a teaspoon of sugar and a pinch of salt into a cup of warm water.

A Willie Wagtail and chicks.

If you're a long way from help, try to give the bird its natural food, but this is really a job for experts. Baby seed eaters can't crack their own seeds and need you to do this for them. If you prefer not to chew seeds, you can also use a mixture of wholemeal bread and plain cake (with lots of eggs).

If a chick falls out of the nest it is usually okay to put it back in – provided the nest isn't too high. If it's a magpie or butcherbird nest, you need to put on some robust headgear to protect yourself from its anxious parents. If the whole nest has blown down in storms, it's still fairly easy to save the day. The babies are usually fine – you just need to make sure you get the nest back into the tree within a few hours of it blowing down. Rebuilding it usually isn't an option. You can nail an ice-cream container or small basket as close as you can to the original site and put the babies in with as much of the nest as you can. The hungry chicks will call for food and it seldom takes the parents long to relocate them.

BIRD REHABILITATION

Getting birds back into their natural environment can take an enormous amount of ability, time and money and is best handled by those who know what they're doing. The intricacies of rehabilitating birds are best illustrated by the example of an abandoned kite chick.

Kites, hawks, owls and eagles require a balanced diet of mice and birds to provide the roughage and nutrients they need to develop properly. Using substitute foods can cause serious damage. Once the kite chick is older it needs to learn to hunt for itself. The ancient European technique of falconry is the best way to teach it.

When the chick can catch mice in a large cage, it is transferred into a 'hacking' cage. This is an enclosure in an area where the bird's natural prey is plentiful. One end of the cage is open so the bird can fly out to hunt. In the cage, food is provided so the bird will be okay if it doesn't catch enough. Usually after a few weeks, the bird will be able to look after itself.

This process, termed 'hacking' the bird back into the wild, can be very successful if sufficient time and expertise is put into it.

Kites and falcons need roughage from fur or feathers to develop properly.

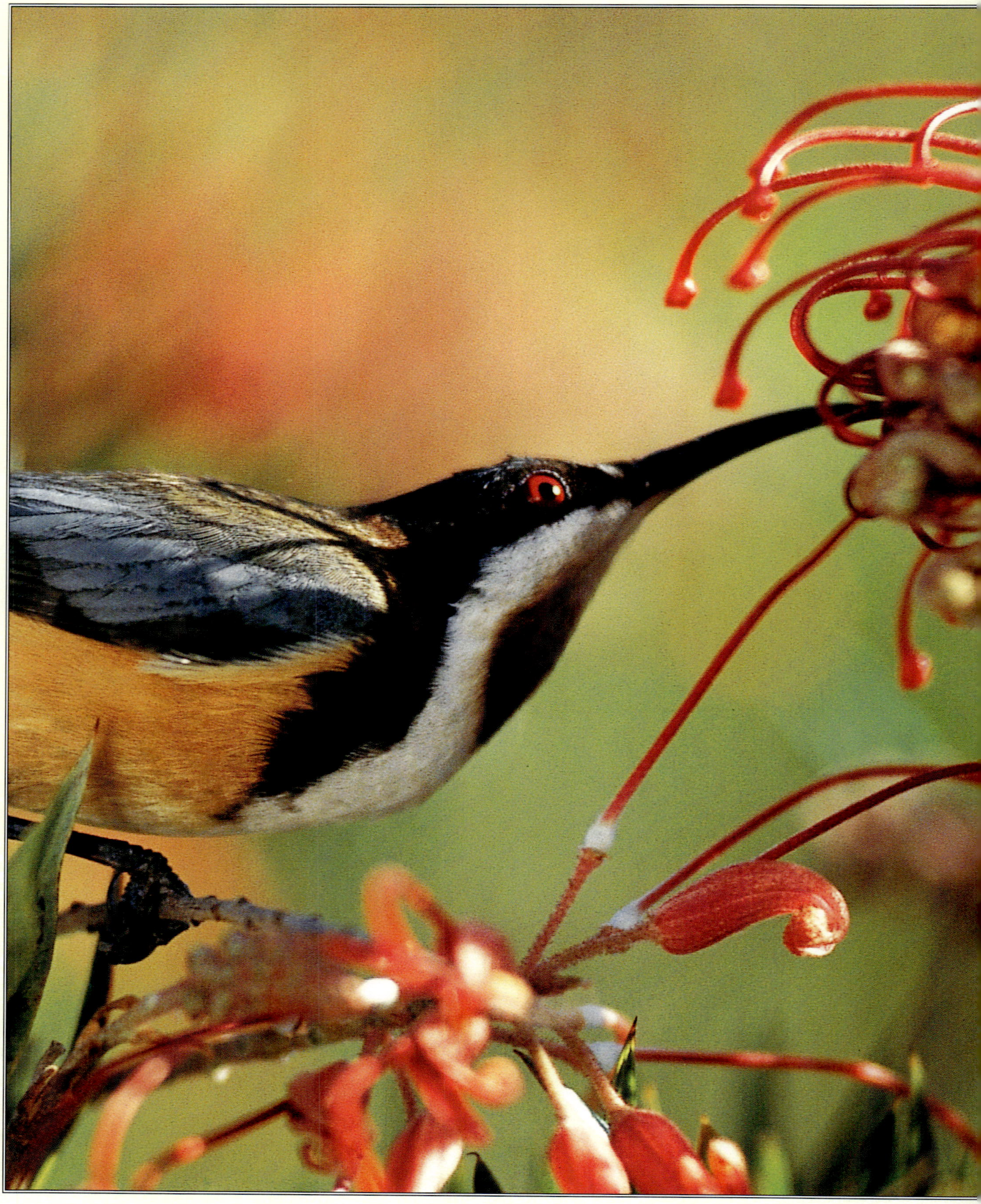

CHAPTER 5

MAINTAINING AN INDIGENOUS GARDEN

There's no shortage of myths about Australian plants, their growth patterns and their requirements. Despite a reputation of being rugged specimens best left alone, most of these plants respond well to care and attention. In many cases, they look a lot better than their exotic cousins – who often make an awkward fit in Australian environments. Native plants are an absolutely vital ingredient in any Australian garden planned to attract birds.

The habits of the Eastern Spinebill are similar to those of hummingbirds.

Until recently, the tradition with Australian plants was to stick them in the ground and leave them to grow naturally. While this can create a wild look, it can also lead to rows of scrawny plants that do little for the aesthetics of the garden and don't offer much to birds either. Both human and bird visitors will be more impressed if the garden has been given a bit of attention.

MAINTAINING AN INDIGENOUS GARDEN

Indigenous plants have been evolving happily on the Australian continent ever since it broke away from the supercontinent of Gondwana about 55 million years ago, so it is no surprise that they have adapted to the vagaries of our erratic climate. If you're a plant, Australia is a pretty tough place in which to live. In many parts of the country plants live an austere life, presenting an endless vista of grey or yellow-green tones and little else. However, there are groups of indigenous plants with fantastic horticultural potential, such as the banksias, grevilleas, hakeas, kangaroo paws and Gymea Lilies.

In recent times selective breeding has produced some outstanding cultivars of Australian plants and there is now a range of stunning grevilleas that flower virtually all year, kangaroo paws that thrive even in the moist eastern States, and banksias with the biggest glowing golden cones you've ever seen. Despite their impressive flowers, these improved varieties still give a garden a wonderful bushland feel and, of course, they are like biological magnets for lorikeets, honeyeaters and other birds.

AUSTRALIAN PLANTS

At one stage it was widely believed that indigenous plants lived only in poor sandy soils, didn't like fertilisers, grew slowly, hardly needed water and made the garden look unkempt – apart from that, they were alright! While there are indigenous (and exotic) plants that like these conditions, most of the ones available from garden nurseries do not.

Horticulturists seldom have the time to propagate plants that have such specific requirements, so cultivated indigenous plants are becoming more and more suited to the conditions found in the average nursery or garden. The idea that indigenous plants are slow-growing is also less than accurate. Plants that grow slowly are not economically viable for most nurseries so they leave them to specialised plant collectors.

The Giant Candles Banksia is renowned as one of the best nectar producers. During winter, many plants literally drip nectar.

MAINTAINING AN INDIGENOUS GARDEN

Australian plants are a great resource for most gardens, whether used solely or together with introduced varieties. Before choosing indigenous plants, find out about the specific requirements of the ones you prefer. For instance, planting a Giant Candles Banksia in a wet area will probably kill it in a few weeks, whereas its close relative, the Swamp Banksia (*Banksia robur*), will certainly thrive. All plants need minimum growing requirements before they do well, and the larger Australian plant nurseries are generally a good place to find out which plants go with what conditions.

MANAGING AUSTRALIAN PLANTS

Indigenous plants can be arranged so that they look either totally wild or more formal and planned.

UNTAMED GARDENS

To many gardeners, especially those of a decade ago, growing a completely untamed garden of local species was the ultimate achievement. Such gardens were great for birds and for conserving the local ecosystems, but they didn't suit everyone. In such a 'hands-off' garden, it's important to select exactly the right species because the aim is to put in the plants and just sit back while they find their own niche in the tangle. Propagating local species is probably the most effective approach for a garden like this and by planting large numbers of them you generally get the best results. For most people, however, the untamed wild look is a thing of the past or only for the wild area of a garden.

Above: *Ned Kelly grevilleas provide shelter and a good supply of nectar for honeyeaters.*
Left: *Bottlebrushes are easily pollinated by birds.*

This untamed garden presents a good lower canopy habitat. Some sunny areas would be useful – with a few nectar-producing grevilleas and banksias to attract the birds.

THE MANAGED INDIGENOUS GARDEN

Those interested in Australian plants and wildlife may have already gone through the stage of planting indigenous shrubs and watching contentedly as they slowly grew to a satisfactory size. You would have seen the plants grow a bit more, then a bit more; and then the lower areas would have become really open and scrawny. At this stage you either pulled them out or chopped them back. These days, most of us recognise that Australian plants, like their European cousins, look a whole lot better when they are given some care as they grow.

Indigenous plants that are sensibly fertilised and watered often produce flowers and a canopy of leaves more effectively than those that are just left to their own devices. They are better for birds, better for the garden and better for your real estate value.

Some Australian plants don't like being pruned. Pinching out the growing tip early in the season or regular light pruning is often the best approach.

Pruning

Many indigenous plants can be improved by pruning. There's a temptation to think that pruning isn't a natural process, but it is. Most plants in the bush are nibbled from time to time by everything from insects to wallabies. In fact, not pruning can lead to all sorts of problems. Apart from creating plants that look scrawny, a lack of pruning on plants that grow in rich soils can lead to them growing minimal roots but lots of top growth. This can be disastrous when a windy day arrives in the middle of a rainy period. You may step outside to find your plant sprawled across the driveway. It is much better to prune your plants, thus ensuring that the roots are able to support the foliage in any weather.

Some species will accept a really heavy pruning, which can be useful if the plant becomes too tall and no longer provides the screen around the base that it once did. However, some species are either killed by such treatment or will sulk for years and stagnate, so the trick is to find out which is which.

Plants that can handle serious pruning include many banksias,

Waratahs are one of the best bird-attracting flowers. Modern cultivars are suitable for growing either in sun or shade.

waratahs (*Telopea speciosissima*), Christmas Bush (*Ceratopetalum gummiferum*), some eucalypts and some bottlebrushes (*Callistemon* sp.). All of these grow from a lumpy root structure called a lignotuber, or have emergency shoots under the bark as a way of dealing with bushfires. With many of these species, you can cut the entire plant off at ground level and it will generally re-sprout, just as it does after a bushfire.

Most eucalypts contain hundreds of these emergency dormant buds under the bark, thus making them resilient to bushfires and other disasters. They can also tolerate heavy pruning – although if a branch is lopped off, the 'epicormic' shoots that sprout from the cut end are seldom as strong as the original branch and are liable to blow off in a storm. Callistemons are also quite capable of sprouting back after radical surgery. Many grevilleas can withstand heavy pruning although they don't always shrug it off as well as other species.

Species that don't like heavy pruning include most wattles (*Acacia* sp.), she-oaks (*Casuarina* sp.), tea-trees (*Leptospermum* sp.), and mint bushes (*Prostanthera* sp.).

The sneakiest way of all to deal with plants that have become too tall and scraggly is not to prune but to bend. Tying branches into new locations is a great alternative to chopping them back. You get the shape you require without having to wait for the branch to regrow. This doesn't always work, but if you have a plant that you're not happy with, have a go at bending it into the right shape before you resort to the secateurs or the pruning saw. Of course if you look after the plants from the beginning, you won't need to resort to chopping or bending.

There are two great ways to prune native plants. The first is to cut back just behind the flowers once they are finished. With callistemons, this means you cut off the shoot that has sprouted from the end of the flower, but it will soon be replaced with several new ones – each of which will flower during the next year or sooner.

MAINTAINING AN INDIGENOUS GARDEN

The second approach is just to pinch off the growing tip when the plant gets to the height at which you would like it to branch. Tip pruning is the most natural approach and the one that has the least impact on plants. All it requires is that you have a vision of how you want the plant to eventually look.

Finally, don't prune if frost is expected in the next few months or so. Any new growth that results from pruning is often frost-tender and encouraging growth when frosts are possible is a recipe for trouble.

Watering

Although some Australian plants can survive for long periods without water in the wild, many of the popular species such as callistemons come from riverside areas and like a lot of water. Even plants that come from drier areas will mostly grow faster if they are watered well.

Young plants like this Silky Oak (Grevillea robusta) *should be watered thoroughly once a week or so to encourage deep root growth, which results in a stronger plant.*

Watering works best if it is done at intervals and enough water is applied to really soak the soil. This method imitates the natural rain pattern and the plant's roots are encouraged to grow deeply into the soil, making it stable and keeping the roots away from the surface where they are vulnerable to rapid drying out. Drip irrigation systems are another way to ensure that watering is done in the most effective way. They direct the water into the soil where it is needed, and not into the air where it is usually wasted. You can even get timing devices that will turn the drippers on and off without you having to remember. Ferns are the main exception to this as they love humidity and water on their leaves, so a misting system is better than drippers in an area featuring a profusion of ferns.

Covering the garden with a thick layer of mulch is a great way to reduce the garden's water needs and it also helps to control weeds. Any of the usual shredded plant mulches are fine as long as they don't contain weeds. Rocks and gravel are also useful as good mulches.

Plants are fairly conservative organisms and once they adapt to a particular watering regime, they don't like changes, so decide how you will approach this aspect of gardening and stick to it. An interesting example of this is when a sewerage system is being installed in a suburb. Instead of all those delicious plant nutrients and water going into the soil via the septic system, they are suddenly carried away down a sewer pipe. If this happens, you need to increase the level of watering in the area where the septic tank used to be for about a year or so until the plants get used to their new environment.

Soil Conditions

Soil conditions are a vital aspect of watering and fertilising. The soil needs to be able to store water without becoming waterlogged. Some soils do this quite well, but sandy or clay soils need a lot of help.

Sandy soils drain well, but also dry out quickly. To combat this, add lots of organic matter like compost, which will help the soil to hold water and also add some nutrients. Clay soils have reasonable nutrient levels but drain badly and don't have any little cracks and crevices to allow the plant roots to penetrate.

Seed-raising mixtures for most Australian plants need to be free-draining.

Digging in lots of organic matter is great for improving these soils. You could also treat them with gypsum which will bind the clay particles together so air and water can penetrate between the clumps.

Another way to combat the problem of bad drainage is to plant clay-tolerant plant species, such as many of the callistemons and melaleucas. Otherwise build up beds of better soil on top of the clay layer – just make sure you don't dig a hole into the clay layer for your chosen plant. The hole will fill up with water and form a deadly underground pool that will kill the roots. In such areas, build up the soil around the plant so it drains well.

Fertilising

As with watering, indigenous plants are more likely to grow better if they are fertilised. Organic fertilisers are best for most indigenous plants, as are the slow-release ones. Well-rotted manure is also good, but it would probably be preferable to avoid chicken manure from battery hens. This can be very high in phosphate and the sawdust residues were probably once treated chemically. Neither of these properties is very good for Australian plants. It is especially important to avoid putting too much phosphate on banksias, grevilleas, hakeas and boronias.

WHEN TO PLANT

Autumn and spring are generally the best times to plant. Most failed attempts at planting are because of a lack of water, so autumn is usually better than spring as the plants will get a chance to establish themselves long before the harsh summer conditions arrive. In higher areas of south-east Australia, winter frosts can also be a problem; as a result spring may be the best time to plant. It's also particularly important to give new plants a chance to adapt to the garden conditions. Remember, they have just come from the nursery where they had a very easy beginning with lots of nutrients, water and just the right temperatures to assist their growth.

If for some reason you do have to sow a plant in summer, you can protect it by placing mulch around it, by creating shade over it with a hessian bag or other material supported by stakes, and by very vigilant watering, preferably every day if it is hot, windy weather. If it is winter, the solutions are similar – lots of mulch and some insulation by using a hessian bag on stakes, possibly packed with straw around the base of the plant.

HOW TO PLANT

Planting successfully is fairly straightforward, so long as you follow a few guidelines. The hole needs to be about twice the size of the plant's root ball and deep enough so that the surface of the soil in the pot lines up with the bed's soil surface. Aerate the soil in the bottom of the hole and for a metre around it using a fork or pick, but don't overdo it and damage the soil's structure by turning it over too much.

Both the ground and the pot need to be moist but not so wet that working the soil creates a texture like mud bricks once it dries. Some potting mixes develop dry spots that are hard to wet again. The best way to deal with this is to soak the pot in a bucket of water for a few hours before planting it. If the garden soil is dry, fill the

When removing plants from pots, hold them as shown so that the root ball is not broken up.

hole with water and allow it to drain away before placing the plant. Hold the pot upside down with one hand placed firmly over the soil to keep it in place and gently tap the rim downwards until the plant pops out into your hand. If the roots are curled around the pot, tease them out straight or cut them off. If you leave them, they'll keep on circling and thickening until they strangle themselves and the plant might die.

Once the plant is in the hole, refill it firmly with the soil you dug out, enriched with well-rotted compost or a slow-release fertiliser. This encourages the new roots to grow into the backfill and eventually into the surrounding aerated soil.

Make a dished area around the plant, a bit larger than the pot was, to ensure that watering penetrates deeply into the root area. The soil forming the dish can be spread out evenly after a year or so. Water the plant well. If you like, you can add some root hormone for the first watering to promote growth from the damaged root ends.

WHERE TO FIND PLANTS

Many of the major garden centres include some indigenous plants, but not always in prominent locations. You may have to do a bit of hunting to find the ones you want. A smaller nursery that specialises in native plants could be the best place to start; you're also more likely to find someone who'll be able to advise which plant will do well in your area. Some State forestry departments and, of course, the Society for Growing Australian Plants might also be able to help.

When you wander around the nursery, beware of plants that are already flowering beautifully. Such plants are probably pot-bound with their roots hopelessly entangled, winding themselves around the inside of the pot. These plants will flower nicely at a small size, but will seldom do very well in the garden. You're better off choosing a plant that is growing strongly and not yet ready to flower.

The other temptation to avoid is buying large plants. If you get smaller ones, you get more plant for your money. More importantly, the plant will handle transplanting much better than the larger ones. This point can be best demonstrated by two of my neighbours who each bought a Sydney Red Gum (*Angophora costata*). The first bought a handsome 60cm plant in a pot, the other a tiny 20cm seedling in a tube. At the end of the first year the 60cm plant was 85cm tall but the 20cm plant had sprouted to 55cm. At the end of the third year, the 60cm plant was 120cm while the 20cm plant was 126cm! Younger plants adjust better to new environments and therefore grow better.

GROWING YOUR OWN AUSTRALIAN PLANTS

Nurturing your own plants from seedlings or propagating cuttings is by far the most satisfying way to get yourself a supply of indigenous plants. It is the cheapest option as well as the best way to produce plants that are often a lot tougher than those grown under the sterile conditions of a commercial nursery.

Although there are some indigenous plants such as geebungs (*Persoonia* sp.) or the Bush Cherry (*Exocarpos* sp.) that are difficult to grow from seed, most are fairly straightforward.

SPROUTING SEEDS

The easiest way to reproduce plants is by using ripe seeds and a good seed-raising mixture. To guarantee ripe seeds, place a paper bag on the seed pod while it is still on the plant until it releases its seeds.

Acacia pods provide a tasty treat for many parrots. Cockatoos are especially fond of them too, whether they're green or mature. Ripe seeds sprout readily once they are treated.

Some plants won't let go of their seeds and need encouragement. The cones of banksias are a good example. They are designed to keep the seeds safe during bushfires and then to release them into the fresh ash bed so they sprout with the first rain. What this means for gardeners is that you have to make the cone think it has been through a fire. To do this put it on a flaming hot barbecue for a few minutes. The cones will soon open and the smoke stimulates the seeds to sprout. In each scale of the cone, there will be two black-winged seeds and between them, a little black partition that is the same shape, colour and size as the seed, but which will never grow, no matter what you do. So make sure you plant the seeds and not the partition.

Eucalypts are similar. Inside the gumnuts are a few dark brown seeds and lots of lighter brown chaff. It is hard to separate these elements but it works well to simply plant the whole lot.

Good seed-raising mixes hold water well, but also drain freely. You can make your own with a mixture of three parts gritty river sand and one part peat moss. Sow the seeds about twice their own depth in the mix or, for really tiny seeds, cover them with a fine layer of pearlite or vermiculite (available from most garden centres). The seed-raising mix needs to be constantly moist, but standing it in a tray of water might attract fungal attacks, so it is better just to water it frequently.

One clever way to make a set of mini glasshouses is to save PET soft drink bottles, saw off their tops or bottoms and place them over the potting mix. This set-up requires little watering and only needs to be put in a cool spot with plenty of light, but not direct sunlight. If any sprouting seedlings go limp, fall over or die, they are probably damping off. This means that they will require a fungicide. Always be careful with any fungicide and carefully follow the directions on the packet to make sure that the cure isn't worse than the disease.

Once most of the seedlings sprout four leaves, take off their plastic tops and let the seedlings harden for a few days before carefully scooping them out singly with a Paddle-pop stick and planting them in containers of potting mix. You can use soil instead of potting mix, but the seedlings won't do as well.

A PET plastic bottle can easily be modified to make a suitable germination chamber for seeds or a mini greenhouse for growing plant cuttings.

GROWING CUTTINGS

Striking cuttings isn't as easy as sprouting seeds, but it is the only way you can preserve particularly good varieties of indigenous plants. This is because unlike seeds, cuttings are genetically identical to their parents. Outstanding grevilleas like Honey Gem or Superb and excellent banksias like Giant Candles always have to be propagated using cuttings.

Cutting media are similar to those for seed raising, and a suitable mix is equal parts of peat moss (for holding water), pearlite (for better drainage and aeration) and coarse river sand.

The best cuttings are taken from new shoots that have lost their soft new look and are beginning to become woody. They usually become available in mid- to late-summer. Cut off enough of the growing tip so that it still has at least six sets of leaves. The cut should be just below the last leaf. The cleaner the cut, the better the chance of the cutting taking, so it's best to use a scalpel or a really sharp knife.

You will need to cut off all leaves except the top one or two sets as the roots will sprout from the nodes – the points where the leaves were attached. If the plant has very large leaves, keep only the top two and cut off half of each of them.

Place the cutting in the medium, leaving about half sticking out, and cover it with an upturned bottle or plastic bag to improve the humidity. The success rate can be improved at the same time by treating the cut stem with root-promoting hormone powders. Gently scrape one side of the bottom centimetre of the cutting with your sharp knife and then

MAINTAINING AN INDIGENOUS GARDEN

Tangled vegetation in the lower levels of the garden provides habitat for scrubwrens and fairy-wrens. A birdbath can be very attractive – as long as marauding cats are kept at bay.

apply the powder. The scraping stimulates the plant's repair processes which will encourage the growth of the roots.

Once the cutting has formed roots, it can then be transferred to a pot with potting mix and grown as usual. Softer plants tend to form roots after two to six weeks while woodier species take from four to 20 weeks. Difficult species like geebungs (*Persoonia* species) have been known to form their first roots only after two years!

Growing eucalypts, acacias and casuarinas from cuttings is either impossible or not worthwhile, but cuttings can be a great way to propagate most other indigenous species.

HARVESTING

Nature has proved to be very successful at sprouting her own seeds and sometimes you can simply harvest seedlings that have sprouted in your garden by themselves. Transplant seedlings at the four-leaf stage and take a large amount of soil with them.

Seedlings should preferably not be taken out of the bush. Although it's an excellent idea to increase the natural value of your garden, robbing natural areas certainly isn't the way to go about it.

THE SEED BITE TEST

Some plants such as wattles and those with pea-shaped flowers have seeds with hard outer coats. These are designed to last for decades in the soil until their competition is wiped out by a bushfire, then they sprout once it has rained. To see if a seed is in this group, bite it! If it is unaffected, it will need special treatment. You can either rub it gently between layers of sandpaper to breach the seed coat or better still, pour boiling water over the seeds and leave them overnight; then plant them as usual.

Acacia oxycedrus seed pods.

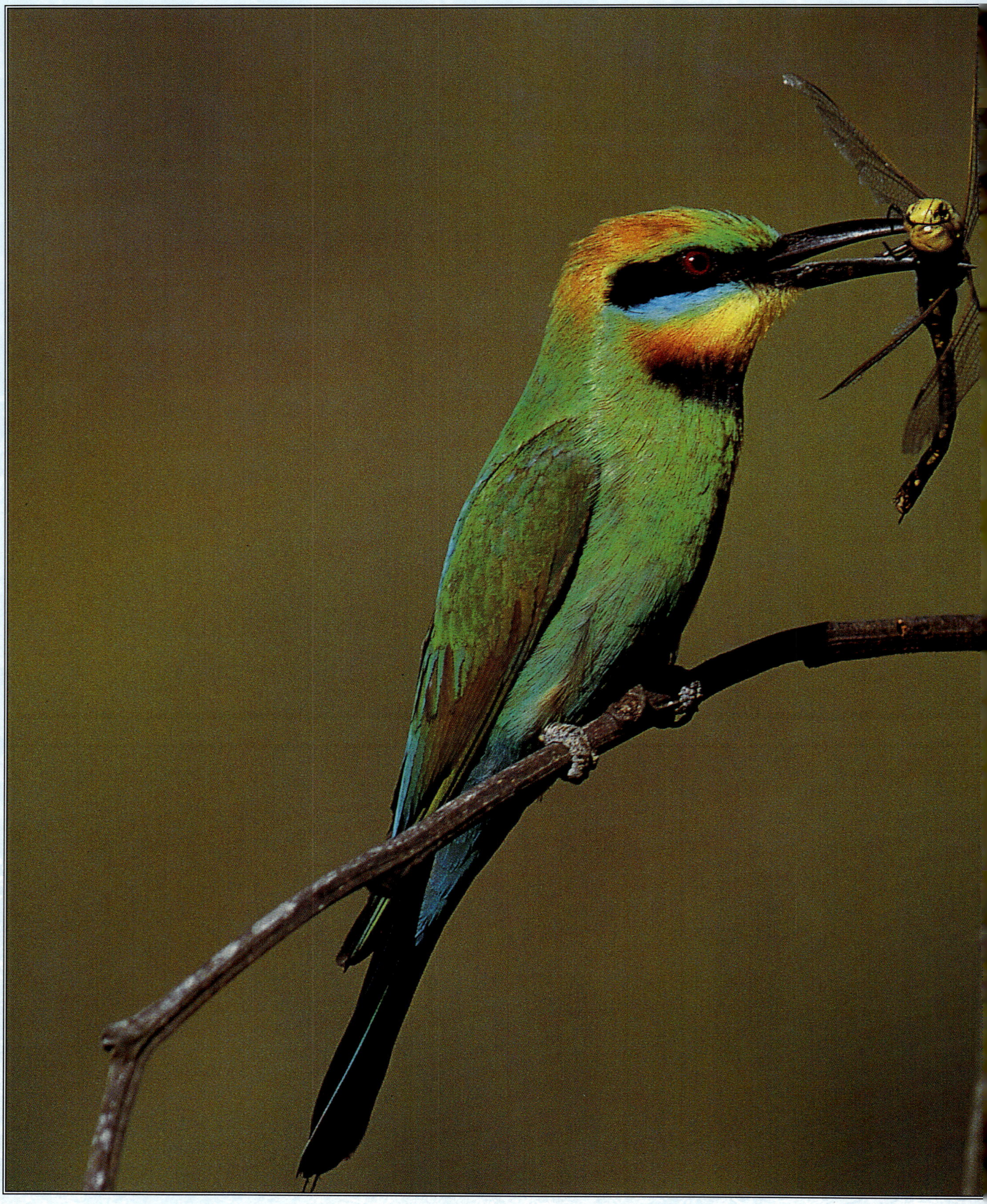

CHAPTER 6

CONTROLLING PESTS

Plant pests, from scale insects, caterpillars, aphids and ants to slugs, snails and possums, have plagued every garden at some time or other. There are natural and artificial ways of dealing with pests, but whatever way you choose, you have to make sure the treatment isn't worse than the cure! Chemical pest controls will eliminate pests, but they can also harm the birds.

Rainbow Bee-eaters are deadly to flying insects.

Attitudes to controlling pests have come a long way. In days gone by, a good pest was a dead one, but people are increasingly realising that tolerating a few pests is a good way to encourage natural predators, and some insects are more interesting than the plants they feed on!

CONTROLLING PESTS

The use and misuse of chemicals has resulted in the deaths of birds worldwide. Birds can learn to survive hazards such as dogs, cats, fences and power lines, but they can't adapt to an invisible poison. Every spring in eastern Australia hundreds of Tawny Frogmouths die a gruesome death, riddled with pesticides that are now banned but still present in the environment. In North America the Peregrine Falcon and Brown Pelican were all but wiped out and pesticides in our own peregrines have been detected at dangerous levels.

Although certain farmers are growing organic produce, many agricultural pursuits are heavily dependent on pesticides and herbicides. At present the unfortunate reality is that agricultural chemicals can't be abandoned altogether. Such chemicals are very rarely needed in the backyard, especially if you allow a natural balance to develop by tolerating a few pests and growing the right kinds of plants.

THE CHEMICAL SOLUTION

There is a vast range of chemical products designed to control backyard pests. Picking the right one for the job is a bit daunting, especially when you read the health warnings on the labels. Rather than wading through all the information, adopt a less toxic but far more satisfying approach to gardening.

Native plants seldom, if ever, need pesticides and by growing fruit and vegetable varieties that need little protection, you can just about completely do away with chemicals. For instance, when was the last time you saw a mulberry with an insect problem, or a lemon tree that needed anything more than an occasional zap with white oil? The best approach is to resist the advertising depicting satisfied gardeners spraying their cares away and take time to consider how pests are controlled in nature.

Scarab beetles feed on the leaves of eucalyptus trees.

BIOLOGICAL CONTROL

One of the things you very rarely see as you walk through the bush is an outbreak of pests. This is because the ecosystem is balanced. An excess of one species upsets the balance, but it is soon returned to normal by that creature's predators and parasites breeding in higher numbers.

You will occasionally see little population explosions of a particular species of creature, for instance, caterpillars or stick insects, but these are mostly controlled by hungry currawongs, caterpillar diseases and by outbreaks of parasitic wasps, which can breed just as fast as their hosts.

In gardens, the balance of nature is less stable, but it is still possible to have natural predators controlling most of the potential pests most of the time.

INTEGRATED PEST MANAGEMENT

Integrated pest management simply means the careful use of chemicals to maximise the ability of natural predators to control potential pests. It is a relatively new approach to agriculture, and one that can be applied to a backyard environment, particularly for those gardeners who find it difficult to give up pesticides.

With this approach, you need to answer a few questions before you reach for the spray-can:
• Are the pests taking over the garden or is their impact only minor?
• How much of the garden is affected? There's no point in treating the whole garden when only a few plants are in trouble. Spot treatment of an individual plant or even a branch can sometimes solve the problem without destroying the rest of the garden. This approach is especially effective when a particularly valuable plant is being attacked by pests that can be dealt with only by chemicals.
• Is there a non-toxic way to deal with the pests – for example, by hand-picking or vacuuming caterpillars, blasting aphids with the hose or trapping snails in a dish of beer?
• How will spraying affect the other garden inhabitants; how can this impact be minimised, and is the impact tolerable?

In answering each of these questions, your aim is to avoid or at least minimise the use of chemicals. Where you are convinced that you have no alternative, try to use a less toxic pesticide that has a short life span. The pyrethroids are less toxic than the organophosphate pesticides, which in turn are less environmentally damaging than the organochlorines, most of which are now banned in this country.

If you have to spray it's a good idea to collect the larger predators like mantises, ladybirds and spiders before spraying and put them back once the toxic effect has worn off. Remember that it's okay to have a few pests around.

The Barn Owl has been adversely affected by the use of rodenticides in urban areas.

Killing them with pesticide would just leave their natural predators and parasites to starve and the coast would then be clear for the next wave of invaders to take over the garden unopposed. Integrated pest management can be a great way to gradually reduce use of pesticides until you can do without them entirely.

UNDERSTANDING PLANTS AND PESTS

Like animals, plants have natural defences against their enemies and it's usually only when they are stressed that they are attacked seriously. So plants that are frequently attacked by mildew, aphids, scale insects or other problems are probably struggling with difficult conditions or are of a weak variety.

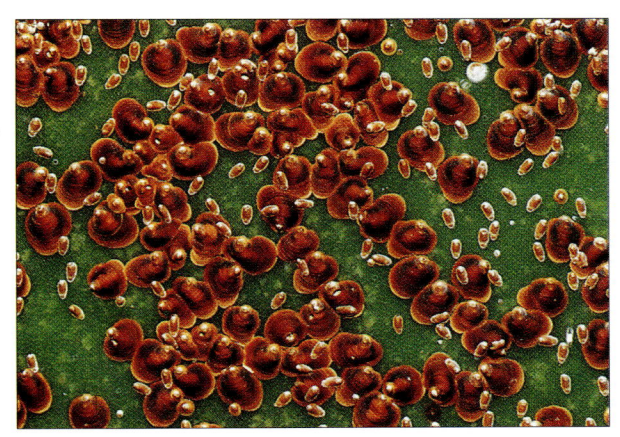

Remove scale insects by scrubbing them with a toothbrush and soapy water. The best control is to ensure that growing conditions are correct.

Plants can be stressed by many factors. Too much or too little shade, the wrong amount of water, rotten soil or soil that contains no nutrition can all contribute.

The answer to these problems is to understand each plant's needs and make sure it is provided with the right conditions.

Some plants will tolerate a wider range of conditions than others and it often pays to use such species to give your garden the best chance of thriving. Many new varieties of grevilleas and kangaroo paws are hardier than their wild cousins, but this doesn't always apply. For instance, sooty mould can be a particular problem with some of the larger-flowered pink tea-trees.

CONTROLLING PESTS

If a plant doesn't thrive, you can try to re-create the conditions under which it naturally grows by moving it, if it is small enough, or by changing the drainage or water supplies. If this fails, it's probably best to replace the plant with a more suitable species or individual as you won't want to spend your time doctoring sick plants.

The trouble often comes when you want to grow a plant outside its natural range. The stress that comes from growing plants in unsuitable conditions can be the factor that predisposes the plant to attack by pests. This can also be a problem with exotic plants which have adapted to conditions different to those in Australia, or become dependent on pesticides through breeding programs that have ignored pest resistance in favour of other attributes.

FOOD PRODUCTION VERSUS BIRDS

Unlike most indigenous plants, calorie-rich items like fruits and vegetables are often subject to attack by insects and other freeloaders – and birds are no exception. While many gardeners are happy to just put in a few extra plants to allow for the consumption by birds, others are keen to take measures to protect their hard-won produce.

One of the best approaches is to use bird netting to keep your fruit and vegetables off-limits to the birds. With vegetable gardens the netting can be draped on a long, 1m-high frame with a triangular cross-section. You can buy netting from most garden centres and from some commercial fishing suppliers. With a large tree, it is possible to protect the choicest items using paper or mesh bags.

If that doesn't work, you can always try water torture. Get someone well co-ordinated (or gullible) to climb to the top of the tree you want to protect and fix a sprinkler there. Then simply turn it on. Birds will like it for a while, but they will eventually get tired of being constantly wet and look for a new place to eat. Bribery isn't a bad idea either, so provide a feeding table well-stocked with fruit pieces as this often (but not always!) keeps birds such as currawongs and Silvereyes off the crop.

For the more creative there is a range of bird-scaring devices which can keep hungry birds out of forbidden parts of the garden. These range from commercially made plastic hawks to rubber snakes, strips of aluminium foil and even plaster owls. In the end the main thing to bear in mind is that birds plus fruit trees are far more interesting than trees by themselves.

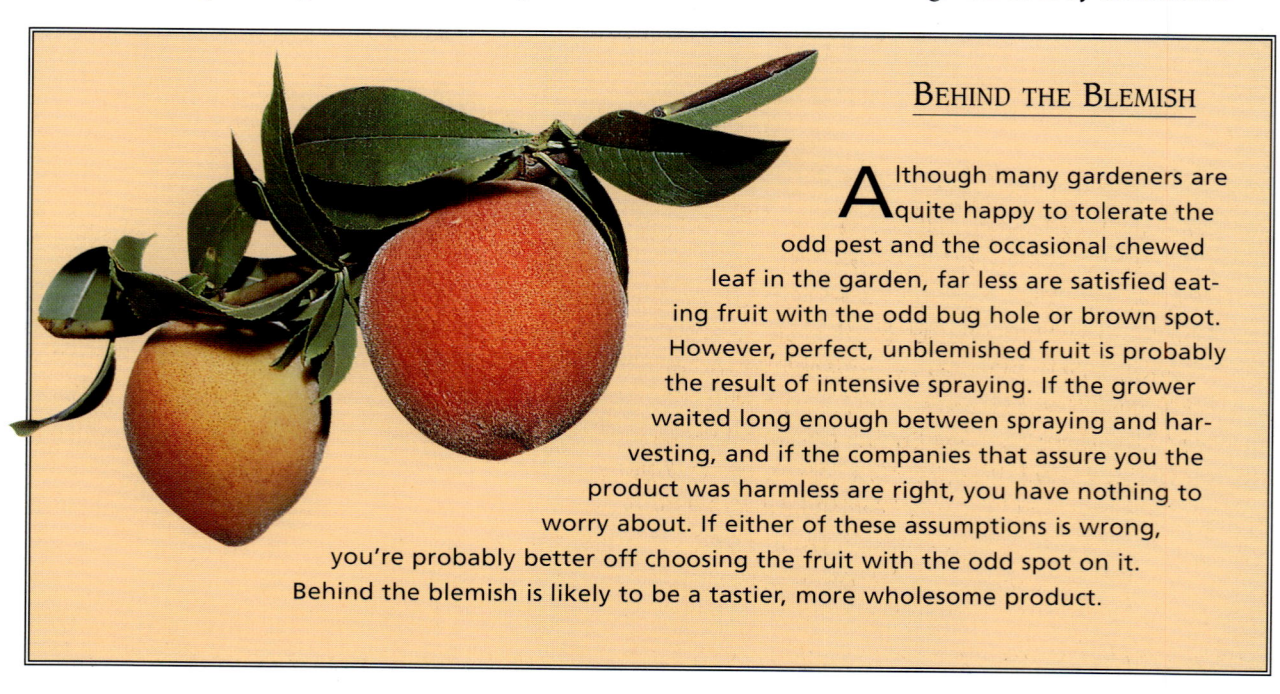

The Figbird feeds on soft fruits.

BEHIND THE BLEMISH

Although many gardeners are quite happy to tolerate the odd pest and the occasional chewed leaf in the garden, far less are satisfied eating fruit with the odd bug hole or brown spot. However, perfect, unblemished fruit is probably the result of intensive spraying. If the grower waited long enough between spraying and harvesting, and if the companies that assure you the product was harmless are right, you have nothing to worry about. If either of these assumptions is wrong, you're probably better off choosing the fruit with the odd spot on it. Behind the blemish is likely to be a tastier, more wholesome product.

'CREAM OF PEST' SOUP

This dubious mixture isn't for everyone, but if you're into biological warfare, it certainly does the trick! Gather up all the pests you can catch or vacuum in the garden, especially any that don't look well. Pop them into a blender with about the same volume of water and turn it on. Mmmm! Strain the mixture and use the discarded bits as fertiliser and the strained bug juice as a spray. This revolting approach probably works by spreading diseases to healthy pests. The caterpillar-attacking bacteria, *Bacillus thuringiensis* (which you can buy as Dipel), was discovered in half-dead caterpillars. You can freeze the juice if you like, but don't get it mixed up with your frozen chicken stock!

ELIMINATING COMMON PESTS

If humans really are the most intelligent life form on the planet, we should be able to outsmart some of the less cerebral creatures instead of just obliterating all insect life in the backyard with an overdose of chemicals! There are simple, non-toxic approaches to nearly all garden pests.

ANTS

Ants are rarely a problem in the garden – they can even be useful in eating insect pests and attacking termite mounds. However, they can also be garden villains – especially when they are scuttling up and down a plant stem. Even though they look innocent, those ants are up to mischief. They are protecting colonies of bugs which drill tiny holes into your plants to siphon the life-giving sap, and they are also spreading plant diseases. The bugs, in return for protection from their enemies, give the ants a sugary solution. It's a great system for the ants and bugs, but not for the plants, which often have wilted shoots and are stained with black mildew growing on the excess sugary residue.

The solution to this problem is to put the bugs off-limits to the ants by greasing their pathways. After blasting the bugs off with a hose, or alternatively, scrubbing them off with a nail brush, cover a few centimetres of the plant stem with petroleum jelly, lanolin or anything else that ants are unable to climb. Although this process allows some of the bugs to return, without their ant protectors, they mostly end up as dinner for other insects.

If you find ant mounds in the paving unsightly, it is usually easy to tip half a bottle of methylated spirits into the holes followed by a good dousing of boiling water. The methylated spirits will rapidly evaporate, leaving no residue.

Ants in pot plants are easier to remove. You simply sink the pot into a bucket of water or a pond. After half an hour, your problems have swum away! The herbs tansy and peppermint are also reputed to repel ants.

APHIDS

Aphids are little bugs that suck the sap from new shoots. Females are able to reproduce without males and they can be blown long distances by the wind, so they can infect healthy plants quite easily.

Water treatment is the best method to repel aphids. Turn the hose into a very fine spray and simply blast the plants. Supporting the shoot with your hand ensures there is little damage to the plant. Aphids are sure to return but in fewer numbers; and if they are met with the water torture every few days, they won't last long.

CONTROLLING PESTS

GARDENER'S FRIENDS

The following visitors to the urban garden are useful because they feed on the harmful pests that are found there.

Praying mantises are active garden hunters who use their excellent vision to snatch a variety of garden pests – but they hate pesticides.

Ladybirds are brightly coloured to warn birds that they taste terrible. Their larvae look like tiny alligators and are deadly predators of aphids.

Tolerating a few pests maintains populations of parasitic wasps whose numbers explode to control outbreaks of insect pests, especially caterpillars.

Without any damaging pesticides, local predators such as the larvae of hoverflies and ladybirds will often make mincemeat of any aphids left in the garden. Marigolds can also be an effective deterrent to aphids and other insects.

BORERS

Borers are caterpillar and beetle larvae and can be especially troublesome in banksias and tea-trees, where they often attack at the fork of branches. While there are pesticide solutions to this problem, more direct methods are less toxic – and more satisfying.

The borer's tunnel is often covered with droppings held together with silk or loose bark. If you sneak out at night, you can often catch the culprit with its head out of the hole. During the daytime, it's easy to probe the hole with a piece of stiff wire to impale the caterpillar. You can also tip some methylated spirits into the tunnel. The liquid will evaporate after disposing of the caterpillar.

One of the most useful approaches is biological warfare. Using the caterpillar disease bacteria, *Bacillus thuringiensis* (Dipel), is a very focused approach that will affect only the caterpillars.

Natural pest controls also include plants. French Marigolds (Tagetes sp.) produce compounds that can be effective in repelling insects from plants.

CONTROLLING PESTS

LEAF-EATING BEETLES

These handsome pests include Christmas beetles which are popular with children, chickens and most things in between, but they can be very damaging to gum trees. Around Christmas, especially in tableland areas, hordes of these beetles can descend on juicy young trees, completely stripping them of leaves. Unchecked, this process leads to eucalypt dieback, a very serious problem that can result in the killing of eucalypts in many parts of Australia.

The best way to protect your trees is to pick the beetles off by hand. For larger saplings where you can't reach the beetles, a long-handled prawn net is an easy way to catch them. These beetles are mostly active at night (although the neighbours might get a bit worried seeing you waving a prawn net around your gum trees in the evening!).

Once you get a good collection of beetles, you can feed them to the chickens, or just turn them into a beetle-mush fertiliser. That way both your trees and chooks will be well-fed and happy!

CUP MOTH LARVAE

Cup Moth larvae are 2cm-long caterpillars which glide along gum leaves, nibbling at the edges and looking quite harmless. Most are dark with rows of yellow spots, but some are green with beautiful pink and white patterns. At each end of the body, and sometimes in between, they have two little bumps that house a cluster of tiny, stinging spikes which sprout at the slightest touch. Like other insect larvae that live in groups, they can have a negative impact on plants simply by eating most of the leaves.

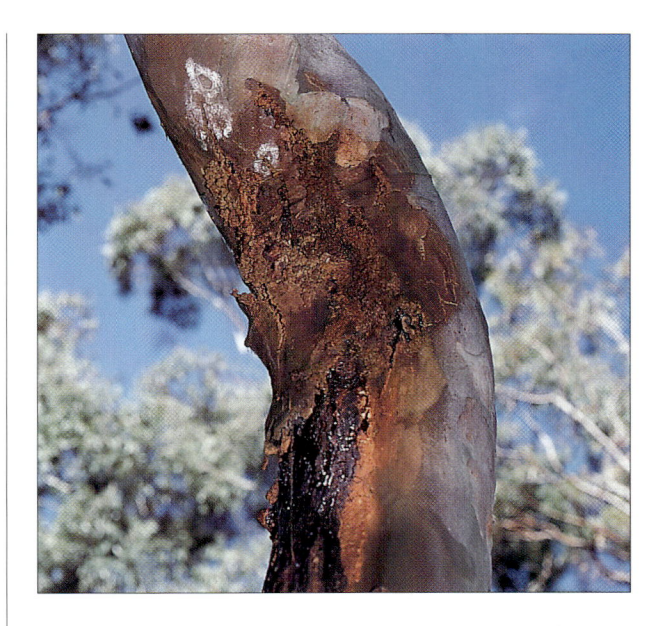

Top: Borers can be a serious problem for some plants. This Sydney Red Gum (Angophora costata) *really needs first aid.*
Centre: Some beetles can cause plants serious problems by defoliating mature shrubs or trees. The solutions are to pick them off and to grow a mix of plants that will disguise the scent of the beetles' preferred species.
Bottom: While a few cup moths can prove to be a fascinating addition to the garden, too many can wreck your gum trees. They can turn previously healthy green leaves into lacy skeletons.

CONTROLLING PESTS

Sawflies live in groups of large larvae; this is fine as long as there aren't too many for the size of the tree.

Hand-picking (with gloves) is the best way to control Cup Moth larvae. This method is very selective and unlike pesticides it allows parasitic wasps to survive. These wasps help control the larvae by laying their eggs on them, with deadly results. *Bacillus thuringiensis* can be effective, but it will also kill all the other interesting caterpillars and butterfly larvae.

It's always good to leave some of the larvae to pupate so you can see the incredible gumnut cases they make as protection from their predators. It takes them about three days to make the case and to coat it with a special fluid that hardens into a wood-like texture. Once they're finished, it's very difficult to tell the real gumnut from the fake one with the little moth hiding inside.

SAWFLIES

Sawflies are dumpy wasps that sip nectar as adults, but eat leaves as larvae. Sawfly larvae look like caterpillars and they live in hungry groups. Some species are large and black with tiny white hairs, others are smaller and green with a little spike on their tail. They are mostly just an interesting addition to the garden, but large numbers of sawflies on a small shrub can strip all its leaves and bring about its demise.

The cure is to pick off the excess sawflies. The black ones are seldom a problem, but the little green ones that attach themselves to melaleucas can be very damaging and you need to be extra vigilant to keep them at bay.

SNAILS AND SLUGS

Both snails and slugs are garden gluttons that will travel up to 10m from their hiding places each night to sample your vegetables and tastiest plants. They are best controlled by a combination of natural predators, trapping and barriers. While ducks and chickens are very effective predators, they will also munch their way through many softer plants. Black rats also like to eat snails, but in this case the cure is rather worse than the disease! A better approach is to encourage natural predators such as blue-tongue lizards, Australian snails and rove beetles.

Snails and slugs are great food for blue-tongue lizards, but not much good for seedlings or other garden plants.

Blue-tongue lizards and indigenous snails love rocks and logs to hide under, while rove beetles enjoy a good, thick mulch layer. Native snails look a bit flatter than your normal garden snail and the centre of the shell's spiral is hollow (have a look underneath at the base of the spiral). Rove beetles are very dark and grow up to 2cm long. They run about with their tails in the air looking dangerous, but they aren't. Their larvae are vicious carnivores, though, who prowl through the litter looking for slugs, snails and other tasty items.

Trapping snails and slugs is very satisfying. You can use a dish of beer with the rim at ground level (at least they drown with smiles on their faces!). Or you can make a snail house. This can be just a wet bag on the ground, a flat piece of wood propped up on snail-sized stones, or an upturned plant pot with space for the snails to enter on one side. Each type of house will be very attractive to snails if placed in a moist part of the garden. You just need to check it each week and dispatch any tenants who have taken up residence.

CONTROLLING PESTS

You go out into the garden after rain to where the snails and slugs are romping around and either take them off to somewhere where they won't get into trouble or dispose of them as you see fit.

TENT CATERPILLARS

By day, Tent Caterpillars live in a silk shelter built against the bottom of the trunk of a wattle or White Cedar, hence their name. By night, they gobble their way through the leaves on the tree, sometimes to the point where there are none left.

Solutions to this are simple. If it is a big tree and a small group of only ten or so caterpillars, don't worry. They will soon wriggle off to find a nice place to pupate into moths. If the leaves are disappearing at a scary rate, then more direct action is needed, but it's really important to avoid touching these caterpillars because the hairs are irritating. Use a stick and gumboots. The stick is for opening up the nest so you can treat it with a bacterial spray containing *Bacillus thuringiensis*. Then put on the gumboots so that you can stomp on the colony without getting the hairs between your toes!

Slugs are quite harmless in most gardens. Following their nocturnal silvery trails to the owner's hiding place is a great detective mystery for younger gardeners.

Setting up barriers can be effective against snails and slugs but some need frequent replacement. Lime or ash from the fireplace works well until it gets wet and sets with a hard crust. A better option is to set up 10cm fences of galvanised iron or copper. You put the fence around the garden bed with the top bent outwards until it is at an angle of about 45° with the upright part of the fence. For particularly susceptible seedlings, a little copper collar at ground level can be quite effective – snails hate copper.

Snail baits will work, but they also kill worms, pets and other useful creatures. The blue pellets are especially dangerous to Satin Bowerbirds whose habit of painting their bowers with chewed-up blue and black objects makes them vulnerable to poisoning. The most satisfying tactic of all is snail hunting. For this you need a torch, boots and a rainy night.

No-one touches Tent Caterpillars twice. Their hairs are particularly irritating and the resulting itch lasts for hours.

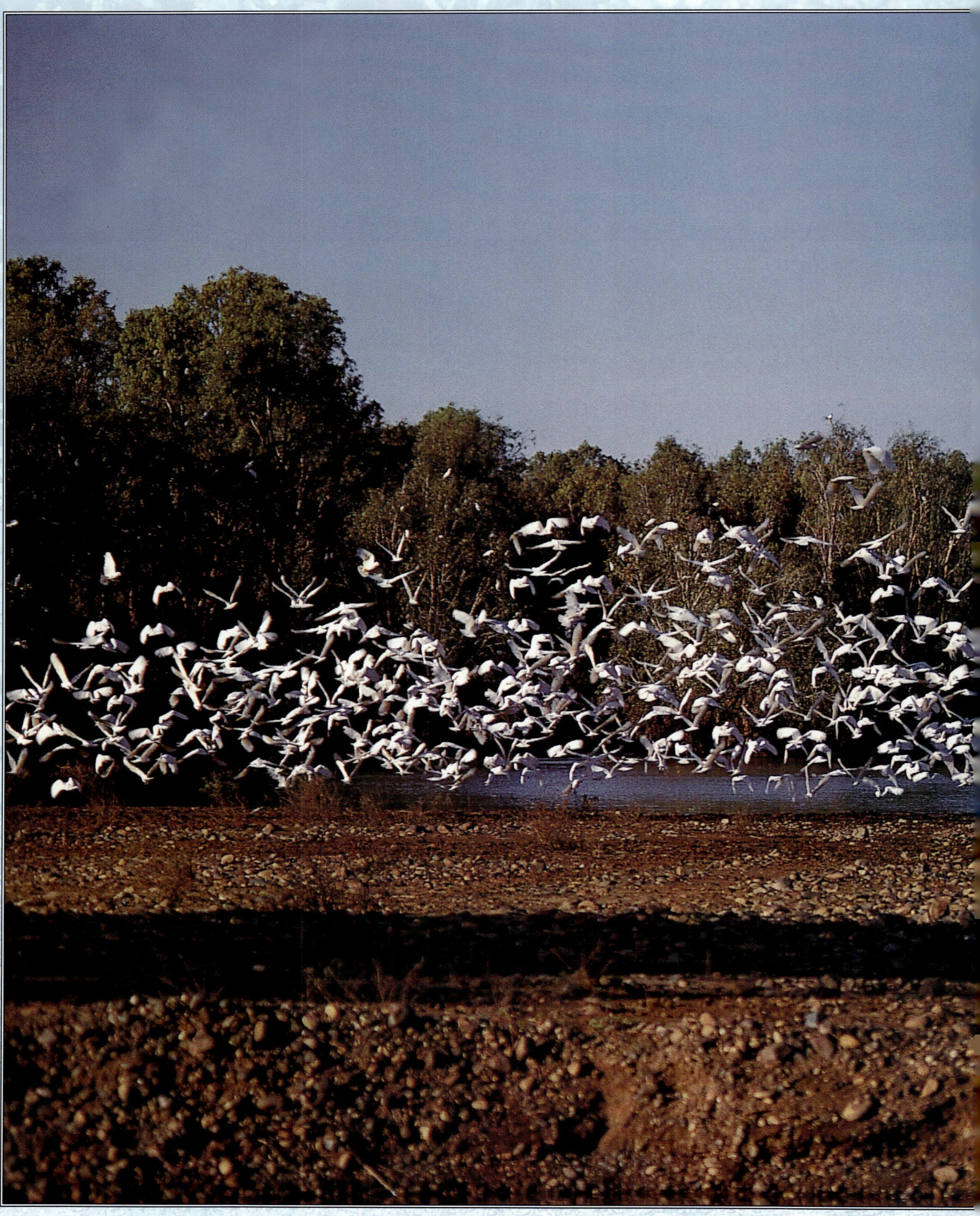

CHAPTER 7

BIRDS ON SMALL FARMS

Unlike urban areas where wildlife habitat has been seriously modified, the countryside often has much higher value for wildlife. Few rural areas are in their original condition, but they usually contain considerably more trees and natural bushland than the more developed parts of the country.

Little Corellas form noisy flocks when travelling between feeding areas.

BIRDS ON SMALL FARMS

Properties on the edges of urban areas can play a vital role in providing a link between the more natural areas and the more developed suburban ones – especially when corridors of natural vegetation can be retained or developed.

BIRDS ON SMALL FARMS

Living on a farm at the edge of a city can be wonderful. The amount of space and the less-developed nature of the land creates an excellent environment for birds and other animals. Living in such an area means you can help wildlife in many ways, from simply excluding harmful influences like shooters or feral animals to major rehabilitation of the area's natural vegetation.

The same basic principles that apply to gardens can be applied to small farms; the difference is that ponds become dams, shrub areas become forests and old monster hollow trees can easily be retained without any risk to the house.

PLANNING A BIRD-FRIENDLY FARM

Whether you are on an expansive rural holding or a tiny inner-city block, the first vital steps are the same; draw up a plan of how you'd like to increase the garden's value to wildlife and take advantage of existing benefits such as established trees and areas of nearby vegetation – whether they are huge national parks or a few grevilleas in a neighbour's garden. When planning an area, aim to have at least as many levels of vegetation and as many species of plants as the local bush. Also think about how the area relates to the surrounding habitat and build on those strengths.

Golf courses are planned with this principle in mind. The most manicured lawns are the greens and these grade through from the longer grass of the fairways to the rough, where ball-eating shrubs lurk. A farm can be planned in the same way. The house and its garden would be the greens with the rest of the area grading into the rough, that is, the natural bushland.

OPEN AREA

A manicured lawn, or at least a green one, will provide protection against bushfires and a pleasant setting for the house, but it can easily adjoin a more natural area of native grasses. These would provide food for a range of finches and parrots, as well as providing a graceful background to the rest of the garden.

You can mow pathways through the grasses to give easy access to the rest of the area, but don't make too many paths and try to leave large areas of unmowed grass to give food and shelter to birds and other wildlife. Birds such as skylarks and Richard's Pipits are especially fond of tussock grass areas where they can find insects and shelter from predators.

SHRUB ZONES

With more space than your suburban colleagues, you can really go to town with this aspect of the property. As with city gardens, it is important to

BIRDS ON SMALL FARMS

Above: *Mistletoe is a great source of nectar and berries for many Australian birds.*
Left: *Black-shouldered Kites like open areas.*

design the plan around existing valuable plants or areas of vegetation. One excellent approach is to start by identifying the local species of trees and shrubs. You don't need to be a botanical expert – ask your local natural history group, the Society for Growing Australian Plants, the National Parks and Wildlife Service or your State forestry department for advice.

Once you've worked out what the local plants are, you can use them to re-create areas of natural bushland that link the house garden to the adjoining bushland. You can enrich the bushland around the house with a range of bird-friendly plants which can be maintained at higher than natural densities by adding extra water and nutrients (low in phosphates for most Australian plants).

It isn't always easy to get local indigenous plants, but taking a few minutes to ring some of the specialist nurseries can pay surprising dividends. If this doesn't work, you can always grow your own (*see* Chapter Five). Propagating your own plants has the added advantage that you don't have to know which plant is which, you just have to find a propagation technique that works for that species!

As a general rule, don't transplant seedlings from the bush to your garden – you are trying to do something positive for wildlife, and damaging the natural areas to improve your garden is a bit like robbing Peter to pay Paul. The exception is when too many plants have sprouted and they can't all survive. This could be when huge numbers of seedlings come up after a bushfire or flood and it would do very little harm to remove some of the seedlings. Don't overdo it, though. Make sure you take only a few and that you choose ones at the two- or four-leaf stage – any later and the plant's chances of survival drop sharply. This is why transplanting mature plants has a very low success rate and is justified only where the bushland is about to be flattened for urban development. Under such circumstances you can try moving the mature specimens, but you will generally get more plants for your efforts if you collect seeds or cuttings and propagate them.

The further away from the house you go, the more the plants will have to look after themselves, so hardy local varieties need to predominate in areas where watering is difficult. The dished-mound-of-earth method of watering plants is useless if watering is infrequent. A better approach would be to have a mound just downhill of the plant with low contour banks tapering off on each side towards the plant to direct any run-off to it. If there is a shed nearby that catches water, one way to make the rainfall last longer is to direct it into a large container, such as a well-washed 200-litre plastic drum, and then construct a drip irrigation system for each of the plants within reach.

The shrub area works best if it is well stocked with rocks and logs that shelter wildlife from predators and the elements. By doing this, the area is made far more interesting where people are concerned and far more productive for birds looking for something to eat. Such shelter can also be useful agriculturally. On cold, wet days fallen logs retained on a property could well be the only thing standing between a new lamb and freezing death.

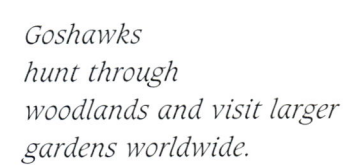

Goshawks hunt through woodlands and visit larger gardens worldwide.

TREE CANOPIES

The tree canopy should link up with areas of bush. Trees are often left along roadsides, travelling stock reserves and watercourses. By retaining and linking such areas, you can do a great deal to improve the wildlife value of the whole district. For information on setting up bush corridors in your area, contact the local office of Greening Australia, Landcare, National Parks, or your local conservation society or forestry department.

Retaining aged trees is so much easier on farms than in the suburbs. These ancient giants may fall over unpredictably but they provide extremely valuable hollows for some of our larger birds such as Powerful and Barking owls, as well as for gliders and other possums.

Australasian Grebes make extraordinary floating nests.

A WATER WONDERLAND FOR BIRDS

Water areas can be an exciting project in any garden, but especially in rural areas where space is not an issue. More than half the wetlands in eastern Australia have been destroyed or seriously modified. By creating water areas on small farms, you can play a part in arresting this decline. Surface water is a scarce commodity in much of Australia so garden wetlands can be especially attractive to wildlife, in particular the seed-eating birds that need to drink once or twice a day. While all farms have dams or other water supplies, these are usually not as useful to wildlife as they could be and some simple changes can pay large dividends.

CREATING A BIRD-FRIENDLY DAM

Apart from adding a wetland upstream, there are plenty of ways of enhancing your dam to make it attractive to birds. Different birds like different depths of water, so variety in this area will be well rewarded. Birds such as grebes will hunt for fish and tadpoles as far down as 2m. Many fish will use the deeper areas as a haven from climatic extremes, and these also ensure the dam will always have reed-free zones for ducks. Handsome birds like Black-fronted Dotterels will enjoy prowling around the shallow edges. Other birds like White-faced Herons, Great Egrets and coots prefer intermediate depths, so the ideal dam is at least 2m deep, grading to very shallow areas.

The edge of the dam is a very productive area and can be expanded by allowing spurs of land to run into the dam instead of cutting them off with a bulldozer as is usually the case. One of the best aspects of a bird-friendly dam is also the presence of an island or two. Islands allow birds to relax without

Flame Robins are found only in the larger gardens. Males are a gaudy crimson colour.

Reed warblers and other birds will feel right at home nesting and feeding in areas like this.

Rural Wetlands

The ideal addition to a farm dam is a swampy area where the water flows in. This is best achieved by placing a low earth wall across the line of water flow, just uphill of the water level in the existing dam. The wall can be a metre or so high, depending on how much space there is and how steep the sides of the gully are.

The extra wall catches enough water and silt to turn the area immediately upstream into a wetland, which can then be further improved and stabilised by adding a range of water plants bought commercially or gathered from nearby dams. The larger water plants such as Bulrushes (*Typha domingensis*) and the larger saw sedges (*Ghania sp.*) are great for such areas where space allows these plants to reach their full potential. Once such an area is established, it acts as a wonderful filter – reducing the amount of silt and excess nutrients that can otherwise reduce water quality in the adjoining dam. Excess nutrients can cause algal blooms which can be toxic to stock and also lower oxygen to levels where fish suffocate.

A wetland acts as a bird magnet, attracting insect eaters such as swallows which like to hawk over the tops of the plants, migratory reed warblers which suspend a neat cup nest between bulrush stems, and seed-eating finches which feast on the tiny orange saw sedge seeds.

The tiny orange seeds of the saw sedges (Gahnia *sp.*) *are favoured by finches, while the plant's elegant structure enhances any water feature.*

fear of a predator sneaking up behind them and are great breeding areas for plovers, moorhens, coots and some ducks. Earth and rock islands are the best, but even a small dam can have a floating island of heavy hardwood planks that are attached to plastic drums and covered with a layer of earth. Wetland plants will grow surprisingly well on such artificial islands, whether floating or stationary.

Rocks and logs along the edge of the dam or on the island are a great place for a bird to sit or for a fish to hide under. If the island is large enough, a few trees can increase its attractiveness – just make sure you choose species like paperbarks (*Melaleuca* sp.) or she-oaks (especially *Casuarina cunninghamiana*) that don't mind wet feet.

Keeping stock away from the dam will improve the water quality. It would be a pity to install a wetland upstream, then have all the good work undone by cattle stomping around in the mud at the dam's edge. Fence the dam and then install a gravity feed

Once stock are fenced out, this newly built dam will soon be colonised by native plants. The dam can still be used for stock by running a pipe to a watering trough outside the fence. The nearly complete island is a great asset.

BIRDS ON SMALL FARMS

FLOODING AND FLIRTING

When flooding fills the parched wetlands along the Murray River or the Macquarie Marshes, something amazing happens. Most of the waterbirds in Melbourne, Sydney, and everywhere in between, leave the coast and turn up in the inland areas with romance on their minds – with good reason. When dry areas are flooded, nutrients are released from the soil in a way that never happens in areas that are constantly under water. This creates a flush of insect life which provides perfect food for ducklings and other baby waterbirds. Ibis, ducks and egrets congregate to breed and continue doing so until the wetlands dry out again.

This system is a very effective way for waterbirds to take advantage of Australia's erratic climate, but it drives birdwatchers nuts – no-one can work out how a duck on Moonee Ponds or in Centennial Park can know that 500km away it is pouring with rain. Theories abound, but none fully explains the situation. Some have suggested that waterbirds can sense barometric pressure and can therefore detect storms. Others say ducks fly very high and so see storm clouds gathering, and yet others suggest that waterbirds are so mobile, they spend a lot of time flying around the country, checking out the wetlands. However they do it, waterbirds certainly rely on floods for most of their breeding.

When it isn't flooding, these birds fly to the coast or other permanent bodies of water where they endure the drought. This is where farm dams come in handy. By providing water during difficult times, they can help waterbirds survive until the next rainstorm breathes new life into inland wetlands. This also means that all is not lost if your dam dries out. When it finally fills again, the flush of insect life that follows can produce all sorts of interesting bird visitors.

Paperbarks like this Melaleuca quinquinervia *provide nesting areas for currawongs, nectar for honeyeaters and wonderful shade for people.*

line to a water trough which is kept full by a float valve. This allows plants to grow to the edge of the dam, keeps the water much clearer and therefore creates a better environment for fish, water plants, birds and the stock.

Consult your local garden nursery (and *see* Chapter Three) for lists of water plants that will make your dam an ideal and peaceful place for you and your bird visitors. Bear in mind, though, that although ducks can rise vertically from the water surface, they prefer to fly to and from the dam at a more gradual angle. This means that trees around a dam need to be planned with at least one fly-way in mind so birds can come and go easily.

Introducing Fish

On a farm, a dam can hold edible fish as well as those that are good to look at. Larger fish like Golden Perch (*Macquaria ambigua*) and Silver Perch

(*Bidyanus bidyanus*) can do well in dams, especially Golden Perch which have been known to breed in new dams (not in older ones). Fingerlings of these and other indigenous species are often available from suppliers contactable through your State fisheries department. The only problem with this is that when it rains, perch move upstream to breed. In the wild, they can travel up to 1000km. But in one particular farm dam, they ended up on a cricket pitch!

While there are several fish that are fine in farm dams, there are a few species that are really worth avoiding. The various varieties of carp are not useful as their bottom-feeding habits stir the water and generally make the dam a less productive place. Mosquito Fish (*Gambusia affinis*) are also on the undesirable list as they will eat everything else in sight, although they are a good source of food for the larger perch.

Fish will feel especially at home in the dam if there are plenty of rocks and logs to hide under. Such shelter is particularly important if cormorants are around. Without shelter for the fish, these birds can nearly clear a dam of fish in a few days.

A Darter (Anhinga melanogaster).

WORKING WITH NATURE

The many reasons for buying a small farm can include the quest to make extra money, to get away from stressful city living or simply for the satisfaction of self-sufficiency. If you're looking for a change of pace, finding space for wildlife is easy. Even if the aim is to get the maximum production from the area, there are methods that can benefit both wildlife and the desire for profits. The most intensive agriculture still allows for a house garden which you can arrange to encourage wildlife, and out in the fields you can set up windbreaks and make the dam as bird-friendly as possible.

Windbreaks may be a bit of a surprise as the more trees, the less crops. Look under a row of trees and

THE SUPERB PARROT'S DEMISE

These beautiful birds used to live in an area stretching from the Namoi River in northern New South Wales to the central districts of Victoria, but these days their distribution has become restricted and their numbers lower. Their stronghold is the Murrumbidgee River between Hay and Canberra.

Superb Parrots breed in the red gum forests along the river and feed on the ground in adjoining areas. They breed in loose groups of several pairs, each needing a very large hollow – preferably over water. Such hollows are formed only in centuries-old trees and as a group of birds needs several hollows within a few hundred metres of each other, breeding sites are limited.

In recent decades, the logging of nesting trees and intensive agriculture in the areas surrounding the forests have reduced both the nesting and feeding resources. What these birds need is conservation of the older trees in the river forests around the border between Victoria and New South Wales, and protection of their natural food from cropping and grazing. Each winter they migrate to the north of their range which means that having natural habitats in the central section of New South Wales is also important.

You might not live in the Superb Parrot's range, but the problems they face are common in rural Australia and everyone can play a role in making an effort to turn things around for our wildlife.

you will see that the grass is spindly and crop plants hardly grow there at all. But what you can't see so easily is that those same trees are affording the crop protection over an area that's up to 15 times their own height. By planting a row of trees specifically as a windbreak, wind speeds are reduced which leads to increased yields of everything from fruit crops to vegetables and grazing land.

Plants for windbreaks shouldn't be too dense but they need to retain their lower branches so they don't allow wind through at the bottom level. Pine trees will suffice, but so will many indigenous trees or shrubs with the right structure. Cypresses are not suitable for windbreaks. Many she-oaks (*Casuarina* sp.), Silky Oaks (*Grevillea robusta*), Lilly Pillies (*Acmena smithii*), Wilga (*Geijera parviflora*), and some eucalypts like tallowwoods (*Eucalyptus microcorys*) are excellent windbreak trees and also provide resources for wildlife.

MANAGING PESTS

The chemical-free approach to controlling pests in the garden can work just as well on the farm. Some of the more intensive techniques, like hand-picking the caterpillars, might have to be reserved for the house garden, but others, like ensuring the plants are growing in healthy soils, can be accomplished anywhere. Using unwanted vegetable matter as mulch can improve the soil, as does growing winter crops like clover, which contribute nitrogen to the soil.

Top: *The edible berries of Lilly Pillies like this* Acmena smithii *add both a visual and a palatable element to the garden.*
Centre: *The Silky Oak* (Grevillea robusta) *is our largest grevillea. It usually retains its lower branches, which makes it highly effective as a windbreak tree.*
Bottom: *If you have one of the taller trees in the area, this will ensure a passing parade of magpies and currawongs, as well as unusual birds like Dollarbirds and Channel-billed Cuckoos.*

BIRDS ON SMALL FARMS

> ## Predator Perches
>
> Top predator birds like goshawks, Peregrine Falcons or Wedge-tailed Eagles don't have to hide from other birds and they love sitting on a high perch surveying their realm. In some parts of Australia, telephone poles along railway lines are the only remaining high perches for these birds. As you drive along some outback roads, falcons and eagles regularly dot the crossbars of power and telephone lines.
>
> If trees are in very short supply on your farm, you might like to erect some 'predator perches' until your seedling trees have grown. Such perches need to be as tall as possible; 6m tall with a 2m crossbar is about right. The best crossbars are about as round in the middle as a very stout shovel handle, grading down to broom-handle thickness towards the ends. Different birds will choose the spot that best suits them. Such structures attract a range of predators including goshawks, eagles, falcons and even owls at night – all of which feed on rodents and other farm pests.
>
> Some birds will even nest on similar structures. From Hervey Bay in Queensland to Kangaroo Island off South Australia there are records of endangered ospreys nesting on platforms built for them on the tops of electricity poles or on other artificial structures like cranes.
>
> *Predator perches can provide Barn Owls with great vantage points for scanning prey.*

Integrated pest management, which aims to encourage a natural balance on the property between pests and their prey, is far more preferable than relying on chemicals. This approach includes tolerating a few pests to ensure that natural predators have something to eat. It also means doing what you can to provide the other resources predators need. If you retain large hollow trees, they will serve as nesting sites for owls who eat rats and mice. If you're really lucky, some of the larger hawks and eagles may take up residence, ensuring a rapid drop in the local rabbit population.

Even in an ecosystem as unnatural as an orange orchard, natural predators can be the main control. A good illustration of this is an orange grower who was convinced, against his better judgement, to spray his crop for pests. He was told that the fruit would look better and he would get a better price for it. He sprayed the crop and saw the pests disappear before his eyes. What he didn't notice was that the predatory insects and mites were also killed. With no predators around, insects that had not previously been a problem suddenly increased in numbers, threatening the crop. He was advised to spray these too. However, he had learnt by then and refused. It took two years for the decimated natural predators to increase in number to necessary levels. These days he doesn't spray with anything stronger than white oil, which he sometimes uses to control scale insects. His farm is profitable and his produce healthy.

If after abandoning the use of chemicals you find that you have unwanted bottles of them in the shed, see if you can give them back to the distributor or manufacturer. They will probably be happy to take them – unless of course the chemicals have been banned in the meantime!

One of the joys of watching feathered friends in your garden is settling into your favourite chair with a set of binoculars and your favourite drink in hand and learning more about the fascinating lives of Australia's birds. Step one for most people is to work out who's who in the bird world.

Directory of Garden Birds

This directory presents over 100 of our most common birds, ranging from everyday species like magpies, which visit almost every garden, to creatures like Topknot Pigeons and Superb Parrots, two species which are most likely to be chance encounters.

To get the most out of having birds in your garden you need a reasonable pair of binoculars. These are described by two numbers, for example, 8 x 40. The first number is the magnifying power and the second is the size of the lens at the bigger end (the objective lens). The power should be between seven and ten. Below seven you won't get a very good view; above ten the field of view is so small that it is hard to find the bird – and once you do, the high power magnifies every slight shake of your hand.

Objective lenses need to be between 35mm and 50mm. Above 50mm tends to be too heavy to carry and below 35mm the picture will be too dim and the field of view too small. Something around 8 x 40 is about the right size.

WHO'S WHO IN THE BIRD WORLD

Identifying birds becomes easier the more time you spend watching them. The first step is to decide what group a bird belongs to, and then to work out which member of the group it is. A field guide is very useful at this stage (*see* Further Reading). Identifying birds is the same as trying to identify anything. For instance, with a piece of fruit it's obvious whether it's an apple, orange or lemon. Apples can be further specified as a Delicious, Jonathan or Spartan, and some people can even tell you that Spartans resist powdery mildew and that the branches of a Delicious need spreading (but not the Golden variety!). It's the same with birds: you already know several groups of birds such as pigeons, ducks and parrots.

In grouping birds, it's the shape that's important, so ignore the colours. Having decided what group of birds your species belongs to, colour then becomes more important in working out which particular member of the group it is. As with people, birds' faces are generally their most distinctive feature and it's often facial colours that separate closely related species, such as the different types of thornbills. These critical differences are called 'field marks'.

Calls are also important. A kookaburra's laugh is quite distinctive and there are many other calls that can be learnt easily, such as the descending two-second trill of the Fantailed Cuckoo, or the pure tones of the bellbird.

Some birds have distinctive habits that set them apart, like the way cuckoo-shrikes shuffle their wings when they land, or the way a Little Raven flicks its wings with each call.

The geographic range can also help to eliminate unlikely possibilities. A brown, bronze-winged pigeon on the coast could be a Common or a Brush Bronzewing, but if it is in the inland it can only be a Common.

So the things to notice in identifying your bird are its shape, colours, field marks, call, habits and range. To keep these key points in mind, try to remember either of the following two phrases:
Sexy Cockies Flirting Can Have a Riot; or
Silly Crows Fighting Can't Hear the Radio.

At first, we all have a very tough group of birds to identify – the little brown bush ones. These include thornbills, warblers, whistlers and some of the honeyeaters. The more you just relax and observe them, the more obvious the differences will become. Soon you will be able to distinguish the male and female rosellas and you will no longer understand how anyone could possibly confuse the slim lines of a honeyeater with the much more robust outline of a whistler. In short, just sit back, relax and let it happen!

GETTING CLOSE TO BIRDS

The closer you get to a bird the more you can see. Playing a tape recording of its call can be an effective way of getting the bird to come very close. During winter and spring some birds will be so angry at hearing an intruder that they just about take the speaker apart. You should use this technique very sparingly.

A bird hide can also be a valuable addition to the garden. It is basically just a high, narrow tent with a variety of viewing slots for binoculars and camera lenses. By making the hide on a frame, you can move it around, leave it until the birds are accustomed to it and then hop in while it's still dark and wait for that great close-up photo opportunity.

For nesting birds, it's important to move the hide closer to the nest in gradual steps. This will ensure the parents aren't unduly alarmed and avoids putting the chicks at risk by scaring their parents away.

It's an excellent idea to join a local bird group so you can increase your knowledge of birds and share your experiences (*see* Useful Addresses). You'll soon be swapping information with like-minded people and before you know it, you'll be talking about 'pishing', 'jizz' and all sorts of obscure bird terms. You'll also be well on the way to deciding whether you're a twitcher, ticking off new species like you might collect stamps; an ornithologist, who is aiming to contribute to science and therefore looks down on the twitcher; or a birdo, who is somewhere in between and thinks the other two should just take it easy.

IDENTIFYING BIRDS

Some people find it helpful to use these labelled bird parts when recording a new species. Take note of a bird's shape, colour, field markings (especially on the face), call, habits and range. It will also be useful to note the type of habitat the bird lives in. The more detailed your notes, the better are your chances of identifying the bird once you check a field guide.

This bird directory aims to provide interesting information about the birds that might turn up in your garden. It will help you identify one species from another and, most importantly, to work out what each species needs to feel at home in your garden. It contains information on a bird's favourite food, its habitat needs and the kind of nesting areas it likes.

The directory is designed for dipping into rather than for reading from end to end, and the birds are listed in the order that scientists use – the taxonomic order. Have fun!

DIRECTORY OF GARDEN BIRDS

Australian Brush-turkey
Alectura lathami

At first sight, male brush-turkeys can look quite silly, as they spend most of their time scraping leaf litter into a huge compost mound that can reach up to a metre or so high.

DIET
Small creatures that they can catch when typically scratching in forest leaf litter.

FIELD NOTES
Brush-turkeys were once seen as birds to pluck and put in a moderate oven. This made them very wary in most areas – numbers have increased only since we grew out of the rather nasty habit of shooting them.

In the last few decades these birds have become much more trusting, to the point where some cafes on the edge of rainforested areas (like the one at Sea Acres Nature Reserve in Port Macquarie) have had to reorganise things to keep turkeys away from their cake display!

Brush-turkeys soon become used to handouts and are quite tame in many picnic areas and campgrounds in eastern Australia. Bread isn't part of their natural diet, so it should be offered in moderation.

Brush-turkeys use their large feet to rake through leaf litter. This is how they find most of the insects they eat.

IN THE GARDEN

HABITAT

If you live in turkey country, a surplus of mulch generally means plenty of brush-turkeys. Shady gardens on the edge of rainforests are especially popular. If their manic scratching is wrecking your garden, mulch fragile plants with big, flat rocks to protect them from drying out as well as from overactive turkeys.

FOOD

These gluttons will eat almost anything – ranging from grain and bread to cake and cheese. They've even been seen in Noosa National Park fighting ravens for a cooked chicken leg!

NESTING

Unlike normal, self-respecting birds, these characters lay their eggs in a mound of mulch where the heat of the compost hatches the 20 or so eggs.

Females find a compost heap irresistible, which is why the males are probably not so silly after all. It explains why they spend most of their time scraping up leaf litter – to attract females.

DIRECTORY OF GARDEN BIRDS

Australian Wood Duck
Chenonetta jubata

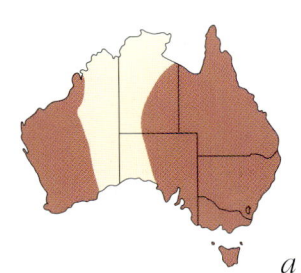

Soft grey plumage, a quiet disposition and the ability to nest in trees a long way from water make these ducks one of the more common waterbirds to grace our gardens.

A female Australian Wood Duck takes her brood out for a morning swim on the lake.

DIET
Most of our other ducks eat small creatures in the water, but these birds prefer green grass – especially if it's short from mowing or grazing.

FIELD NOTES
Telling who's who in the Wood Duck world is easy. It's the females who have the white-stripe eye make-up (*below*), while the boring old males have a plain, dark head.

IN THE GARDEN

Habitat
Swimming pools with lawns nearby are very popular with these birds. Munching on the juicy grass is a Wood Duck's delight and the pool is always handy if unwanted visitors like dogs or small children turn up.

Baby ducklings take a while to develop their adult colours. In the meantime they travel around in the soft camouflage patterns common to many waterfowl.

Food
Grass near water – especially sprouting grain and leafy vegetables like lettuce.

Nesting
Australian Wood Ducks breed in hollow trees, sometimes more than a kilometre from water, and at a considerable height above the ground. The chicks leave home almost as soon as they hatch, and well before they can fly. To get to the ground, they simply jump out of the tree. When they hit the ground they just bounce like fluffy tennis balls, and waddle off with mum and dad to the water.

The female sits on her eggs (normally 10) until they hatch, which is in approximately four weeks.

DIRECTORY OF GARDEN BIRDS

Australasian Grebe
Tachybaptus novaehollandiae

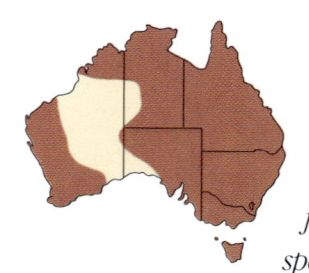

Australasian Grebes, one of our most delightful little waterbirds, spend their time floating or diving in lakes and reedy farm dams where they hide from predators and hunt for food.

Baby grebes are so small and vulnerable that they need the very best of camouflage colours. Their stripes help them to vanish into the vertical shadows provided by the reeds that border their pond.

Grebes seldom fly in the daytime. They are usually seen floating or swimming.

DIET
Small fish, insects and other water creatures.

FIELD NOTES
Grebes like swimming peacefully on small areas of water such as lakes, dams and reservoirs. Creeping up on them is an interesting experience – when you get too close, there's a sudden splash of water and instead of flying away, the grebe just disappears.

Wait five minutes and you can guarantee you are being watched – but finding the grebe is another matter. Scan around the edge of the reeds and you just might spot the bird floating with only the top of its head out of the water like a biological submarine, keeping a watchful eye on you.

IN THE GARDEN

Habitat
Grebes need quite a large pond but they can be a wonderful addition to larger country gardens. They like deep water for hunting and reeds or rushes to hide in.

Food
The best way to provide grebes with food is to have deep, clear water with plenty of water weeds, sunken logs or rocks as well as places for other food sources to live in such as tadpoles, snails or fish.

You can keep water clear by having grass and shrubs on the banks of the pond. It is especially important to avoid pesticides, as many of the grebe's food sources are easily killed by chemicals.

Nesting
Grebes make an extraordinary floating nest out of water weeds. When the sitting female bird leaves the nest, she pulls weeds over it so amateur egg collectors and other predators think the nest is an old one.

Grebes breed from September to March. The four to six eggs probably take about three weeks to hatch.

The parents usually cover up their eggs when they are away.

DIRECTORY OF GARDEN BIRDS

Little Pied Cormorant

Phalacrocorax melanoleucos

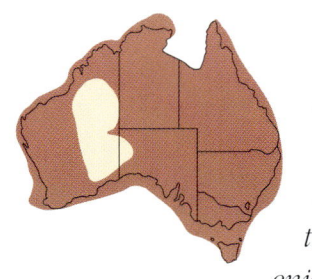

Of the five cormorant species in Australia, the Little Pied Cormorant is the most widespread, enjoying inland and coastal areas alike. You can see them around almost any body of water, holding their wings out to dry after a morning's skindiving.

Little Pied Cormorants, with their short stubby wings, have to flap quite hard to get into the air.

DIET
Yabbies, other crustaceans and fish.

FIELD NOTES
Although cormorants have nice oily feathers, the structure of their plumage lets water in, so they aren't too buoyant – which is why they have to sit and dry out.

Despite their dumpy wings, cormorants can fly hundreds of kilometres and will often turn up at farm dams and large ponds.

Although they are good at fishing, there is no truth in the rumour that the birds are showing the size of the one that got away by how widely apart they hold their wings!

The dark face distinguishes this species from the Pied Cormorant.

IN THE GARDEN

Habitat
A large country garden pond or farm dam is a perfect spot for Little Pied Cormorants.

Food
These birds have a shorter beak than other cormorants which allows them to specialise in feeding on prey such as yabbies, other crustaceans and fish, which they catch in short dives of less than 20 seconds in farm dams and larger garden ponds.

Broken terracotta plant pots or small concrete pipes provide a great shelter for yabbies when placed on the bottom of a pond or dam. By attracting yabbies you're likely to see cormorants on the water.

Nesting
These cormorants build nests in colonies during spring and summer in the south, or during autumn in the inland. Surprisingly, there is little information on how long the four or so eggs take to hatch. With dozens of colonies in south-east and south-west Australia, here's a golden opportunity for you to push back the frontiers of science by employing some patient observation!

White-faced Heron

Egretta novaehollandiae

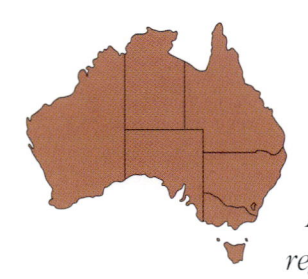

White-faced Herons live in most parts of Australia except desert regions. With their powder-soft plumage and subtle grey tones, they provide a classy addition to any area.

DIET

Fish, insects, crustaceans and other creatures that live on mudflats, in shallow water or grassy areas.

FIELD NOTES

White-faced Herons usually hunt by sitting still or stalking slowly along mudflats, zapping their prey with a quick thrust of the bill.

Feeding in such wet, shiny areas has disadvantages because of the sun's glare, but hunting herons minimise this problem by walking quickly towards the sun and then slowly away from it to get a clear view of their prey. This makes it hard for sharp-eyed crabs and fish to spot approaching herons, since they now have the sun in their eyes.

IN THE GARDEN

Habitat

Open grassy areas near a large pond will attract these herons, especially if there are medium to tall trees for roosting nearby.

A White-faced Heron.

Adult White-faced Herons are easy to tell from reef herons because of their light faces, but grubby-faced juveniles are much harder to separate. To tell them apart, you need to notice the thinner beak of the White-faced Heron, or the dark trailing edges to its wings in flight.

Food

White-faced Herons love goldfish, which gives rise to a garden dilemma. Both goldfish and herons are great to have around but can you have your goldfish, at the same time allowing the herons to eat them too? The answer is yes.

All you need to have is plenty of places for the fish to hide, such as waterlilies or sunken rocks and logs. That way the herons might zap an unwary fish, but usually a balance will be struck, leaving you with both fish and the odd heron to make your garden pond more interesting.

Snails are a last resort for hungry herons.

Nesting

These herons build a thin stick nest in trees, away from other herons and up to 4km from water. From what we know, it looks like they lay about five eggs and it takes about four weeks for the noisy babies to hatch.

SACRED IBIS

Theskiornis molucca

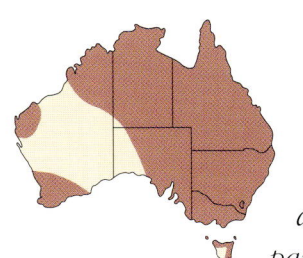

With a taste for ham sandwiches and the ability to nest in city parks and gardens, these birds have adapted very well to life in the suburbs. They can fly long distances and are found in most parts of Australia.

Sacred Ibises have recently adapted to life in our city parks – so much so that in many areas there are rather more of these freeloaders than visitors would like.

DIET

Insects, crabs, yabbies, fish, worms and, of course, ham sandwiches (and any other leftovers they can get their beaks into).

FIELD NOTES

Since 1950, the Sacred Ibis has spread into urban areas in south-east and south-west Australia.

You can see them wandering along mudflats and grassy parks, probing into the mud and water, or pecking at food items on the surface.

The adult ibis doesn't wander much, but juveniles travel thousands of kilometres. One juvenile that was banded in Victoria made the 3000km trip all the way to Papua New Guinea.

IN THE GARDEN

Habitat

Ibises like lakes and ponds near open flat areas of lawn or sticky mudflats. While mud might not be a popular option in today's gardening fashions, large gardens and farm pastures can be great for these birds.

Food

If you really want these vandals around, you could leave out a ham sandwich or two, or a spot of dried pet food if you'd rather have the sandwich yourself.

Nesting

Ibises nest on wetlands in colonies ranging in size from a few individuals to tens of thousands. The two to four eggs are brooded by both parents and take about three weeks to hatch.

Ibises breed when inland wetlands are flooding. Breeding colonies are especially vulnerable to sudden drops in water level, so the diversion of water from wetlands to irrigation areas must be managed very carefully.

DIRECTORY OF GARDEN BIRDS

BLACK-SHOULDERED KITE
Elanus axillaris

This is one of our most handsome hawks and also one of the most widespread. You can see them floating effortlessly over grassy paddocks in most parts of the country.

Black-shouldered Kites like a room with a view and usually nest in the taller suburban trees. In a good season all the eggs will hatch and the chicks will survive until they leave the nest.

In flight, the clearly visible under-wing pattern of these handsome birds makes it easy to distinguish them from the closely related Letter-winged Kites.

DIET
Mice, grasshoppers, lizards and even frogs.

FIELD NOTES
Like most mouse-hunting hawks, these birds move around the country as the numbers of their prey wax and wane. One bird caught in the early 1970s at Lithgow near Sydney had flown nearly 1000km from Redbanks near Adelaide.

In recent decades, more people than ever can enjoy seeing these snazzy birds, as they have spread into the south-western areas of Western Australia and also into parts of inland Victoria.

IN THE GARDEN

HABITAT
These birds hunt over long, grassy areas that have the odd tall tree to roost in. Larger gardens or those on the edge of parks can be great for Black-shouldered Kites as long as the lawn isn't mowed too often! Short grass isn't a very good place for a mouse or grasshopper to hide in and doesn't offer these kites much in the way of food reserves.

FOOD
Black-shouldered Kites hunt by hovering in one spot, then dropping on their prey. Just keep pesticides and lawnmowers away from the grass and nature will supply everything a hungry kite needs.

NESTING
Tall trees on the edge of open grasslands are an ideal site. The mottled brown babies spend about five weeks in the nest, making their distinctive begging calls. The two to four eggs are brooded by the female for about four weeks.

DIRECTORY OF GARDEN BIRDS

Nankeen Kestrel

Faclo cenchroides

Only three hawks in Australia can hover in one spot for any length of time: the Letter-winged Kite which lives in the far inland, the Black-shouldered Kite which is fairly common, and the Nankeen Kestrel which you can find everywhere, from the biggest cities to the hottest deserts.

Kestrels fan their tails and wings for gliding.

Female Nankeen Kestrels are only small birds, but they still have powerful talons and beaks that make quick work of prey.

FOOD
Mice, lizards, insects and smaller birds.

FIELD NOTES
As with many hawks, the female is bigger than the male and in this case, rather more glamorous. Males have a grey head and only one band on their grey tail, while their female counterparts have a brown head and lots of bands on their brown tail.

Kestrels will nest in all sorts of places, from the abandoned nest of another bird, to hollow trees and even ledges on city buildings.

IN THE GARDEN

Habitat
Larger areas of grass and other open areas with a few big trees for the kestrels to survey the landscape.

Food
Kestrels mostly hunt for their own food but can grow to like handouts of little meat titbits. Straight meat isn't all that good for them unless it's dusted with calcium carbonate (from the chemist). Otherwise, prepared pet food is nutritionally balanced but don't overdo this as they need fur or feathers as part of their diet.

Nesting
Like nearly all our falcons, these trim little raptors don't build a nest. Instead they use the old nest of a raven or similar-sized species, or they'll nest in a tree hollow, cliff ledge or even niches in city buildings.

The four eggs hatch after almost four weeks of incubation by the female.

DIRECTORY OF GARDEN BIRDS

Masked Lapwing (Plover)

Vanellus miles

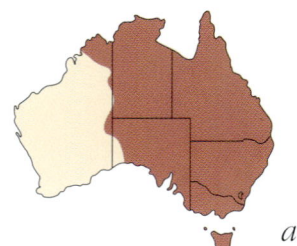

The strident calls of Masked Lapwings in the middle of the night and their flashing brown and white shapes swooping over parks and ovals make these birds relatively hard to miss.

DIET

Insects, worms, crabs and the odd bit of vegetable matter make up the lapwing's diet.

FIELD NOTES

Civilisation has been both good and bad for lapwings. The extra grasslands, such as playing fields, airports and pastures, have given them more habitat, but the dogs, cats and foxes haven't been too good.

Masked Lapwings love open grassy or gravelly areas where they can get a clear view of approaching predators.

IN THE GARDEN

Habitat
Large areas with short grass, protection from dogs, cats and lawnmowers, and some nearby water will create a lapwing paradise.

Food
These birds will find their own food, as long as you can provide the right habitat without any pesticides.

Nesting
Lapwings live and nest on the ground; you never see them in a tree. Four eggs are laid in a scrape in the ground, or often on a rise or even on a pile of gravel to afford the birds a good view of dangerous creatures or approaching children.

If you wander up to a lapwing sitting on the eggs, the bird will usually just slink away. The young birds hatch after about four weeks and are led to a feeding area by the parents. At this stage, if you wander up to them, you'll be met by a screaming banshee of a bird with outstretched wings that display centimetre-long spikes. Although lapwings rarely hit anyone, their threatening display is usually enough to convince all but the keenest naturalist to bug off.

Baby lapwings have such good camouflage, you just won't see them – when they stop moving they disappear.

SILVER GULL

Larus novaehollandiae

A taste for everything except vegetables coupled with impressive powers of flight (they can crash into planes) make Silver Gulls our most common seabird. There are probably a lot more of them than there used to be and this leads to all sorts of problems. They tend to prowl around nesting colonies, trying to eat other birds' eggs or chicks.

Silver Gulls eat anything from fish to tasty morsels from the local garbage tip. They have adapted rather too well to living with people.

DIET

Carrion, crustaceans, worms, insects, plankton – and a lot more.

FIELD NOTES

You can see Silver Gulls almost anywhere in Australia, even in some of our desert regions.

Large groups roost in open areas on the ground. The birds on the outside of the group are the first to spot intruders, and they share guard duty by swapping places with the inner birds. Late-night visitors to city parks and airports often notice swirling flights of these gulls as they swap guard duty and grab insects around light poles.

You can't tell the sex of the adults but it's easy to separate the brown beaks and eyes of the drab young birds from their sparkling white parents with their bright red beaks and white eyes.

IN THE GARDEN

HABITAT
Open areas of grass, sand or pebbles are fine for gulls, especially if there are large areas of water nearby.

FOOD
Gulls will eat a very wide variety of non-vegetable food from old prawn heads and chicken wings to meat; they also eat potato chips.

NESTING
Nearly all the gulls in our larger cities nest on islands or sandspits a long way from where you usually see them. Near Wollongong, the birds nest off the coast on the Five Islands, and commute daily to the local tip where dinner is nearly always available.

Most gulls breed in southern Australia in winter, and in eastern areas in spring. They are especially active in the southwest, where they can breed in both spring and autumn.

The gulls nest on the ground or occasionally on a quiet boat or pontoon. The two eggs hatch after just over three weeks' incubation by both parents. The young leave the nest after about four weeks.

Adult Silver Gulls have white eyes.

Rock Dove (Feral Pigeon)

Columba livia

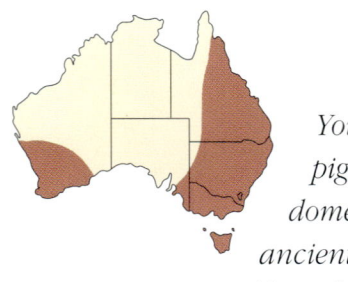

You can't miss these pigeons. They were domesticated by the ancient Egyptians at least 3000 years ago and have been living in most of the world's cities ever since. Their colours vary, but many have a white rump which is visible when they fly.

DIET
Seeds and anything that is based on grains, like bread.

FIELD NOTES
Rock Doves are also called Feral Pigeons. They have spread across the world, nesting on building ledges just as their ancestors used to nest on cliff faces in England and the rest of Europe. Pigeons aren't always welcomed; neither are their droppings, which decorate buildings.

Male pigeons perform quite a dance for their female friends. They fly up high, spread their tails and glide down with their wings held high in a V shape, saying, 'Look at me, I'm handsome and I'm not scared of falcons'. They also walk around after the females, bobbing their heads up and down to show off their beautiful neck feathers.

IN THE GARDEN

HABITAT
All these birds need is a building to perch on and some open ground for feeding.

The sun glinting off the large iridescent chest patch reveals that this bird is a male.

Feral Pigeons have taken to living in the bush in many parts of Australia. They are also found in woodland and around coastal cliffs and beaches.

FOOD
One study in the northern suburbs of Canberra found that the birds ate 40% grain, 31% garden and weed seeds, 28% bread and 1% other foods. Mixed seeds in a feeding tray are an easy way to attract pigeons if you really want to!

NESTING
Feral pigeons are experts at nesting on buildings. If they nest at your home, it can be fascinating to watch their matrimonial antics.

To provide a nesting habitat you will need to put a 15cm wall around a window ledge and place some food near it. Pigeons are fussy about nest sites, but if they are in your neighbourhood and nesting sites are in short supply, a boxed-in window ledge might be just the thing. The two eggs hatch after about two and a half weeks and the chicks leave the nest after about five weeks. The two chicks are often a male and a female – in fact, the origin of the expression a 'pigeon pair'.

WHITE-HEADED PIGEON

Columba leucomela

It's likely that the population of these pigeons dropped dramatically after the over-zealous clearing of rainforest last century. This handsome bird has made a comeback in the past 50 years probably due to the spread of the South American weed tree, Camphor Laurel (*Cinnamomum camphora*).

These days, White-headed Pigeons are not often seen in the suburbs, but they are making a comeback in many parts of their range.

DIET

Rainforest fruits and seeds taken mostly from smaller trees and occasionally the ground.

FIELD NOTES

This pigeon is one of the most difficult to see in the rainforest. It flies like a stealth bomber and seldom calls. Feeding birds don't even give their presence away by spitting out seeds like other pigeons.

They feed in the early morning and roost during the hotter part of the day, generally in rainforest areas.

IN THE GARDEN

HABITAT

Despite their shyness in the rainforest, these birds are becoming increasingly common in open country where rainforest species or the introduced Camphor Laurels are growing.

On the north coast of New South Wales, there are recent records of them nesting in gardens and they're commonly seen feeding in areas where the right trees are growing.

FOOD

The best way to provide food for these birds is to include the trees they feed from in your garden plan.

Unlike other rainforest pigeons, these birds have a muscular gizzard which grinds up seeds as well as fruits.

The White-headed Pigeon's favourite trees are quite obscure and include bollywoods (*Litsea* sp.), Blush Walnut (*Beilschmeidia elliptica*) and some of the Cryptocaryas.

They also like the fruit of some more common trees such as Lilly Pilly (*Acmena* and *Syzygium* sp.), Cheese Tree (*Glochidion ferdinandi*), achronychia (*Achronychia oblongifolia*) and Sweet Pittosporum (*Pittosporum undulatum*).

Pittosporum undulatum.

NESTING

White-headed Pigeons lay only one egg in a typically frail pigeon's nest between 2 and 20m from the ground. They like dense tangles of vegetation, and unruly clumps of lawyer vines (*Calamus* sp.) are great if you can find a place in your garden for them to scramble over some trees.

The egg takes just under three weeks to hatch and the chick can fly after about another three weeks.

SPOTTED TURTLE-DOVE

Streptopelia chinensis

These soft brown doves are the source of the peaceful cooing sounds that you often hear in the suburbs. They were brought to Australia last century from China, Malaysia and possibly India.

DIET
Like their relatives, the Feral Pigeons, these doves like to eat seeds on the ground.

FIELD NOTES
There is some evidence that Spotted Turtle-doves have thrived at the expense of indigenous birds like Bar-shouldered and Peaceful doves. However, it is also possible that the indigenous birds were displaced by the development of suburbs and the Spotted Doves simply moved in as the natives moved out.

Turtle-doves, who do well in the suburbs, have thankfully not been able to invade natural bushland.

Spotted Turtle-doves are one of the species that adapt readily to extra food being provided in the garden.

IN THE GARDEN

HABITAT
Spotted Turtle-doves like dense bushes between 2 and 5m high, near open areas with short grass.

FOOD
Seeds of garden plants and scrounged sandwich crusts. Near zoos, most of their diet consists of purloined animal pellets.

NESTING
Turtle-doves build a silly excuse for a nest that you can just about see through when the bird is not sitting. Despite this, the eggs seldom roll off or fall through and the birds even seem to be expanding their range.

Most nests are in bushes, like those of normal birds, but they have also been found using the cross arms on electricity poles and even the orange light on a set of Sydney traffic lights!

If they're not eaten by currawongs, the two eggs take just over two weeks to hatch and the chicks leave the nest after a further two weeks.

CRESTED PIGEON

Ocyphaps lophotes

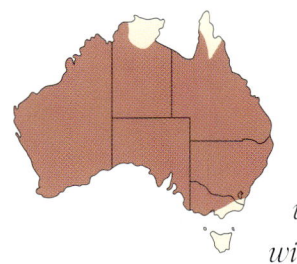

Very few Australian birds make more noise with their wings than with their voices, but the Crested Pigeon is one that does. You won't hear the soft cooing call unless you're very close. When they fly, the wings make a unique whistling sound that carries much further and is probably made by the very narrow third primary feather. Perhaps this functions as an alarm signal to other Crested Pigeons.

While many of the other bronze-winged pigeons are found only in their natural environments, Crested Pigeons have spread successfully from their former inland homes to many Australian suburban areas.

DIET

Mainly seeds and greens, but they also eat the odd insect or other little creature.

FIELD NOTES

This is one of the success stories of wildlife in Australia. Before 1920, you had little chance of seeing a Crested Pigeon anywhere outside the semi-arid parts of Australia. These days they are quite common in coastal districts northwards from about Sydney. This is probably due to the clearing of coastal forests to provide pasture and the extra water supplies created by bores and dams in arid zones.

The attractive bronze wings of these handsome birds make them a welcome addition to parks and open gardens in many parts of Australia.

IN THE GARDEN

HABITAT
Crested Pigeons need areas with short grass near water, with a few nearby trees for nesting. These days pastures, parks, large gardens and golf courses provide a good habitat.

FOOD
These birds are able to eat a very wide variety of food and are often found around farms where they help themselves to chook pellets or other food. You can attract them by putting out pellets or sprouted grain.

Letting the lawn get long enough to grow seeds can also be very attractive for this pigeon.

NESTING
They build the usual hopeless pigeon nest with a few twigs roughly placed in a tangle of branches, for example, where a eucalypt branch has broken off and dozens of new shoots are sprouting.

The two eggs hatch after about two and a half weeks and the young leave the nest after about three weeks.

DIRECTORY OF GARDEN BIRDS

Peaceful Dove
Geopelia striata

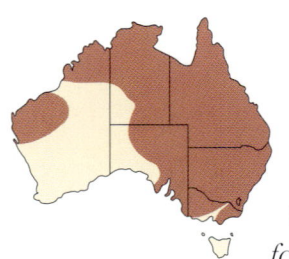

Just as the call of the Bar-shouldered Dove typifies Australia's coastal forests, so the musical 'doodle-oodle' of the Peaceful Dove permeates the woodland areas of the inland.

DIET

Grass seeds.

FIELD NOTES

Peaceful Doves prefer drier, more open places than the more luxuriant habitat of their close relatives, the Bar-shouldered Doves.

You often see Peaceful Doves feeding quietly along country roadsides or flying in an undulating way close to the ground.

Despite their name, these little creatures aren't exactly peaceful. They are quite aggressive with each other during the breeding season and with other birds at drinking places.

Peaceful Doves spend a lot of time on the ground where their subtle colours blend into the surroundings.

IN THE GARDEN

HABITAT

Peaceful Doves need open, grassy areas dotted with trees for roosting and nesting.

Don't mow the lawn if you want to help these pretty birds; the grass-seed heads are an important food source.

FOOD

These doves will appreciate a seed mix designed for smaller birds. They also like chook pellets and sprouted grain.

Right: *Mixed poultry grain can also be fed to garden birds – doves and parrots in particular.*

NESTING

A typical Peaceful Dove nest has only about 25 to 35 twigs and can be found in a wide variety of places within 5 or 6m of the ground.

The two eggs hatch in about two weeks and the young leave the nest after around a further two weeks.

Like most pigeons and doves, the male and female of this species are difficult for humans to distinguish. The female's colouring is only slightly duller than the male's.

Bar-shouldered Dove

Geopelia humeralis

If one thing typifies the feeling of being in the moist forests around the New South Wales–Queensland border, its the 'whoop-a-whoop! whoop-a-whoop!' call of the Bar-shouldered Doves. These handsome little birds live on the edges of rainforests and other places where there is a nice shrubby understorey.

DIET

Bar-shouldered Doves eat the seeds of grasses, sedges and other plants. They don't mind extremely small ones; near Port Moresby, their staple diet is a daisy seed less than one-hundredth of a millimetre across!

Bar-shouldered Doves have beautiful iridescent colours that can only be appreciated when the bird is in the full sun, a characteristic they share with many other Australian pigeons. These birds usually live in small groups.

FIELD NOTES

These doves have done reasonably well from the way humans have changed Australia. In some areas, clearing has resulted in dozens of forest 'islands', each with its population of Bar-shouldered Doves on the edges.

IN THE GARDEN

Habitat

This bird's preference for a reasonably dense understorey, grass seeds and a nearby water source means that many gardens provide suitable habitats.

Although Bar-shouldered Doves spend much of their time perched in trees, they are not afraid to come to the ground for food.

Food

Like several other pigeons and parrots, these characters will help themselves to chook pellets and other grains. If Bar-shouldered Doves live in your area, some mixed seed or sprouted grain offered on the ground will usually attract them.

Nesting

Two eggs are laid in the pigeon's usual frail nest. They take about two weeks to hatch and the little ones leave the nest after about three weeks.

DIRECTORY OF GARDEN BIRDS

Wonga Pigeon
Leucosarcia melanoleuca

These stately birds stroll through rainforest and similar areas looking very much like lords of the manor surveying their realm. They are quite large but get around with surprising agility.

Once shot in large numbers for the table, these regal birds are now strictly protected. They eat fallen fruit and berries on the forest floor.

DIET

Wonga Pigeons feed on fruits, seeds and the odd bush cockroach, snail or worm, with almost all their food taken from the ground.

FIELD NOTES

The Wonga Pigeon's huge breast muscles enable it to surge away from predators such as goshawks and goannas, but this also makes them popular shooting and trapping targets.

In 1865, the famous ornithologist John Gould, who generally wrote about birds' habits in the wild, felt obliged to comment on the eating qualities of the Wonga Pigeon with: 'the whiteness of its flesh rendering it a great delicacy for the table'. Thankfully most of us have now grown out of the unpleasant habit of shooting our wildlife.

IN THE GARDEN

Habitat
Wonga Pigeons need a fairly dense forest canopy with an open forest floor for easy walking, and bushes that produce fruits and seeds.

Food
The fruits of Blueberry Ash (*Elaeocarpus reticulatus*), Ash Quandong (*Elaeocarpus obovatus*), the Bush Cherry (*Exocarpos cupressiformis*) and inkweed (*Phytolacca octandra*) are all eaten by Wonga Pigeons, as are the seeds of acacias.

You can attract the pigeons with corn, sprouted grain or fruit pieces. Better still, grow the plants that provide their natural food so that when your neighbours inquire politely about your inkweed-infested garden, you can point out that you are providing food for passing Wonga Pigeons!

Nesting
The two eggs are laid in a nest that varies from flimsy to substantial. The incubation time is not known but the young seem to leave the nest after approximately four weeks.

Wonga Pigeons like areas where dense plants like this Acacia fimbriata *provide cover from aerial predators.*

TOPKNOT PIGEON

Lopholaimus antarcticus

One of the first Europeans to see this snazzy bird was Captain Cook. While he and his crew were stuck in the Endeavour River, repairing their coral-damaged ship, parties of men went ashore for food and to study the area. The botanist Joseph Banks wrote that they would sometimes shoot 10 or 12 birds which, from his description, must have been Topknot Pigeons.

DIET

These pigeons prefer bite-sized fruits between 5 and 25mm in diameter, and although they like to feed in the top of the forest, they will happily descend to lower levels if they need to.

Huge flocks of Topknots numbering in the thousands once flew up and down the east coast of Australia, providing one of our more spectacular wildlife events.

FIELD NOTES

Topknot Pigeons move along the ranges and up and down the coast, depending on what's fruiting at the time. They make a distinctive picture, often sailing high overhead looking for their next fruit salad, with their long tails and slower wing beats making them easily distinguishable from Feral Pigeons.

Flocks of 3000 in the Lismore area were once common during winter, but today you'd be lucky to see 30.

IN THE GARDEN

Habitat

Topknots are forest birds and don't cross open country unless there is a tasty tree fruiting in the open.

The bigger your trees and the closer the rainforest, the more these pigeons will like your garden.

Food

The key to attracting these stately birds is to plant local fruiting trees, since Topknots will arrive in a specific area because of the fruiting of the trees.

Topknots love large fruit trees, especially Bangalow Palms (*Archontophoenix cunninghamiana*) and Cabbage Tree palms (*Livistona australis*), as well as Lilly Pillies (*Acmena* and *Syzygium* sp.), Cheese Trees (*Glochidion ferdinandi*), figs and a wide variety of other rainforest fruits. They're also partial to the weed tree, Camphor Laurel, but the local species are much better as garden plants.

Nesting

Most nests discovered in recent times have been perched very high up, around 30m or more, although in earlier days, some of the nests that were recorded could be examined from horseback.

The Topknot Pigeon's nest varies from flimsy to substantial and is probably built by the female from material that the male collects.

Only one egg is laid, which hatches after about three weeks' incubation by both sexes. The young bird leaves the nest after nearly four weeks.

Yellow-tailed Black-Cockatoo

Calyptorhynchus funereus

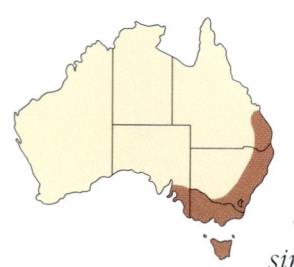

Sounding like a cross between a set of bolt-cutters and an air-raid siren, these large cockatoos are one of the more remarkable birds in Australia. In Western Australia, their relatives have white tails and many authorities there recognise two separate species, the White-tailed and Long-billed black-cockatoos.

Male Yellow-tailed Black-cockatoos have a pink eye-ring while females and juveniles do not. Fledgling birds can be easily distinguished by their frequent begging calls.

DIET

Seeds from pine cones or indigenous plants with similar structures, such as banksias, are the preferred diet. Wood-boring moth caterpillars are also popular.

FIELD NOTES

For a large bird, yellow-tailed blacks fly very well through the tangled branches of our eucalypt forests, using their huge tails to change direction suddenly.

Giant Candles Banksias are a great source of nectar for cockatoos who delicately shred them to get the sweet juice.

IN THE GARDEN

Habitat
These birds like forests with a continuous tree canopy but they will cross open areas to feed on pine trees or to reach the next bit of forest.

Food
Using their massively powerful beaks, these birds extract seeds from the cones of banksias, pines and hakeas, something a person can't do with a pair of pliers. But cones are child's play compared to wood grubs which they somehow locate through 8cm of solid wood, and then dig out.

In Western Australia, the two species seem to have shared these extraordinary talents. The White-tailed Black-cockatoo busts open cones and the Long-billed Black-cockatoo goes for grubs to supplement its staple diet of seeds from Marri trees (*Eucalyptus calophylla*).

Nesting
These birds nest in very large hollows or vertical nest boxes (which the female often enters backwards).

They lay two eggs, but usually rear only one chick which hatches after about four weeks' incubation by the female. The chick leaves the nest after a further three months of feeding by both parents.

DIRECTORY OF GARDEN BIRDS

Gang-gang Cockatoo
Callocephalon fimbriatum

These endangered cockatoos live in the coastal ranges of eastern Australia where their penchant for fruits sometimes brings them into gardens on the edge of forested areas.

FIELD NOTES

During the summer, Gang-gangs remain in the mountains where they breed. When the cool weather comes, many of them move down to lower levels and there is a marked influx of birds into areas like Canberra and to coastal forests where they enjoy the nuts of the Black Ash (*Eucalyptus sieberi*).

Birds feeding in hawthorn (*Crataegus* sp.) are very obvious and can be easy to approach closely. They can be much harder to find in eucalypts and their 'rusty hinge' call or their constant snapping of gumnuts are the best clues to their presence.

IN THE GARDEN

Habitat
Gang-gangs need large areas of forest within about a kilometre or so of the garden. The closer you are to natural forest, the better your chance of seeing these birds.

Male Gang-gangs are unmistakable. Their crimson heads contrast with their softly scalloped grey bodies.

With a call like a rusty gate hinge and brilliant red feathers on the male's head, Gang-gangs would seem to be fairly obvious, but their finely scalloped patterns blend into the foliage making them easy to overlook.

Food
The best way to attract these quiet little cockatoos to your garden is to introduce trees with the berries and seeds they like to eat. Gang-gangs pick eucalyptus nuts to extract the tiny seeds; they are partial to ripening wattle seeds and they just love introduced pyracantha and especially hawthorn berries.

They also eat the odd caterpillar and are one of the very few birds that attack sawfly caterpillars (they're the black ones which get around in a big mass and exude green, eucalyptus-smelling fluid at predators).

Gang-gangs will also eat apples and other orchard fruits and can sometimes be attracted to a feeding tray carrying these fruits.

Nesting
The female Gang-gang chooses the nest site – which is normally very high in a hollow eucalypt, and often situated near water.

The two eggs hatch in just over four weeks and the young leave the nest after a further seven weeks.

DIRECTORY OF GARDEN BIRDS

Galah
Cacatua roseicapilla

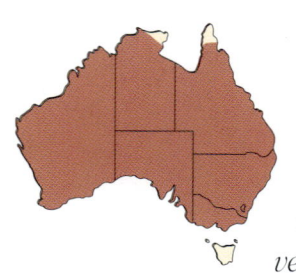

Like Crested Pigeons, these rascals have done very well in recent decades; there are now a lot more of them than there used to be. Changes to the face of Australia that have been good for Galahs have been disastrous for many other birds which are now rare in many parts of the country.

DIET
Grass and shrub seeds, especially ripe ones that have fallen to the ground.

Like most cockatoos, Galahs are too smart for their own good. Watching their antics can be great entertainment though – they love hanging upside down in rain and will even do it when the weather's fine.

FIELD NOTES
Although they are quite common, Galahs are among Australia's most beautiful parrots. Flocks wheel together in the sunlight, their colours appearing to turn from grey to pink as they change direction.

Unfortunately, there are rather too many Galahs in some places and they can sometimes be a crop pest.

It's easy to tell males and females apart. The females have light brown eyes and the males' are dark and mysterious. Young birds have eyes like the adult females and their breast feathers are pink but washed with more grey than the older birds.

IN THE GARDEN

Habitat
Galahs need open areas for feeding and a few large trees with hollows for nesting and resting in during the heat of the day.

Food
They love wheat and other seeds and they commonly come to inspect any seeds that are put out for them.

A male Galah.

Nesting
Large hollows or nest boxes do the trick here. Nest boxes should be upright to imitate a large tree with a hollow trunk, so the bird goes in the side and then drops down onto the base of the box.

Galahs often bite the bark off the tree around their nest site. This may be a signal to other Galahs that the nest is occupied, or to make it harder for nest-robbing goannas to get a grip.

The two to five eggs take just over four weeks to hatch and then the chicks spend another six to eight weeks in the nest. After this they are taken to a creche where they spend a further five or six weeks being fed by the parents.

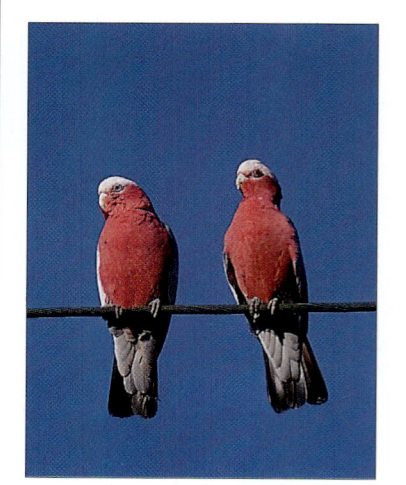

A pair of Galahs, perched on overhead electric wires, keep an eye out for predators.

DIRECTORY OF GARDEN BIRDS

LITTLE CORELLA

Cacatua sanguinea

The natural range of these corellas traditionally covered much of inland Australia but they have recently expanded their population beyond the limits of their former range. In recent decades, populations have appeared in southern coastal areas, probably the result of escaped cagebirds.

DIET

Little Corellas eat the seeds of grasses, shrubs and trees, as well as corms of plants like onion weed and blossoms.

FIELD NOTES

Sightings of Little Corellas are among the very first to have been reported from Australia. On 22 August 1699, 71 years before Captain Cook sailed for the south seas, Englishman William Dampier reported them as 'white parrots which flew a great many together' from what is now called the Dampier Archipelago. If you go there today, you can still see them, flying a great many together.

IN THE GARDEN

HABITAT
In the inland, their stronghold is the treed country along watercourses, and they seem to like similar areas in the suburbs. The arrival of Europeans has probably helped these corellas – forests have been turned into treed parkland, and around homesteads, the inland plains have been scattered with trees.

Large gangs of Little Corellas travel around together. All those watchful eyes make it hard for predators to catch them unawares and the large group gives its members endless scope for social interaction.

FOOD
Like Sulphur-crested Cockatoos, these characters like to eat mixed parrot seed and will also sometimes be tempted by bits of fruit.

NESTING
Corellas use some wacky nesting sites. In north-west Western Australia, they nest in boab hollows, niches in sea cliffs or even in broken termite mounds. In southern areas they are a bit more traditional, generally nesting high in hollow eucalypts.

The two eggs are incubated by both parents who can sometimes be found in the nest at once. The eggs probably take about four weeks to hatch.

Although corellas have small crests, they still use them in their interactions with members of their flock.

DIRECTORY OF GARDEN BIRDS

Sulphur-crested Cockatoo

Cacatua galerita

Seen as overactive vandals, Sulphur-crested Cockatoos are not the sort of bird everyone wants to attract to a garden – unless of course it's one that's a thousand miles from theirs!

Sulphur-crested Cockatoos are the archetypal bird rascal. An overactive brain, deafening voice and bolt-cutter beak give them endless opportunities to make mischief.

DIET

These cockatoos eat the seeds of grasses and trees, fruit, roots and insects. They can cause problems in farming areas by eating grain crops and ripening corn.

FIELD NOTES

Each flock of these cockatoos roosts together in the same area each night. At dusk they squabble noisily as they jostle for position and it is often long after sunset before they settle down.

In the morning, they have a drink, and then cruise off to a feeding area, where they munch away before taking a midday rest in nearby trees. During the afternoon they feed again before returning to their roost.

While the flock feeds, a few birds stay in the trees rising and screeching at any disturbance, at which the rest of the flock will also take off to escape the intruders.

IN THE GARDEN

HABITAT

Cockatoos like feeding in open areas that are surrounded by forest trees.

FOOD

Some of their favourite foods are ripening wattle seeds, pine cones and cedar (*Cedrus deodara* and *atlantica*) cones which you can find shredded in Canberra and other towns on the Great Dividing Range.

Like other parrots, cockatoos are mostly left-footed and you can see them holding a cone in their left foot as they bite chunks out of it to get to the seeds.

If you really want to attract these destructive characters, put out some parrot seed – but not if anyone in your street has cedar timber on the outside of the house. Bored cockatoos just love sinking their powerful beaks into soft wood. Forty thousand dollars later, your neighbours might not be so friendly!

NESTING

Sulphur-crested Cockatoos need a very large tree hollow high off the ground and near water. They also nest in holes in cliffs on the banks of the lower Murray River.

The two eggs hatch after just over four weeks' incubation by both parents, and the young leave the nest after a further 10 weeks.

The spectacular crest of the Sulphur-crested Cockatoo.

DIRECTORY OF GARDEN BIRDS

Rainbow Lorikeet
Trichoglossus haematodus

Raucous screeching calls and extraordinary flashing colours mean that your garden has been invaded by Rainbow Lorikeets. These gaudy parrots do very well in the suburbs.

DIET
Nectar and pollen from flowers as well as seeds, fruits and the occasional insect.

FIELD NOTES
This is the most common lorikeet on the Australian east coast where its iridescent colours and raucous voice make it very easy to see.

Flocks of lorikeets make an incredible noise when they all roost together in one tree, which they do mostly along the coast in the evening. No-one knows why they do this – perhaps it keeps them safe from cats, owls and other predators. These hunters can only eat one bird at a time, so by roosting together the birds maximise their odds of survival.

IN THE GARDEN

HABITAT
These lorikeets are birds of the forest canopy and need lots of trees, especially nectar-producing ones.

FOOD
To help them eat pollen, lorikeets' tongues have dozens of little bumpy bristles. As they feed, they spread pollen from one plant to the next, and so play

Rainbow Lorikeets are the largest and boldest of Australia's seven species of lorikeet. They monopolise feeding trays in many parts of the country.

their part in nature by helping to pollinate the plants, thereby ensuring their own breakfast!

In the canopy, Rainbow Lorikeets feed on eucalypts, the larger banksias, melaleucas, callistemons and Silky Oaks (*Grevillea robusta*). Although they prefer the upper branches, they will descend to flowering grevilleas, the smaller banksias and to bird feeders in backyards.

Lorikeets will also sit quietly in she-oaks (*Casuarina* sp.), picking the seeds out of the cones.

(*See* Chapter Two for some good formulas to make your bird feeder attractive to these birds.)

NESTING
Rainbow Lorikeets nest in a horizontal hollow in a large branch or a vertical one in the main trunk of the tree – usually a eucalypt or paperbark – near water.

The two eggs hatch after nearly four weeks' incubation by the female, and the young are fed by both parents for a further eight weeks before they are ready to leave the nest.

DIRECTORY OF GARDEN BIRDS

SCALY-BREASTED LORIKEET
Trichoglossus chlorolepidotus

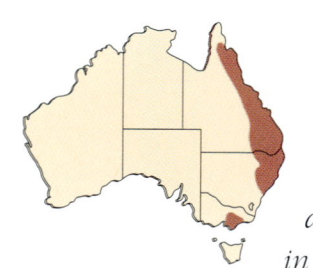

These birds are smaller than Rainbow Lorikeets and much less common in the suburbs, perhaps because the larger rainbows tend to monopolise all the feeding trays set out for birds.

FIELD NOTES

Ironically, for such a brightly coloured, noisy bird, Scaly-breasted Lorikeets are ridiculously hard to see. You can sit under a flowering gum for ages – with bits of flowers falling all around, the air filled with squawking – and still not see them until one actually flies down to another part of the tree.

IN THE GARDEN

HABITAT

Like other lorikeets, these birds are residents of the treetops. They like forest areas, especially where there are flowering trees, and will travel long distances to find good nectar supplies.

FOOD

Nectar-producing trees such as eucalypts, banksias, melaleucas and grevilleas are a proven method of attracting these classy visitors to your garden.

They don't mind the nectar of coral trees (*Erythrina indica*) and in gardens near heathland, lorikeets will feed from the 2m flower spikes of grass trees (*Xanthorrhoea* sp.).

They also like nectar mix, but in the end this is never as good for them as their natural food.

NESTING

Scaly-breasted Lorikeets nest in a hollow eucalypt branch usually at a great height; both parents are normally involved in establishing the nest.

The two eggs take nearly four weeks to hatch after incubation by the female. Young take about seven weeks to leave the nest. They mature slowly, perhaps due to their nectar diet.

As old trees are removed from most suburban areas, birds such as the Scaly-breasted Lorikeet become increasingly dependent on nest boxes or hollow trees that can be retained

DIET

Pollen and nectar from flowers as well as seeds, fruits and probably the occasional insect.

Melaleuca fulgens provides good supplies of nectar for both lorikeets and honeyeaters.

Australian King Parrot

Alisterus scapularis

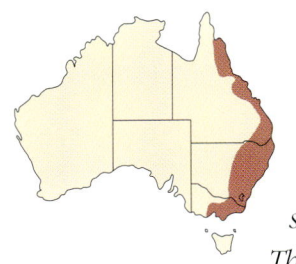

These beautiful parrots are among the most striking birds that visit suburban gardens. The red colour of the adult male seems to shine as though there is a light glowing from within.

DIET
Seeds, berries, nectar and even leaf buds.

FIELD NOTES
Australian King Parrots are much quieter than lorikeets and less frantic in the way they go about their lives.

They feed early in the morning and spend the hotter part of the day perched in a leafy tree canopy. Tall forest eucalypts offer little shade, so King Parrots will often perch in understorey plants, such as Sweet Pittosporum (*Pittosporum undulatum*), only a few metres from the ground, offering a rare sight to anyone lucky enough to spot them.

IN THE GARDEN

Habitat
King Parrots are equally at home in rainforest and eucalypt forest. They will cross open country to get to a good source of food, but are never spotted far from tall trees.

Diet
The King Parrot's staple diet is seeds from eucalypts, angophoras and wattles, so growing these species in forest areas is the perfect way to attract these birds. They also like the berries of introduced hawthorn, pyracantha and cotoneaster, as well as poplar buds in spring and acorns of Pin Oaks (*Quercus palustris*).

Wild tobacco fruits are also popular, especially in the northern areas.

King Parrots are surprisingly difficult to see, despite their bright colours. It's often easier to find them by listening for their high-pitched 'eeeek!' call.

King Parrots are one of the easiest parrots to attract to a feeding tray. Mixed bird seed does the trick (don't include too many sunflower seeds), and they also enjoy pieces of fruit.

Although these birds have been seen feeding on potatoes that lie around on the ground in country areas, it doesn't mean you should put french fries out for them!

Nesting
King Parrots nest in a really deep hollow, usually in the trunk of a eucalypt. In one particular instance, the entrance to a bird's nest was 10m from the ground but the hollow was so deep, the eggs were only a metre or so above ground level. Nest boxes need to be grandfather-clock-shaped with the entrance high on one side. The four eggs hatch after about three weeks' incubation by the female and the chicks take about five weeks to leave the nest.

Superb Parrot

Polytelis swainsonii

This stylish bird lives only in a small part of New South Wales and adjoining parts of Victoria. The mature males are among the world's most beautiful parrots and are a welcome addition to gardens throughout their range.

DIET

Seeds, berries and blossoms.

FIELD NOTES

Superb Parrots breed in ancient red gums growing next to rivers. They need a large hollow high above the ground for nesting – the kind that only forms in trees that are more than 100 years old. Because they like to nest in loose groups, these parrots need several such hollows near each other. With the logging of some of the older trees for railway sleepers, the chances of finding an ideal nesting habitat are slim.

IN THE GARDEN

Habitat
They favour open grassy areas for feeding with some trees nearby for shade as well as protection from predators.

Food
Seeding grasses are a favourite food of Superb Parrots, so leaving sections of your lawn unmowed is a good idea.

Striking contrasts between the green, gold and crimson colours of the male Superb Parrot make this one of our most beautiful species.

Ripening acacia seeds are great food for Superb Parrots.

They will forage on the ground for wattle seeds under acacias. In spring, these parrots also like to eat the blossoms of eucalypts including Yellow Box (*Eucalyptus melliodora*) and Sugar Gum (*E. cladocalyx*).

They like any sort of grain and will visit farms or gardens to pick up spilled wheat and other cereals.

Nesting
They typically nest in a large hollow branch over water. The female broods the eggs for nearly three weeks, after which both she and the male feed the young until they leave after a further six weeks.

Although Superb Parrots prefer to feed on the ground, they will sometimes visit flowering eucalypts to supplement their diet of seeds and berries.

CRIMSON ROSELLA

Platycercus elegans

This common parrot varies widely through its range – many forms have local names: Crimson Rosella in northern and eastern Australia, Yellow Rosella along the Murray and Murrumbidgee rivers and the Adelaide Rosella in parts of coastal South Australia. In Tasmania, it is represented by the Green Rosella which is generally regarded as a separate species.

This young bird is searching for nectar, which it will extract by chewing the banksia cones. The camouflage-green colours of young birds contrast with the red of their parents and may help them to survive their first year.

DIET
Seeds, berries, blossoms and occasionally insects.

FIELD NOTES
Despite their extremely variable colouring, Crimson Rosellas have one feature that tells them apart from other parrots – they all have blue cheek patches. They also have a trick for novice birdwatchers. In late spring, groups of nearly all-green, rosella-type parrots fly around defying identification – it took the author quite some time to work out that these pesky birds are just juvenile rosellas.

You can solve the mystery by watching them until late summer, when you will have the satisfaction of seeing them moult into their true adult colours.

IN THE GARDEN

HABITAT
Crimson Rosellas are forest birds that like areas where the treetops form a continuous canopy. They will feed on the ground but prefer trees or shrubs.

FOOD
Seeds of eucalypts, acacias and grasses are a favourite food, as are the berries of the introduced hawthorn, pyracantha and cotoneaster. They also like the funny little fruits of the Cheese Tree. They are readily attracted to a feeding tray if it contains mixed seeds and a variety of fruit pieces.

Feeding stations for rosellas need to be designed so that they can be cleaned by hosing.

NESTING
Crimson Rosellas nest in a hollow tree trunk or branch that stands between 2–16m above the ground. The four or five eggs take nearly three weeks to hatch and are brooded by the female. Once the chicks hatch they are fed for a further five weeks. Like kingfishers, rosellas are sometimes the losers in nest competitions with Common (Indian) Mynas.

EASTERN ROSELLA

Platycercus eximius

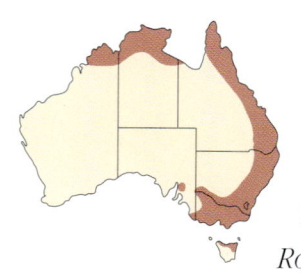

The widespread Eastern Rosella, like the Crimson Rosella, has several plumage patterns each of which has a different local name. Known as Eastern Rosellas in eastern and southern areas, and Northern Rosellas in the north, in the northeast the birds are known as Pale-headed Rosellas.

DIET
Seeds of grasses, eucalypts, wattles and shrubs, as well as berries and blossoms.

The pale-headed form of this species lives in northern New South Wales and most of coastal Queensland.

FIELD NOTES
This is the first bird to which the name rosella was applied. The early colonists called them 'rose-hillers', after the original settlement near Parramatta, which was then shortened to rosella. Eastern Rosellas live in more open areas than the crimson ones. Calls are similar but the former have a slightly higher pitched one.

IN THE GARDEN

Habitat
Trees with open grassy areas in between are great for Eastern Rosellas.

Food
Eucalypts provide seeds and blossoms; wattles can be a very useful source of seeds.
Seeding grasses are probably more important to Eastern Rosellas than to their crimson cousins so it's a good idea to let the grass grow tall enough to produce seed. They are easy to attract with mixed seed and fruit pieces.

Eastern Rosellas' colours are variable; males are generally brighter than their mates, especially on their breasts.

Nesting
Eastern Rosellas nest in a hollow branch or tree trunk from almost ground level to 15m. The female broods the eggs for nearly three weeks and the young leave the nest after a further five weeks.

WESTERN ROSELLA

Platycercus icterotis

These birds look similar to their white-cheeked eastern cousins but they are smaller and the males are markedly different to the females. They are also less active than Eastern Rosellas.

Western Rosellas are the only parrot of their type living in Western Australia, so they are easy to identify.

DIET
Seeds, berries and fruits.

FIELD NOTES
These rosellas are fairly common but their quiet habits make them difficult to find.
During the heat of the day, they sit unobtrusively in the forest canopy – usually in a eucalypt. The female is easy to tell by her more sombre colours, compared to the vibrant red head and breast of the male. During the breeding season, their feathers become ruffled from sitting in the snug nest hollow.

IN THE GARDEN

HABITAT
Open areas for feeding, with trees nearby for shelter, provide an ideal habitat for these birds.

FOOD
Seeding grasses and shrubs are the foods favoured by Western Rosellas. Like other Australian Rosellas, they are also partial to sampling various fruits, especially apples.
Offering mixed parrot seed and fruit pieces is a good way to attract them too.

NESTING
Western Rosellas prefer a hollow branch, usually in a tall eucalypt. They lay about five eggs on a coarse bed of debris from the walls of the hollow. The eggs hatch after nearly three weeks' brooding by the female. The chicks leave the nest after a further five or so weeks. For a short time afterwards, they travel around in family parties.

The Western Rosella nests in hollows, which are in increasingly short supply in most suburban areas.

Australian Ringneck

Barnardius zonarius

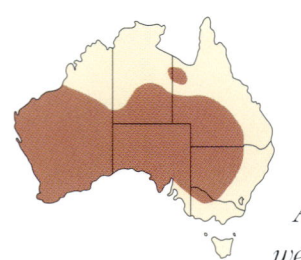

Although these birds are widely distributed in Australia, it is only the western sub-species, known as the Port Lincoln Ringneck, that has successfully adapted to the changes effected in the country since the arrival of Europeans.

DIET
Seeds, berries and blossoms, as well as some insects taken on the ground or in tree canopies.

FIELD NOTES
Like other green birds, the colours of ringnecks come from the microscopic structure of the feathers – they have no green pigment, it's the way the feathers reflect the light that makes them appear green. This means the brighter the sunlight, the more brilliant the green appears. For this reason, ringnecks look so much better in the wild than in photographs. In the blazing inland sun, they can really make the drab Australian bush sparkle. It's hard to forget your first sighting of this species.

IN THE GARDEN

Habitat
These adaptable birds favour everything from forests to lines of trees along watercourses, with the critical ingredient being trees that are the biggest in the area.

Ringneck parrots feed in trees, but they will also descend to the ground for seeds that have fallen from shrubs.

Food
A good way to attract these parrots is by growing Marri trees (*Eucalyptus calophylla*), as they love to rip into the half-ripe gum nuts produced by the trees.

Ringnecks also like the berries of White Cedars (*Melia azedarach*), introduced from eastern Australia.

They are insectivorous parrots, eating lerps, sawflies and other bugs. You can turn this to your advantage by avoiding pesticides, and therefore encouraging insects that the birds enjoy eating.

Putting out a mixture of fruit pieces and grains will also encourage ringneck parrots.

Nesting
The nest hollow can either be low or high, in a branch or a tree trunk. The female broods the four eggs until they hatch after nearly three weeks. Then both parents feed the young until they leave the nest five weeks later.

This variable parrot has four separate forms in different parts of the country. Although the ranges of the different forms now overlap, they probably arose during times when the birds were separated by climatic barriers.

Red-rumped Parrot

Psephotus haematonotus

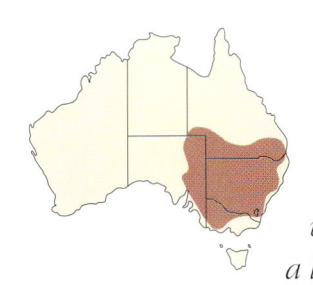

The little Red-rumped Parrot is surprisingly well camouflaged and is a lot more common that many people think. As forest areas are cleared for grazing, they have expanded their range, but only in some areas.

The brilliant green plumage of male Red-rumped Parrots allows them to blend into the grasslands, but doesn't act as camouflage against areas of exposed earth.

DIET

Grass seeds, some leaves and occasionally blossoms.

FIELD NOTES

There is something relaxing and reassuring about watching these little parrots. They feed by walking quietly along the ground in a calm, unruffled way.

The bright, grass-green males tend to be difficult to see, but the brownish females are almost invisible when feeding on the ground – certainly an advantage when a goshawk comes by.

IN THE GARDEN

Habitat
A mixed lawn of seeding grass, dotted with trees for shelter, is ideal for Red-rumped Parrots.

Food
Partial to the seeds of thistles, these birds offer a great excuse to go easy on the weeding and to leave the lawnmower in the shed!

Mixed seed left on the ground will help to entice these parrots and can also produce a little forest of seed plants which are highly attractive to them if you don't mind the appearance of your lawn!

Nesting
Red-rumped Parrots like to nest in a hollow branch or tree trunk, usually near water. They will also nest in hollow fence posts and in the eaves of farmhouses. In Adelaide they have been found nesting in crevices in suburban and city buildings.

The five eggs are brooded only by the female and hatch in nearly three weeks. The chicks are fed by both parents and leave the nest after about four weeks.

A pair of beautiful Red-rumped Parrots visits a quiet waterhole at dusk for their evening drink.

DIRECTORY OF GARDEN BIRDS

Pallid Cuckoo
Cuculus pallidus

With a range that extends across the whole country, these cuckoos lay their eggs in the nests of at least 80 other species – that's more than any other Australian cuckoo.

DIET
Hairy caterpillars, beetles and other insects.

FIELD NOTES
Pallid Cuckoos have a long, barred tail that sets them apart from most similar birds – a feature they share with other middle-sized cuckoos.

You generally hear, rather than see, the Pallid Cuckoo. Its main call starts with a few notes which descend the scale rapidly and then slowly rise, semi-tone at a time, for about eight to 12 notes.

IN THE GARDEN

Habitat
These birds live in open woodland where the tree canopies are separate from each other. They will also live on the edge of dense forests and even in dry inland areas where trees are scarce.

Food
Being insect eaters, the best way to provide for these birds is to ensure your garden is a healthy place with no pesticides and a wide variety of indigenous plants.

Cuckoos belong to one of the few bird groups that will happily eat caterpillars covered in extremely irritating hairs. After a hearty caterpillar meal, the bird's stomach is lined with hairs that would drive most animals nuts.

Nesting
Pallid Cuckoos' favourite foster parents are middle-sized honeyeaters like the yellow-faced and the white-plumed species. If your garden has a well-developed shrub layer and trees, you might be lucky enough (or your honeyeaters unlucky enough) to have Pallid Cuckoos lay their eggs in your garden.

The Pallid Cuckoo is one of the many species that like to call from an open perch. These birds live in most inland areas where their soft grey colours add a subtle note to any garden setting.

DIRECTORY OF GARDEN BIRDS

Fan-tailed Cuckoo
Cacomantis flabelliformis

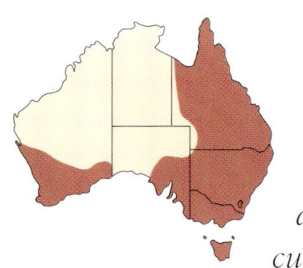

On the coast and in the ranges, the happy downward trill of these cuckoos heralds the arrival of spring each year. Like most cuckoos, they are very vocal as they set up their territories.

Fan-tailed Cuckoos like to advertise their ownership of an area by singing from an exposed perch. This makes them vulnerable to being hassled by the other birds in the forest, but it's often a successful way for them to attract a mate.

DIET
Caterpillars, beetles and other insects.

FIELD NOTES
These birds live in the lower levels of the forest canopy in rainforest, eucalypt forest and even in coastal heathland. They feed by sitting quietly on a branch, watching for an unwary caterpillar to move. Once they have their prey in sight, they swoop gracefully from their perch to snaffle it.

IN THE GARDEN

HABITAT
Being generally forest-dwelling birds, these cuckoos are attracted to gardens with plenty of trees.

FOOD
You can maximise the number of caterpillars and other insects in your garden by growing a wide variety of indigenous plants and avoiding pesticides.

NESTING
These cuckoos lay their eggs in the nests of at least 50 other species – mostly smaller birds that build a spherical nest with an entrance in the side. Thornbills, scrubwrens and fairy-wrens are favourite hosts.

One of the mysteries surrounding Fan-tailed Cuckoos is how they time their egg production with that of their host species. It's also a fascinating challenge to work out how they get their eggs into the enclosed nests of their much smaller victims.

Fan-tailed Cuckoos show the slim lines and finely barred tails that distinguish this group of cuckoos from similar birds. Although adults always have dark grey backs, the buff colour on their fronts can cover just their throats or the whole of their breasts.

DIRECTORY OF GARDEN BIRDS

Common Koel

Eudynamys scolopacea

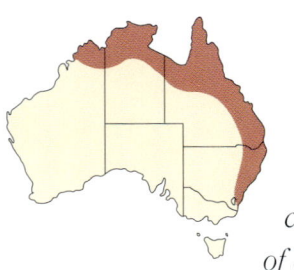

These birds are the classic example of cuckoos not being very visible but being very audible. Each spring they drive people on Australia's eastern seaboard crazy with their 'coo-ee' calls at four o'clock in the morning.

DIET
Fruit, berries and even the odd insect.

FIELD NOTES
Each spring, Common Koels arrive from Indonesia to breed. To attract females and to repel rivals, males have to be obvious. But, being cuckoos, they are hated by other forest birds who attack them on sight. Koels avoid their enemies by being well-camouflaged but remain obvious to other koels by being very noisy – a tactic which is effective, but it doesn't do much for gardeners' tempers.

Male koels are a sinister jet-black colour while females have beautiful mottled brown patterns and black caps.

IN THE GARDEN

Habitat
Common Koels need forest areas – those with large trees are especially popular.

Food
Fruit and berry trees are great for Common Koels. They love large fig trees – the bigger the better, with species such as Moreton Bay Fig (*Ficus macrophylla*), Port Jackson Fig (*F. rubiginosa*) or Green-leaved Moreton Bay Fig (*F. watkinsiana*) being the most suitable – if your garden is large enough.

Berry fruits from trees such as Blueberry Ash (*Elaeocarpus reticulatus*), Lilly Pilly or domestic mulberries are also very attractive.

Nesting
Common Koels generally lay their eggs in the nests of larger forest birds. They prefer Red Wattlebirds, Magpie Larks and Blue-faced Honeyeaters as foster parents for their hatchlings.

The female usually lays one egg in each of several nests. After only a two-week incubation period, the egg hatches and the baby cuckoo monopolises all the food brought by the parents – probably pushing other eggs or chicks out of the nest in the process.

The feathered legs and unique colours of the female make the bird look like a falcon – perhaps to ward off attacks by other birds.

DIRECTORY OF GARDEN BIRDS

Channel-billed Cuckoo

Scythrops novaehollandiae

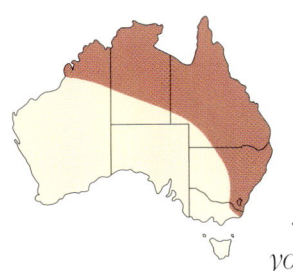

You almost always hear these birds' awful squarking cries before you see them. They really do have Australia's worst bird call, which at least makes them easy to locate.

Although Channel-billed Cuckoos only used to be seen rarely in eastern Australia, in the last five to ten years numbers have increased, especially around Sydney.

DIET
Fruit, berries and insects.

FIELD NOTES
These birds are our largest species of cuckoo. With their monstrous curved beaks and long tails used for manoeuvring in the forest canopy, they have been compared with a flying walking stick by one of Australia's leading bird artists, Peter Slater.

IN THE GARDEN

Habitat
Like Common Koels, these birds need forests with large trees, especially figs.

Channel-bills prefer dense, coastal forests where the tree canopies produce substantial habitat, but they readily travel to tableland areas where they inhabit eucalypts.

Food
Channel-billed Cuckoos are partial to the same plants as Common Koels and can often be seen gobbling down figs. They also prowl the outer foliage for larger invertebrates such as stick insects.

Nesting
These cuckoos usually lay their eggs in the nests of the largest forest birds, for example, ravens, magpies, currawongs and White-winged Choughs.

DIRECTORY OF GARDEN BIRDS

Southern Boobook
Ninox novaeseelandiae

Last century, before modern spotlights became widely available, argument raged about whether the 'mo-poke' call belonged to this owl species or the Tawny Frogmouth. These days, groups of naturalists light up the bush like a Christmas tree to confirm that it is the Southern Boobook which gives this distinctive call.

DIET
Small birds, mammals the size of mice, and insects.

FIELD NOTES
This is Australia's most widespread owl, and the one that has taken most readily to civilisation. You can find boobooks in nearly all Australian cities, where their calls echo around bushy gullies in winter and spring.

IN THE GARDEN

Habitat
Boobooks are most common in areas with a reasonable number of trees – especially dense trees for hiding in during the day, and hollow ones for nesting.

Food
Birds, mice and other prey will be attracted to a wild garden with layers of vegetation and no pesticides.

Nesting
Boobooks need a hollow tree trunk or a nest box at least 20cm wide. Three eggs are laid and hatch after four weeks' brooding by the female, who is fed by the male while she sits. The chicks hatch after about five or six weeks' feeding by both parents.

Top: *The open area of the garden, where insects or rodents may be found, is the hunting ground of this predator.*
Above right: *Owls are powerful creatures with few enemies, so they don't mind an open nest box. Although this box is built for Barn Owls, boobooks may also use it.*
Left: *Eucalypts have to be many decades old before they form hollows large enough to shelter owls.*

132

BARN OWL

Tyto alba

Barn Owls are found not only in Australia but throughout the world. They tend to adapt successfully to new environments.

In common with many other owl species, Barn Owls hide in trees during the day to avoid the unwelcome attention of other birds that attempt to drive them away.

DIET
Small mammals, birds and some insects.

FIELD NOTES
A Barn Owl has such acute hearing that even the rustling sounds a mouse makes in a pile of leaves are enough to locate it accurately in total darkness.

Soft plumage and a row of tiny teeth on the leading edge of each wing ensure silent flight that does not interfere with its sense of hearing.

These owls don't call very often but when they do, it's blood-curdling – something between the tearing of canvas and a scream, if you can imagine that!

IN THE GARDEN

HABITAT
Barn Owls live throughout Australia but prefer open, wooded country with hollow trees for nesting, and dense trees – if possible – to hide in during the day.

FOOD
In the garden, these owls eat insects, mice and small birds, which can be attracted with a variety of vegetation layers, and by avoiding the use of pesticides.

Owls have specially soft plumage to aid their silent, predatory flights through the forest at night in search of prey.

NESTING
True to their name, Barn Owls usually nest in barns and other buildings, as well as in hollow tree trunks or nest boxes. The five or so eggs are brooded by the female and hatch after about five weeks. Chicks are fed by both parents and leave the nest after about nine weeks.

DIRECTORY OF GARDEN BIRDS

Tawny Frogmouth
Podargus strigoides

Looking more like a tree stump with eyes, these birds have extraordinary camouflage and have adapted to most Australian habitats. They use their large beaks to capture insects.

The nests built by Tawny Frogmouths are extremely well camouflaged and are just as difficult to spot as the bird.

DIET
Insects, spiders and other little creatures, together with the odd mouse, mostly taken on the ground.

FIELD NOTES
Frogmouths are quite common in the leafier suburbs but are rarely seen. In the centre of Sydney, they nest each year in the Botanic Gardens.

IN THE GARDEN

Habitat
Although frogmouths can survive throughout Australia, they do prefer areas with plenty of trees – especially in the more densely settled parts of the country.

Food
These birds will find their own food in a healthy garden, but are extremely sensitive to pesticides, particularly the organochlorine ones. These chemicals are now banned in nearly every part of Australia but their toxic legacy lingers – they still poison frogmouths in late winter when food supplies are short.

Nesting
Frogmouths build a scrawny excuse for a nest in a horizontal fork, towards the top of the forest canopy.

The two eggs hatch into fluffy white chicks after about four weeks' incubation by both parents. The chicks leave the nest after a further four weeks.

Frogmouths have huge eyes to see in the dark and very soft feathers that enable them to hunt silently.

LAUGHING KOOKABURRA
Dacelo novaeguineae

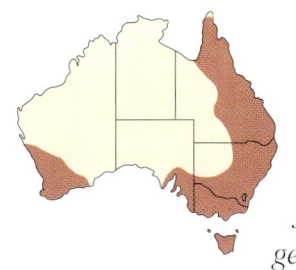

These birds are one of our continent's most famous creatures. In general, people find their laughing call endearing – but not when it's heard in the early hours of the morning.

DIET
Insects, lizards, small snakes, mice, nestlings and anything else they can catch on the ground.

FIELD NOTES
Kookaburras like to live in family groups where the hatchlings are looked after by their older siblings. In early summer, you can sometimes see the youngsters hopping around after a group of older birds. The very young birds have short tails and make rasping, begging calls all day long, usually in summer.

IN THE GARDEN

HABITAT
Kookaburras enjoy forests and woodlands with open ground between the trees for hunting.

FOOD
Although they are quite capable of finding their own food, you can tempt them

Kookaburras are happy to perch in the open.

As any pack of Australian playing cards shows, Kookaburras kill snakes. Although the bird on the right has a Red-bellied Black Snake, they usually only attack smaller reptiles and probably catch more lizards than snakes.

with mealworms, pet food, cheese and meat (dusted with calcium carbonate to balance the phosphate in it).

NESTING
Kookaburras need a large horizontal hollow for nesting. This can be anything from a hollow branch, a shallow hollow in a tree trunk or nest box to a tunnel dug into a termite nest, or even an airconditioning duct.

Two or three eggs hatch after just over three weeks' brooding time by the female, who is assisted by the older siblings. The young leave the nest after five weeks.

Like many newly hatched birds, young kookaburras won't win any beauty contests. But it only takes about five weeks for the 'ugly duckling' chick to be transformed into a handsome juvenile kookaburra.

DIRECTORY OF GARDEN BIRDS

Sacred Kingfisher
Todiramphus sanctus

Kingfishers are a well-represented group, with some 90 species found worldwide. Only 10 occur in Australia. Although many enjoy wetlands, some species are content a long way from water.

DIET
A carnivorous diet of insects, lizards, fish and crabs.

FIELD NOTES
Kingfishers hunt by sitting motionless on a branch before pouncing suddenly on their prey on the ground or in the water. After grabbing the food with their beak, they fly back to their perch to eat it.

You won't see kingfishers in southern areas in the winter, as they spend their holidays in the sunny north, where the high temperatures help to ensure a good food supply.

Sacred Kingfishers are vulnerable to nest competition from Common (Indian) Mynas. In many urban parts of their range, their numbers seem to be dropping.

IN THE GARDEN

Habitat
These kingfishers like open woodland where the treetops don't quite meet, but they can also live quite happily in much denser forests. Like kookaburras, these birds need open ground between the trees where they can go to hunt for their food.

Above: Larger water features can be popular with kingfishers and gardeners alike. The birds enjoy perching on lower branches and watching for prey.
Left: A bowl of wriggling mealworms can be attractive to kingfishers.

Food
Although they like to catch their own food, kingfishers might be tempted if you put out a couple of wriggly mealworms regularly. They will also snatch the odd goldfish – especially from ponds that don't have protective plants floating on the surface.

Nesting
Kingfishers sometimes build nests in a hollow tree, but they usually dig a horizontal nest hole in a creek bank or especially in a termite mound in a tree. Watching this procedure can be quite alarming, as the birds start the hole by flying headfirst into it!

They lay between three and six eggs which are white. The eggs hatch after about two and a half weeks' incubation by both parents and the young leave the nest after a further four weeks.

Rainbow bee-eater

Merops ornatus

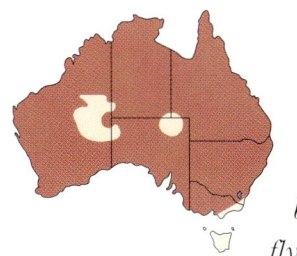

Rainbow Bee-eaters, among Australia's most beautiful birds, look like flying jewels as they flash through the air in pursuit of insects. These birds are very agile in flight and have a beak like a pair of forceps for snatching prey in midair.

DIET
Wasps, bees, dragonflies and other insects.

FIELD NOTES
You rarely see Rainbow Bee-eaters on their own. They feed together, breed together and even look after each other's chicks. Early in the season, it's easy to identify the males by their two long, thin tail feathers. As the feathers wear, this difference isn't so easy to see.

Rainbow Bee-eaters use their impressive powers of flight to catch insects on the wing – even high-speed specialists like dragonflies are fair game.

FOOD
These birds will catch their own flying insects in a healthy, pesticide-free garden environment.

NESTING
Bee-eaters burrow for a metre or so into vertical creek banks and lay their four to five eggs in a chamber at the end of the tunnel that has been created.

The eggs hatch after about three weeks' brooding by the parents and their helpers, who are usually young male bee-eaters. The chicks leave the burrow after a further four weeks.

Dead branches are often chosen as perches to give an all-round view.

IN THE GARDEN

HABITAT
Bee-eaters like trees with lots of open space between them. They are very fond of perching in exposed locations to survey the surrounding area for flying insects. Once they grab one, they often return to the same perch to devour their catch.

DIRECTORY OF GARDEN BIRDS

Dollarbird
Eurystomus orientalis

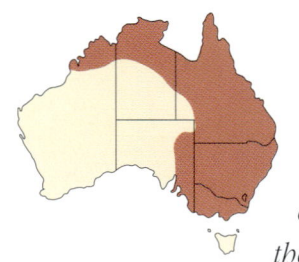

The noisy and peculiar-sounding maniacal cackling in spring signals the Dollarbird's arrival.

Dollarbirds love to survey their realm from a lofty vantage point and they are often visible high up on electric wires or exposed dead branches of trees.

DIET
Cicadas, moths and other flying insects.

FIELD NOTES
The name 'Dollarbird' is derived from the white circles on the wings (only visible when the bird is in flight) which resemble dollar coins.

Dollarbirds are one of Australia's more obvious migrants and it is hard to miss the spectacular aerobatics and other noisy antics of a breeding pair.

Flying ants don't last long with a pair of Dollarbirds about.

IN THE GARDEN

HABITAT
Dollarbirds need a garden of tall trees with open spaces in between. They are birds of the canopy and seldom come anywhere near the ground, so they don't mind whether there is a shrub layer or not.

FOOD
A healthy, pesticide-free garden will provide all the insects a Dollarbird needs.

NESTING
This species needs a shallow hollow in a tree trunk, large branch or a nest box. The birds lay three to five white eggs on the unlined floor of the hollow. Both parents incubate the eggs and both help to feed the hungry chicks.

Large trees are very good for Dollarbirds, but only where there is a lot of space in between the canopies.

DIRECTORY OF GARDEN BIRDS

Superb Lyrebird

Menura novaehollandiae

An extraordinary ability to imitate other sounds, as well as an impressive courting display, make the Superb Lyrebird one of Australia's most famous species.

Above: *Lyrebirds find most of their food by scratching through the leaf litter on the forest floor. Nature has given them particularly powerful legs and feet for this purpose.*
Below: *Spiders form part of the lyrebird's diet, but fast-moving, long-legged creatures often escape.*

DIET
Insects, spiders and small creatures caught on the floor of the forest.

FIELD NOTES
The Superb Lyrebird fills the forest with its incredible song during winter and spring. These birds will imitate any sound – from another bird's call to a barking dog or even a chainsaw. They tend to copy birds that don't sing during the winter and spring months. A constant stream of bird calls coming from one spot is often the only way of identifying this most accurate Australian mimic.

IN THE GARDEN

HABITAT
Lyrebirds live in the denser forest gullies. They do venture into adjoining gardens during dry times, particularly if there is suitable deep mulch to dig in.

FOOD
They may take small pieces of cheese and mealworms.

NESTING
The female lyrebird builds a large, round nest usually near ground level, and looks after the chick by herself. A single egg hatches after six weeks. The mother feeds the chick for a further six weeks.

Lyrebirds are one of our most spectacular species. A displaying male is an extraordinary sight in a dim forest gully, with his impressive lyre-shaped tail feathers framing his strutting song and dance routine.

DIRECTORY OF GARDEN BIRDS

Superb Fairy-wren

Malurus cyaneus

Superb Fairy-wrens, often called Blue Wrens, are one of Australia's favourite birds. The male and his 'harem' of females are a welcome addition to any garden.

The iridescent blue colours of a male fairy-wren are one of the more striking reasons for turning your garden into a mini national park.

DIET
Insects and sometimes berries.

FIELD NOTES
Many people who see a brilliant blue male Superb Fairy-wren surrounded by some half a dozen brown birds assume that the attendant birds are part of the male's harem of females. Unfortunately for male chauvinists, the brown birds aren't females at all but young males who hang around as part of the family group and help raise the chicks.

IN THE GARDEN

HABITAT
These wrens need clumps of dense bushes to hide in and open grassy areas for hunting.

FOOD
They will find their own insects but will also take small pieces of cheese, mealworms and, sometimes, finely chopped fruit.

NESTING
These birds build a dome-shaped nest from grass and spider webs. It is placed in a dense bush usually within a few metres of the ground. The three white, spotted eggs take about two weeks to hatch and the young leave the nest in just under two weeks.

Above: *Female Superb Fairy-wrens have a reddish colouring around the eyes and a brown bill.*
Below: *An unusual view of a Superb Fairy-wren's eggs. The fact that the nest has a side entrance often means that the eggs are difficult to see but, in this case, the unusual angle of the opening lets us peep inside.*

DIRECTORY OF GARDEN BIRDS

Variegated Fairy-wren
Malurus lamberti

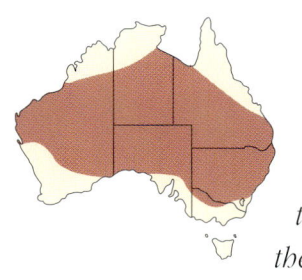

Although not as common in gardens as the Superb Fairy-wren, the range of these little birds covers more of the country. The rufous strip on the male's flank makes it very handsome.

DIET
Flies, beetles and other insects.

FIELD NOTES
Like other fairy-wrens, these birds have a great way of tricking predators intent on nest-robbing – called rodent running. The bird hops through the undergrowth looking for all the world like a deranged mouse. Once the cat or other predator has followed it away from the nest, it gives up and flies off!

The bright rufous patch on the male's back clearly distinguishes Variegated Fairy-wrens from other fairy-wren species.

IN THE GARDEN

Habitat
They like dense shrubs, but more open terrain than that preferred by Superb Fairy-wrens.

Food
Variegated Fairy-wrens, like Superb Fairy-wrens, will find their own food in the garden, but will also take mealworms and small pieces of cheese. They will sometimes pick at fruit slices too.

Nesting
Variegated Fairy-wrens build a dome-shaped nest made from grass and spider web. It is usually placed close to the ground in the densest bushes or grass tussocks. The three or four eggs are white with reddish spots at the larger end. They take two weeks to hatch and the young leave the nest in just under two weeks.

In many cases, the young birds' chances of survival are increased by being cared for by their parents and the previous year's offspring.

While the male fairy-wrens strut about in their blue finery, the females have a more sensible, camouflaged brown colouring.

Red-backed Fairy-wren

Malurus melanocephalus

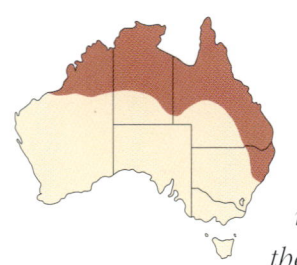

These wrens replace the Superb Fairy-wren in northern areas, where their loud warbling calls advertise their presence during the winter, spring and summer months.

Red-backed Fairy-wrens relish a grassy habitat where they can hop and flutter about after caterpillars and other juicy treats.

DIET
Insects, such as flies and caterpillars.

FIELD NOTES
These wrens aren't as brightly coloured as other species, but what they lack in plumage, they make up for in ingenuity. For example, courting males carry red petals to increase their attractiveness to females. This is a clever idea – it allows the males to be attractive to females when it is safe to do so, but also lets them hide by dropping the petals and remaining motionless when a hungry currawong appears.

IN THE GARDEN

Habitat
Areas of long grass containing Queensland Blue Grass (*Dichanthium sericeum*), Feather Spear Grass (*Stipa elegantissima*), Kangaroo Grass (*Themeda triandra [australis]*), or other tussock-forming species are great for Red-backed Fairy-wrens.

Food
These wrens forage through grassy layers, catching insects at ground level. They will sometimes approach a feeding table on or near the ground for mealworms.

Nesting
Red-backed Fairy-wrens build a dome-shaped nest with a side entrance in a grass tussock or low bush.

They lay three to four eggs which are white with reddish spots. They probably hatch in about two weeks.

Red-backed Fairy-wrens nest in grassy areas including those on the fringes of wetlands. They also inhabit forests and other areas as long as there is a grassy understorey.

Spotted Pardalote

Pardalotus punctatus

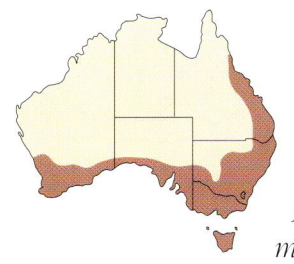

The 'sleep, ba-by' call of the Spotted Pardalote punctuates the air across most of Australia during late winter and the spring months.

Male pardalotes are quite striking birds with the black-and-white plumage on their backs contrasting with the soft grey tones of their breasts and their brilliant yellow throats.

DIET
Insects, especially the sap-sucking bugs which cover themselves with sugary coatings known as 'lerps'.

FIELD NOTES
Pardalotes spend most of their time flying vertically up or down. They feed in the canopy where they dodge aggressive honeyeaters, but nest under the ground. They are only as big as a gum leaf and are more often seen than heard. Sometimes you can hear the soft clicking of their beak as they snip lerps off gumleaves.

IN THE GARDEN

Habitat
Spotted Pardalotes like areas where the tree canopies nearly touch – even in the inland where forests tend to be more sparse.

Food
A healthy forest canopy in your garden will provide all the insects these birds need.

Nesting
To escape from predators, pardalotes nest underground. They dig a 30cm tunnel into an earth bank or pile of topsoil and build a cosy nest chamber at the end. The nesting chamber is lined with strips of stringy bark or similar material and looks a lot like a hairy grapefruit. These birds will sometimes use a nest box with a suitable entrance tunnel. They may even nest in a hanging basket or the end of a drainage pipe.

The four eggs hatch after just over two weeks' brooding by both parents.

Female birds have more subtle colouring than their male counterparts, but they still show the heavily spotted patterns that give these birds their scientific names: both pardalotus *and* punctatus *mean spotted.*

WHITE-BROWED SCRUBWREN

Sericornis frontalis

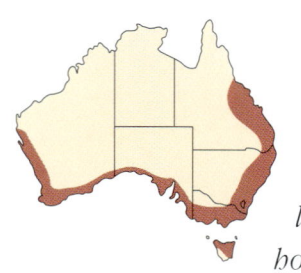

These birds spend most of their time in the lowest levels of the forest, hopping along very close to the ground. The males have dark faces which give them a constant frowning expression.

DIET
Insects, spiders and the occasional seed.

FIELD NOTES
Although these birds are difficult to see in their dense undergrowth homes, they are one of the easiest species to call up by making 'psht psht' or other squeaking noises. During winter and spring, you can often find them looking at you from only a few metres away.

Scrubwrens very rarely perch out in the open. They prefer to skulk around in the dense forest understorey.

Like many baby birds, the White-browed Scrubwren chicks produce droppings in a jelly sac, which the female removes.

IN THE GARDEN

HABITAT
Scrubwrens need a fairly dense understorey, with forest cover above, to feel at home. In rainforests they are generally replaced by the closely related Yellow-throated Scrubwren.

FOOD
These little characters will find their own food in the garden, but can often be enticed with tiny pieces of cheese or mealworms. They will also accept breadcrumbs but since this is not their natural food, it is best to avoid introducing it into their diet.

NESTING
Scrubwrens lay two to three eggs in a dome nest with a side entrance. Their nests are usually found in a dense shrub or grass tussock.

These birds can become quite tame around pcinic areas and in bushy backyards. Here they will take small pieces of cheese.

SPECKLED WARBLER

Chthonicola sagittatus

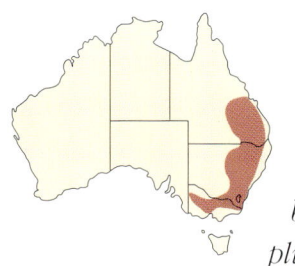

When they don't want to be seen, these inland birds use their mottled plumage to advantage by keeping very still. They are therefore more common than many people realise, but will retreat to trees if approached too closely.

DIET
Insects, spiders, other small creatures, and seeds.

FIELD NOTES
Speckled Warblers are accomplished vocal mimics, including over 40 calls of other birds in their songs. They have the extraordinary habit of singing when under stress – for instance, while being banded for research.

Above: *Speckled Warblers enjoy being in an environment that includes a variety of trees and shrubs, including the* Callitris *pines found in the interior.*

Left: *The nests of these warblers are often built on the ground and nearly always feature a side entrance.*

IN THE GARDEN

Habitat
These warblers choose open woodland with a fairly clear understorey.

Food
The best way to provide food for Speckled Warblers is to allow them access to their favoured habitat – open woodland – and to keep pesticides and cats away. They may also take mealworms from a feeding table.

Nesting
Speckled Warblers lay three or four eggs in a domed nest with a short entrance tunnel. The nest is set into the earth so the entrance is at ground level. Some males will have two mates, each with their own nest. There are claims that Speckled Warblers build a false nest in front of the real one to fool cuckoos, but there is only limited evidence that this occurs. It certainly does little to stop Black-eared Cuckoos from frequently laying their eggs in Speckled Warblers' nests.

Male Speckled Warblers have a black streak bordering a white eyebrow, while females of the species exhibit a brown streak above the eyebrow.

DIRECTORY OF GARDEN BIRDS

WEEBILL
Smicrornis brevirostris

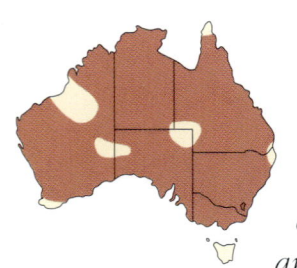

This is Australia's tiniest bird – it is even dwarfed by gum leaves – and is also one of our most widespread birds. It thrives in most regions.

DIET
Insects, spiders and other small creatures.

Weebills' colours vary. In the south, they are brownish yellow while in the north, pure yellow tones predominate.

FIELD NOTES
Weebills forage restlessly in woodlands. Their small size and constant movement make them difficult to separate from thornbills, but their short bills, yellowish colours, pale eyebrows and distinctive shrill call are the best identifying characters.

IN THE GARDEN

HABITAT
Weebills like open woodland and are not common in forests. They hunt in the outer canopy where you can sometimes see them hovering or fluttering after insects.

FOOD
Weebills will find their own food in gardens providing them with a suitable woodland habitat.

NESTING
These birds build a wonderful soft nest which resembles a baby's bootie hanging by the heel, usually in the outer foliage of a tree or shrub. The female does most of the nest building and broods the eggs which hatch in just under two weeks. Once the chicks hatch, they are fed by both parents and other birds in the group. The chicks leave the nest after about 10 days.

Weebills build a tiny nest constructed from plant fibres and held together by spider webs. They sometimes use the egg sacs of Huntsman spiders to decorate their nests.

DIRECTORY OF GARDEN BIRDS

Brown Gerygone
Gerygone mouki

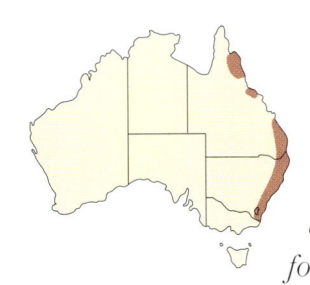

These small birds – they aren't much bigger than a Weebill – love the dense forests the Weebills avoid. Their constant chattering tones are a feature of many forested areas along the eastern seaboard.

DIET
Insects and spiders caught in trees and shrubs.

FIELD NOTES
One of the distinctive sounds in eastern Australia's dense forests is the 'what-is-it, what-is-it' call of the Brown Gerygone. Even in the middle of the day when most birds are napping, these creatures are still active.

Brown Gerygones are best separated from thornbills by their lack of facial streaks and from Weebills by their longer beaks and busier calls.

Their constant calling makes them easy to find – unless they are in the middle of an impenetrable patch of spiny lawyer vines!

IN THE GARDEN

Habitat
Dense forests hung with vines and other tangled vegetation are ideal for the Brown Gerygone.

Food
As they forage in the middle levels of the forest, these birds don't come down to feeding stations readily. They will happily find their own food in a healthy garden.

Nesting
The female broods two eggs inside her dome-shaped nest which hangs in tangled foliage from 1–15m from the ground. The chicks hatch in two and a half weeks and leave the nest after a further two weeks.

Brown Gerygones are also known as Brown Warblers. They are common in gardens that border dense forest and are usually found in pairs or in small groups.

White-throated Gerygone
Gerygone olivacea

The beautiful trilling song of this migratory bird, rising up the scale and cascading down again, heralds the arrival of spring in south-east Australia.

These birds build a substantial nest using finely shredded bark from rough-barked trees. The nest is held together with spider web and placed in the outer foliage.

DIET
Insects and spiders.

FIELD NOTES
The White-throated Gerygone forages actively within tree foliage in woodland areas. It avoids dense forests, except where these consist of narrow strips along inland waterways.

IN THE GARDEN

Habitat
These birds need woodlands in which tree canopies don't touch each other, so an ideal garden habitat shouldn't be too dense.

These gerygones constantly scan their surroundings for predators – a habit they share with many other small birds.

Food
A White-throated Gerygone will find its own food in a healthy garden, but may be attracted to a tempting bowl of wriggly mealworms.

Nesting
Like some other warblers, these birds tend to build their nests near paper wasps' nests or in trees infested with ants – probably as a way of deterring predators. Therefore, if you want to attract these handsome birds, you should also welcome wasps into your garden – unless they are European wasps (they nest in a hole in the ground instead of in a hanging honeycomb-like structure). The female broods the two eggs for about two weeks, then feeds the chicks for a further two weeks until they leave the nest.

DIRECTORY OF GARDEN BIRDS

Brown Thornbill
Acanthiza pusilla

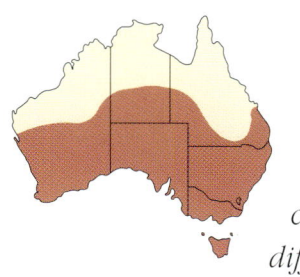

Brown Thornbills are characterised by sombre colouring and are quite difficult to spot as a result. They are commonly found in forests with a reasonably dense understorey.

DIET
Insects, spiders and occasionally seeds and nectar.

FIELD NOTES
The best way to detect the presence of these active birds in your garden is to learn to recognise their sounds. Although they vary, almost all Brown Thornbills' calls include a one-second downward trill.

Brown Thornbills are one of the most common forest thornbills and one of the easiest to identify. Their streaked fronds and brown colours separate them from similar species.

Brown Thornbills can be enticed by a birdbath or tray of mealworms placed in the shrub layer. A bird feeding station in amongst tangled shrubs can also be attractive to these birds. They are one of the few Australian species that can forage successfully in pine trees – possibly because the pine needles resemble the needle-like stems of she-oaks (Casuarina sp.).

IN THE GARDEN

HABITAT
Brown Thornbills need a fairly tall, dense shrub layer between 2–5m high, beneath a forest of taller trees. They are adept at moving swiftly through tangled shrubs to hunt for insects.

FOOD
These birds will find their own food in a healthy garden, but they can also sometimes be tempted to a feeding tray stocked with wriggly mealworms and bite-sized pieces of cheese, placed in the shrub layer.

NESTING
Like other thornbills, the female builds a dome nest with a side entrance. She uses grass, bark fibres and other plant materials to build the nest which she places in dense foliage within a few metres of the ground. The two to three eggs take about three weeks to hatch. The young thornbills leave the nest after about two weeks.

DIRECTORY OF GARDEN BIRDS

Yellow-rumped Thornbill

Acanthiza chrysorrhoa

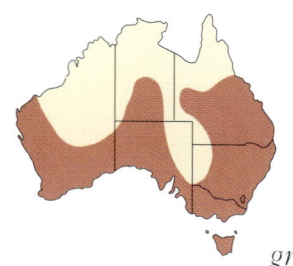

The Yellow-rumped Thornbill is a tiny bird that bounces along open grassy areas in many parts of eastern Australia.

IN THE GARDEN

Habitat
These birds need large open grassy areas dotted with trees or shrubs for feeding. They also inhabit the zone where forest gives way to cleared country.

Food
As long as pesticides are not used and cats are kept at bay, these birds will find their own food in the grassy layer of larger gardens.

Nesting
Yellow-rumped Thornbills sometimes build a false nest on top of the real one, which may be a means of fooling the bronze-cuckoos that occasionally lay their eggs in the thornbill's nest – or it may just be the male thornbill's overactive nest-building instinct at work.

The three eggs hatch after about two and a half weeks. Although chicks are fed by many members of the group, they still take about two and a half weeks to leave the nest.

Yellow-rumped Thornbills are one of the easier thornbills to identify – especially in flight as they display their yellow rump and tail, which are bordered with black. At rest, their speckled dark heads are also distinctive.

DIET
Seeds, insects, spiders and other small creatures.

FIELD NOTES
Yellow-rumped Thornbills may be part of an elaborate camouflage scheme. As they fly away from you, their yellow, black-bordered rumps, can be clearly seen. A very similar pattern is visible on flying grasshoppers, which may have evolved to mimic the thornbills in order to stop the birds preying on them.

Yellow-rumped Thornbills eat a variety of insects and other creatures such as this tasty grasshopper. Although they prefer to feed on the ground, they are unlikely to pass up on such a nutritional snack – even if it is in a tree.

Yellow Thornbill

Acanthiza nana

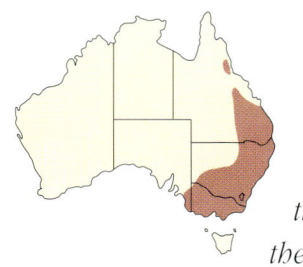

Active groups of Yellow Thornbills occur high in the forest canopy where they drive birdwatchers crazy because they are so small, so far away and so impossibly difficult to spot.

DIET

Insects and spiders.

FIELD NOTES

The Yellow Thornbill's 'chiz chiz!' calls are buzzier than those of other thornbills and easy to identify once you are familiar with them.

As its name implies, the Yellow Thornbill is a warm yellow colour, which makes it look similar to a Weebill.

IN THE GARDEN

HABITAT

These birds are one of the few Australian species that don't like eucalypts. They much prefer canopies of she-oaks, wattles (*Acacia* sp.) and native cypress (*Callitris* sp.). In many areas you can find them in the she-oaks that border streams in eucalypt forests.

FOOD

A healthy garden provides all the insects and spiders a thornbill needs.

NESTING

These thornbills lay their three eggs in a dome nest with a side entrance. When the chicks hatch, they are fed by many members of the group. As the parents usually start moulting soon after the last clutch leaves the nest, having other birds in the group to look after the chicks helps to increase their chances of survival.

A Yellow Thornbill forages through the outer foliage of a fig (Ficus sp.). The ripening figs might be tasty to a range of other birds but the thornbills are only interested in the insects feeding on them.

DIRECTORY OF GARDEN BIRDS

Red Wattlebird
Anthochaera carunculata

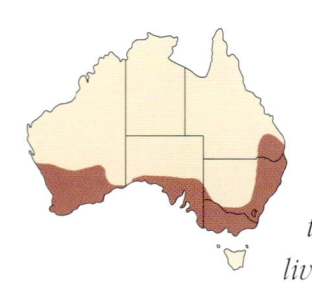

The Red Wattlebird, the largest honeyeater on the Australian mainland, lives successfully in parks and gardens. Its raucous 'rok-aark!' call resounds through many Australian suburbs in late winter and spring.

DIET
Insects, spiders and nectar.

FIELD NOTES
This bird gets its name from the red wattles (yellow in Tasmania) on either side of the neck. Like other honeyeaters, it has a very long tongue with bristles on the end for extracting nectar from flowers.

IN THE GARDEN

Habitat
Red Wattlebirds need forests that have large nectar-producing trees, such as eucalypts and Silky Oaks, in order to survive. They will also descend to garden shrubs, for example, grevilleas and bottlebrushes (*Callistemon* sp.), in search of nectar.

These birds may look like Little Wattlebirds but they are easily distinguished by their red wattles and yellow bellies.

As these birds have few predators, they make little effort to hide their nests which are usually built between 4–10m above the ground. Although up to three eggs can be laid, most nests only produce one or two chicks.

Food
These birds enjoy nectar mix, mealworms and fruit.

Nesting
Wattlebirds build a large untidy cup in a dense part of the tree canopy. The two or three eggs hatch in about two weeks. The young leave the nest after approximately two and a half weeks.

Although Red Wattlebirds' colours blend into the forest background, their noisy habits make them easy to locate.

DIRECTORY OF GARDEN BIRDS

Little Wattlebird
Anthochaera chrysoptera

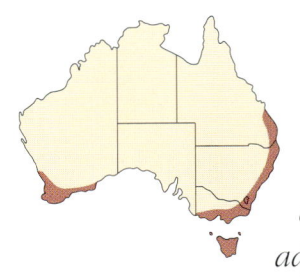

These active wattlebirds are most common in coastal heaths and in adjoining forests with a banksia understorey. They are successful in coastal habitats on both sides of the continent.

These birds use twigs to build a messy nest in the shrub layer or low in the canopy. The nest is lined with finer materials such as feathers or animal fur.

Little Wattlebirds probably once occurred across the whole of southern Australia before the continent drifted north into the desert latitudes and the barren Nullarbor Plain was formed.

DIET
Insects, spiders and nectar.

FIELD NOTES
On the New South Wales north coast, Little Wattlebirds are affectionately known as 'poop-cackers' after their three-syllable call. On the border between Victoria and New South Wales, they sound as if they're saying 'I've got it!' They move around their range according to what shrubs are in flower. Differences in eye colour and other aspects may make the western and eastern groups separate species.

IN THE GARDEN

Habitat
Nectar- and insect-producing shrubs like banksias, grevilleas and bottlebrushes are perfect for Little Wattlebirds. Examples include large grevilleas, such as Silky Oaks, and banksias, including *B. integrifolia* and *B. serrata*.

Food
Wattlebirds enjoy nectar mix, mealworms and fruit, although their natural food from nectar-producing plants is best.

Nesting
They build a cup-shaped nest in the outer foliage of tall shrubs or in small trees. The female broods one or two eggs for just over two weeks, after which both parents feed the chick for a further two weeks.

Large Banksias like this B. ashbyi *are great for Little Wattlebirds – although this particular plant needs very good drainage in eastern Australia.*

Spiny-cheeked Honeyeater

Acanthagenys rufogularis

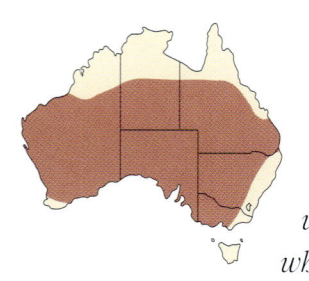

These highly aggressive honeyeaters replace the wattlebirds in the inland, where they are common in parks, gardens and woodlands. They are capable of excluding other species from a food tree.

DIET
Insects, berries and nectar.

FIELD NOTES
Due to their aggressive nature, Spiny-cheeked Honeyeaters will not tolerate other birds in their breeding or feeding territories. Their noisy efforts to expel intruders often make them very easy to spot.

IN THE GARDEN

Habitat
These birds live in dense inland thickets. They like trees or shrubs and don't mind crossing open areas to find a suitable, sheltered spot.

Spiny-cheeked Honeyeaters are common in many inland areas where their noisy calls are hard to ignore.

Food
The berries of saltbush (*Atriplex* sp.), emu bush (*Eremophila* sp.) and mistletoe (*Amyema* sp.) are a source of food for these honeyeaters. They hunt for insects in the canopies of wattles and other inland trees such as Wilga (*Geijera parviflora*), and gather nectar as well as insects in eucalypts. They will also visit the shrub layer, especially if there are flowering grevilleas or outbreaks of tasty caterpillars.

The large hybrid grevilleas such as Honey Gem, Misty Pink and Ned Kelly can be attractive to Spiny-cheeked Honeyeaters – especially if they are planted in areas where other nectar supplies are limited.

Nesting
The female broods her two eggs for about two weeks in a nest that hangs between branchlets in a tree or shrub. The nest is held together very strongly by plant fibres bound with spider web. The young are attended to by both parents as well as other members of the family, and they leave the nest in just over two weeks.

Mistletoe provides a regular supply of nectar and berries which Spiny-cheeked Honeyeaters find very attractive. Although mistletoe is a plant parasite, it is worth tolerating.

DIRECTORY OF GARDEN BIRDS

Noisy Friarbird

Philemon corniculatus

As their name implies, these raucous, cackling birds spend many hours chattering away to each other in forested areas. It is almost impossible to miss a group of these characters.

True to their descriptive name, Noisy Friarbirds are one of the more obvious birds in the inland and in the ranges. Like most birds, they call frequently in the morning, but can also be pretty loud at midday.

DIET
Nectar, insects and fruit.

FIELD NOTES
With their constant calling, Noisy Friarbirds warn others that they own a particular food supply. They also call at dusk as a way of maintaining the flock when its members are roosting apart from each other.

IN THE GARDEN

Habitat
These friarbirds choose forest or woodland areas where they spend most of their time in the canopy.

Food
Friarbirds require nectar-producing trees, such as eucalypts and Silky Oaks, for survival. In coastal areas, they will move into the shrub layer to obtain nectar from banksias and large grevilleas.

They will take nectar mix, fruit pieces and mealworms from garden feeding trays.

Nesting
The female broods her three eggs in a cup-shaped nest, which is built in a tree or shrub from a few metres above the ground up to 17m.

*Although Friarbirds prefer plants that are native to Australia, they will sometimes feed on berries from the hawthorn bush (*Crataegus sp.*). They often chase other birds away from feeding areas.*

DIRECTORY OF GARDEN BIRDS

BLUE-FACED HONEYEATER

Entomyzon cyanotis

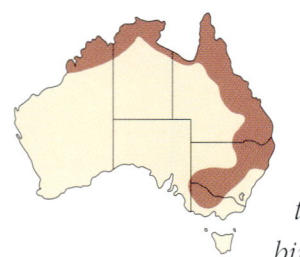

Gaudy Blue-faced Honeyeaters are one of the very few Australian birds with blue markings on them. Adults have luminous-blue bare skin on their faces, while immatures' faces are green.

DIET
Insects, nectar and fruit.

Nectar from bottlebrushes provides a major food source for many honeyeaters, including the blue-faced. Bottlebrushes are specially adapted for pollination by birds.

As a general rule, red tubular plants are great for honeyeaters. Blue-faced Honeyeaters are large and aggressive and are quite happy to feed in the open.

These birds prefer eucalypts and large bottlebrushes (*Callistemon* sp.), paperbarks (*Melaleuca* sp.), banksias, and also grevilleas.

FIELD NOTES
Blue-faced Honeyeaters are one of the more gregarious bird species, hanging around in groups of up to ten or more. They actively forage through the foliage and hawk insects unwary enough to fly past.

IN THE GARDEN

HABITAT
Blue-faced Honeyeaters are birds of the canopy; they also inhabit the tops of larger shrubs.

FOOD
As a supplement to their natural food, these birds will readily accept nectar mix, fruit pieces and mealworms.

NESTING
Blue-faced Honeyeaters build an untidy cup nest, but will use the abandoned nests of other species, especially babblers.

They lay two eggs. When the chicks hatch, they are probably fed by most members of the group.

Blue-faced Honeyeaters have adapted well to urban environments where they feed from flowering plants and bowls of nectar mix.

DIRECTORY OF GARDEN BIRDS

Noisy Miner
Manorina melanocephala

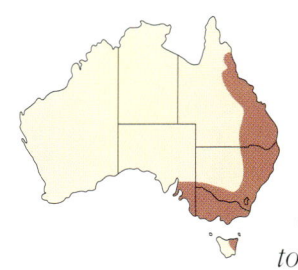

These vandals are one of the species that have adapted very successfully to life in leafy suburbs. They tend to live in groups that consist of more males than females.

As one of our most aggressive honeyeaters, Noisy Miners are able to exclude many other birds from an area and to monopolise their food resources.

DIET
Insects, nectar and fruit.

FIELD NOTES
Noisy Miners are one of the most gregarious and aggressive species to visit your garden. They are especially noisy when a predator such as a goanna or raven is in the vicinity. They fly around the intruder calling loudly and pecking at it when it isn't looking, which gives the miner its other name of Soldier Bird.

IN THE GARDEN

Habitat
Noisy Miners inhabit the upper and middle levels of the forest, especially tall, dense eucalypt forests in well-watered parts of the country.

Food
Although these birds find most of their food while hunting insects in the canopy, they also enjoy nectar and fruits and will readily descend into the shrub layer for these foods. They will just as readily accept nectar mix, fruit pieces and mealworms from a feeding tray.

Of the fruits that appeal to Noisy Miners, the soft flesh of pawpaw is particularly inviting.

Nesting
Female miners build a cup nest in the canopy of a large shrub or small tree. The three eggs are brooded by the female who is visited at the nest by many of the males in the group. When the chicks hatch after just over two weeks, they are fed by 20 or more males until well after the two-week period it takes for them to leave the nest.

Of all Australian birds, baby Noisy Miners receive some of the best care. They are looked after by their many older uncles as well as by their parents.

157

YELLOW-THROATED MINER

Manorina flavigula

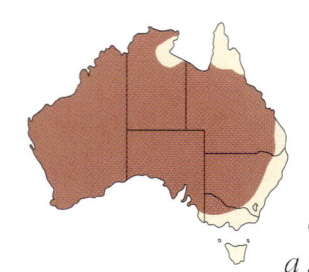

This species replaces the Noisy Miner in inland areas, where it leads a similar life.

FOOD
Yellow-throated Miners are partial to the nectar from grevilleas, bottlebrushes (*Callistemon* sp.) and eucalypts. They will also accept fruit pieces, nectar mix and mealworms.

NESTING
Like their noisy cousins, Yellow-throated Miners live in close-knit groups in which most of the members help feed the young, but don't breed themselves.

The breeding females lay three or four eggs in a bulky twig nest built in the outer canopy.

Yellow-throated Miners live in pairs or noisy, aggressive groups that move from tree to tree annoying other bird species, searching for insects or sipping nectar.

DIET
Insects, fruits and nectar.

FIELD NOTES
This species looks very similar to the Noisy Miner. The best way to identify these yellow-throated birds is not by the colour of their throat but rather by their white rump, which is easier to see especially in flight.

IN THE GARDEN

HABITAT
Yellow-throated Miners need a woodland of wattles or eucalypts. They will also visit large shrubs such as tall grevilleas and Wilgas (*Geijera parviflora*).

Yellow-throated Miners seek out tree canopies for nesting and feeding in the inland parts of Australia.

Lewin's Honeyeater

Meliphaga lewinii

The rapid, repetitive 'chew-chew-chew-chew' call of this species is one of the characteristic sounds of the dense forest gullies in eastern Australia. It is common in many parts of its range but is rarely seen in the tangled undergrowth.

DIET
Insects, nectar and fruit.

FIELD NOTES
Lewin's Honeyeaters are aggressive towards other birds, including their own species. Their dense forest homes provide shelter, but make them difficult to see.

IN THE GARDEN

Habitat
Lewin's Honeyeaters need very dense plantings to feel at home. They live mostly in the understorey, where they hop actively through the foliage.

Food
Plants producing nectar and fruit are excellent food sources for these birds. They can become tame around houses built on the fringes of suitable habitat. Here they will take full advantage of fruit pieces and nectar mix.

Banksias provide excellent nectar supplies for Lewin's Honeyeaters.

Nesting
Lewin's Honeyeaters build a cup nest suspended from the outer twigs in a dense tree or large shrub. They lay two eggs that take about two weeks to hatch. The chicks leave the nest after a further two weeks.

These honeyeaters will readily visit gardens near dense bushland. The closer your garden is to the bush, the higher the chance of seeing these shy birds.

Large hybrid grevilleas are also very attractive to Lewin's Honeyeaters. Some of the best are Honey Gem, Superb and either Ned Kelly or Robyn Gordon.

DIRECTORY OF GARDEN BIRDS

YELLOW-FACED HONEYEATER
Lichenostomus chrysops

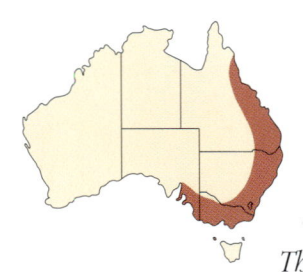

These slim honeyeaters make a good living in open forests and gardens. Their 'chip-chop chip-chop' calls are a common sound in eastern Australia during the spring months.

DIET
Insects, nectar and fruits.

The call of the Yellow-faced Honeyeater is commonly heard in gardens that have an abundance of grevilleas, eucalypts and other flowering plants.

FIELD NOTES

The Yellow-faced Honeyeater is a conspicuous migrant species in Australia. From March to May the birds travel north in flocks, calling to each other as they fly past. Mysteriously, these honeyeaters are less obvious to the observer on their return trip to breeding areas.

In some parts of the Yellow-faced Honeyeater's range, such as the Blue Mountains in New South Wales, its annual migrations attract an influx of predators, such as currawongs which prey upon stragglers in the flocks.

Yellow-faced Honeyeaters breed in spring and early summer. The nest is sometimes camouflaged with pieces of bark or lichen, or sometimes left unadorned. The tiny naked babies in this nest will have feathers within a week.

IN THE GARDEN

HABITAT
Yellow-faced Honeyeaters like forests where the tree canopies touch each other, or woodlands where the canopies are separate. Either way, tall trees tend to be a favoured habitat.

FOOD
Nectar from eucalypts and shrubs is a favourite of these birds. Plants such as Leucopogon, bush cherries (*Exocarpos* sp.) and Lilly Pillies (*Acmena* and *Syzygium* spp.) have bite-sized berries, which the birds enjoy too. You can also try a menu of nectar mix, a bowl of mealworms or chopped fruit pieces.

NESTING
These honeyeaters need a fairly dense large shrub or small tree for nesting. The nest is a neat cup of grasses and other plant fibres bound with spider web. It takes about two weeks for the two eggs to hatch and the young leave the nest after a further two weeks.

DIRECTORY OF GARDEN BIRDS

VARIED HONEYEATER

Lichenostomus versicolor

In tropical parts of Australia, this species of honeyeater is common in parks and gardens. Its appearance varies from the dark southern form to the lighter, yellowish northern form.

DIET
Nectar, insects, spiders and other small creatures.

FIELD NOTES
These honeyeaters are fond of mangroves and nearby gardens, where their restless habit of foraging through trees and shrubs makes them easy to notice but hard to study at close range.

IN THE GARDEN

HABITAT
Large shrubs and trees are about right for this species. They also inhabit mangroves, a valuable asset if you happen to live on the coast.

Mangrove forest such as this is a popular habitat for these honeyeaters, providing both food and shelter.

A bird of the northern race of the Varied Honeyeater calls from the sanctuary of a bottlebrush. Such plants provide food and some shelter.

FOOD
Nectar-producing shrubs are just what Varied Honeyeaters require to feed. They may also accept nectar mix and bowls of wriggly mealworms.

NESTING
Varied Honeyeaters build a cup-shaped nest in the outer foliage of larger shrubs or trees – seldom less than 4m from the ground.

The female lays two eggs that probably take about two weeks to hatch. Both parents, as well as other birds in the group, feed the young once they hatch.

Medium to large grevilleas are great nectar sources for Varied Honeyeaters and other species. These plants perform best when they are pruned carefully just after flowering.

161

DIRECTORY OF GARDEN BIRDS

Yellow Honeyeater
Lichenostomus flavus

Australia's yellowest honeyeater is also one of the noisiest and most active species. Its hard-edged whistles and chatters are a conspicuous sound in north Queensland gardens and parks, where it can be seen singly and in pairs.

DIET
Insects, spiders, nectar and fruit.

FIELD NOTES
Last century, leading ornithologist John Gould wrote that very little was known of this species. He said he hoped he had 'thrown out a sufficient hint to those who may visit its native country ... that contributions to its history are very desirable.' Despite this appeal, we still don't know much, even though this bird is found in many suburban gardens.

This species can be identified by its size and fairly uniform yellow colouring.

A Yellow Honeyeater takes a breather from feeding on this large grevillea to check out the surrounding area for predators or other honeyeaters.

FOOD
Trees and shrubs that produce nectar and fruits can be very useful when attempting to attract this nomadic species to your garden. Chopped fruits, nectar mix and mealworms can also be very popular.

NESTING
These birds lay two eggs in a suspended, cup-shaped nest in the outer foliage of a tree or shrub. They use coconut fibre or paperbark, binding it together with spider web into a sturdy structure.

IN THE GARDEN

HABITAT
Yellow Honeyeaters choose trees as their residences, especially eucalypts and paperbarks. They live in woodland regions, but seem to prefer forests where the trees are fairly close together.

Gardens near a tropical forest like this one have great potential to attract a wide range of fascinating birds.

DIRECTORY OF GARDEN BIRDS

White-eared Honeyeater
Lichenostomus leucotis

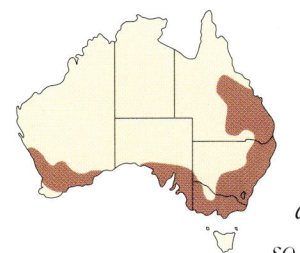

These trusting birds don't mind people being around. In fact, they are so at ease around humans that they have even been recorded plucking hair from passing bushwalkers to line their nests!

DIET

Insects, spiders, nectar and fruit.

FIELD NOTES

These honeyeaters spend a lot of time probing for insects in the bark of eucalypts. They don't partake of nectar as often as some other honeyeaters.

White-eared Honeyeaters are one of the many hosts of cuckoos. Here an adult bird is feeding a fully grown Pallid Cuckoo chick.

A garden water feature can be enticing for White-eared Honeyeaters. Although they can get water from their insect food, they still appreciate a regular bath.

IN THE GARDEN

HABITAT
Eucalypt forests with a fairly dense shrub layer provide the right habitat for these birds.

FOOD
Rough-barked eucalypts (or smooth-barked species with strings of hanging bark) provide the best foraging areas for insects and spiders.
Nectar mix and bowls of mealworms can also serve to attract these birds.

NESTING
The White-eared Honeyeater builds a neat cup nest lined with fur or feathers in a low shrub or grass tussock. The two eggs hatch in about two weeks. The young leave the nest in a further two weeks.

Most White-eared Honeyeaters lay two eggs, but three can be laid in a good year.

DIRECTORY OF GARDEN BIRDS

White-plumed Honeyeater

Lichenostomus penicillatus

One of Australia's more variable honeyeaters, this species lives in noisy family parties from the tropical north to the wet forests of Victoria and the deserts of the arid inland.

Their penchant for woodland forests makes White-plumed Honeyeaters an obvious addition to gardens with a well-developed tree canopy.

DIET
Insects, spiders, nectar and fruits.

FIELD NOTES
White-plumed Honeyeaters are often referred to as 'greenies' in country areas. Their call note, which descends over two syllables and then ascends over one or two, is commonly heard in forests and woodlands. They also produce a shrill piping call on one note when a predator such as a goshawk passes over. Often this call is taken up by other birds.

IN THE GARDEN

HABITAT
White-plumed Honeyeaters like trees either in woodlands or forests. They are especially attracted to clumps or lines of trees in open country.

FOOD
These birds collect most of their insect and nectar food in the canopy of eucalypts, but they will also descend into the shrub layer and even onto the ground.
They will often happily help themselves to nectar mix, chopped fruit and mealworms.

NESTING
The nest is built anywhere from a low shrub to a tall tree. Grass and bark fibres are woven with spider web to support the structure. The two eggs hatch in about two weeks and the young leave the nest after a further two weeks. They are fed by both parents and by other birds in the group.

Many honeyeaters have tufts of feathers decorating the sides of their necks, but don't have the exact colouring of the white-plumed.

DIRECTORY OF GARDEN BIRDS

Brown Honeyeater

Lichmera indistincta

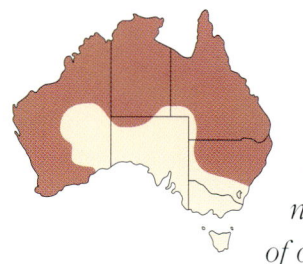

Widespread through most of Australia, this noisy honeyeater is one of our most successful species, also ranging north through Indonesia's Aru and Lesser Sunda islands and New Guinea.

DIET
Insects, spiders and nectar.

FIELD NOTES
You can hear the musical warbling notes of this species at most times of the day, especially around flowering bottlebrushes, (*Callistemon* sp.), eucalypts and other nectar-producing plants. They sound surprisingly like Reed Warblers.

With the ability to survive in parks and gardens and a musical voice that produces a range of complex songs, Brown Honeyeaters are a feature of many suburbs.

IN THE GARDEN

Habitat
These active birds like forests and woodlands. They are especially attracted to groups of trees and they also love mangroves. Generally, they prefer living in clumps of vegetation that are more dense than the surrounding bush.

Food
Nectar-producing plants are perfect for Brown Honeyeaters. They are especially fond of bottlebrushes and will hunt for insects in a wide variety of shrubs, generally favouring those with fairly dense foliage.

Nesting
The female builds a messy cup nest that hangs in the outer foliage of a dense shrub within a few metres of the ground.

The two eggs take about a fortnight to hatch and the young leave the nest two weeks later.

To attach its hanging nest to a tree, this honeyeater used large amounts of spider web and insect cocoons. The nest is lined with fur, feathers and other soft material.

DIRECTORY OF GARDEN BIRDS

New Holland Honeyeater

Phylidonyris novaehollandiae

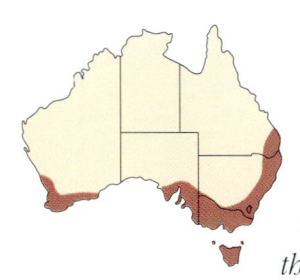

These active, aggressive birds are very common in heathland areas where they are easy to hear but difficult to see as they flit rapidly between the dense bushes. During the spring and winter months they impress the opposite sex by indulging in spectacular song-flights above the vegetation.

DIET
Nectar and insects.

FIELD NOTES
New Holland Honeyeaters expend more energy catching tiny insects than they gain from eating them, but they make up for the energy loss by sipping the abundant nectar in their heathland home. This way they get both the protein and carbohydrates they need.

IN THE GARDEN

Habitat
These birds need plenty of dense, nectar-producing shrubs. They will visit gardens near heathland areas during summer and other times of the year when the heath plants aren't flowering.

Food
Nectar production is often low during summer, so banksias such as *B. serrata* and *integrifolia*, which flower in summer, are very useful.

New Holland Honeyeaters love gardens with a dense shrub layer of banksias and grevilleas. They replace White-cheeked Honeyeaters in southern areas.

Banksia ericifolia, callistemons, grevilleas and *Darwinia fascicularis* are also great food plants for these honeyeaters. Nectar mix can be attractive to them, but their natural food plants are far better.

Nesting
They build a tidy cup nest, often in dense bushes that are tall in relation to the surrounding ones (generally within 2m of the ground). There is a record of them nesting in a garden cabbage, but it's probably not worth waiting for them in the vegie patch!

The pair of eggs takes two and a half weeks to hatch. The young leave the nest in just over a fortnight.

These honeyeaters use their long beaks like a pair of forceps to snatch insects on the wing.

White-cheeked Honeyeater
Phylidonyris nigra

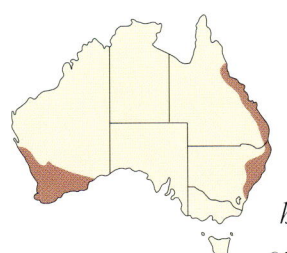

Like their New Holland cousins, these heathland honeyeaters are constantly on the move, travelling between bushes and also between areas of heathland as flowers become available.

White-cheeked Honeyeaters replace New Holland ones in northern areas. They prefer gardens with a dense shrub layer that resembles their natural heathland home.

DIET
Insects and nectar.

FIELD NOTES
These birds are similar to White-cheeked Honeyeaters, although it's easy to tell them apart if you count the white bits on the birds' head. In profile, the White-cheeked has two white patches (and a dark eye) while the New Holland species has four (and a white eye).

IN THE GARDEN

Habitat
These honeyeaters need dense heathland bushes to feel at home. They will also venture into forest areas if there is a dense understorey of nectar-producing plants such as banksias and, in the west, dryandras.

Food
Plants that supply food for New Holland Honeyeaters are also excellent for the White-cheeked variety. It's worth noting too that the hybrid grevilleas like Robyn Gordon and Ned Kelly can be a good choice as they often flower when local heath plants don't. During such times, heathland honeyeaters will readily travel to nearby gardens where they are welcome visitors.

Nesting
The female honeyeater builds a cup-shaped nest in a concealed part of a dense shrub, usually within 2m of the ground.

The two eggs hatch after just over two weeks' brooding by the female. Both parents feed the chicks, who leave the nest after a further two weeks.

White-cheeked Honeyeaters nest in the denser parts of the shrub layer where their nest is hard to find, even though it is close to the ground.

DIRECTORY OF GARDEN BIRDS

Rufous-throated Honeyeater
Conopophila rufogularis

Nomadic bands of this pugnacious honeyeater range across Australia's tropical north, forever on the lookout for flowering trees. They frequently appear in parks and gardens.

DIET
Insects, nectar and bite-sized fruits.

FIELD NOTES
These honeyeaters use their rufous throats to great effect during their frequent, aggressive encounters with each other and with similar-sized species. They puff out their feathers to make themselves look bigger and also raise their wings to show off their yellow wing colours.

A large amount of spider web is used to suspend this honeyeater's nest from a near-horizontal fork. It is one of the deeper honeyeater nests.

IN THE GARDEN

Habitat
Clumps of trees such as eucalypts and Bauhinias (*Lysiphyllum caronii*) can be attractive to this species, especially when near creeks, rivers or lakes. These birds like to bathe in water but also hunt for insects there.

Food
With insects and spiders being their favourite items, the best way to provide food is simply to have a healthy garden with a wide variety of plants. Flowering eucalypts, callistemons and grevilleas are also attractive to these honeyeaters.

Nesting
The female lays her two eggs in a cosy cup-shaped nest in the foliage of a large shrub or small tree. The eggs are off-white with pink to brown spots. They hatch in about two weeks and the young leave the nest after about 12 days of feeding by both parents, especially the female.

Both adult male and female birds have rufous throats but immatures have light-coloured throats and paler bills.

Eastern Spinebill

Acanthorhynchus tenuirostris

This charming species is one of our most popular garden birds. With its active noisy habits and striking plumage, the Eastern Spinebill is hard to miss. Its long beak and brush-tipped tongue make it well suited to sipping nectar.

Eastern Spinebills use their impressive beaks to probe the deepest flowers, such as correas and epacris, to penetrate cracks in bark and also to snatch tiny insects.

DIET
Nectar and insects.

FIELD NOTES
This is one of the few species of honeyeater where it's fairly easy to tell the females from the males. Apart from the different colouring, males also have slightly longer beaks which may enable them to take slightly different food items.

IN THE GARDEN

Habitat
Spinebills need a dense shrub layer where they find nectar and fly after insects. They don't mind forest, as long as it has a dense understorey of flowering plants.

It is especially important to grow a good number of plants with tubular-shaped flowers or those shaped like bottlebrushes or grevilleas.

Food
Spinebills extract nectar from large flowering indigenous vegetation such as banksias, callistemons and eucalypts, but they are also fond of the smaller plants – grevilleas and others such as Correa, Darwinia, kangaroo paws (*Anigozanthos* sp.) and the Mountain Devil (*Lambertia Formosa*).

They use their agility to pursue insects through dense shrubbery where their flashing colours provide a stylish display.

Nesting
The female uses grasses and plant fibres to build a cup nest in a fork anywhere from a low shrub to a tall eucalypt, 15m from the ground. The two eggs are brooded mostly by the female and hatch in about two weeks.

Male Eastern Spinebills have glossy black feathers on their crowns while the females' crown feathers are grey. Immatures lack the stylish contrasting colours of their parents.

DIRECTORY OF GARDEN BIRDS

YELLOW ROBINS

Eastern – *Eopsaltria australis* • Western – *E. griseogularis*

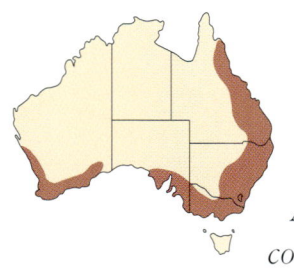

There are a few yellow robins in eastern Australia, with the most common one being the Eastern Yellow Robin. In Western Australia there is only one species – the Western Yellow Robin.

DIET
Insects, spiders and other little creatures.

FIELD NOTES
Yellow robins are often seen perching sideways on a vertical tree trunk, surveying the ground for items to eat. Their 'chew-chew' call punctuates the pre-dawn darkness of most eastern Australian forests.

There are two races of the Eastern Yellow Robin. The southern one has a dull olive-green rump. The northern race has a bright yellow rump.

Western Yellow Robins were probably once part of a single population spread across southern Australia.

IN THE GARDEN

HABITAT
Both yellow robins live in forests, although the Western Yellow Robin can live in more open conditions than its eastern cousin. They both like gardens with a canopy of tall shrubs or small trees and an open understorey where they can nest and hunt.

FOOD
These trusting birds are partial to little pieces of cheese or mealworms. The best way to present the food is to flick it onto the ground close to the bird.

NESTING
Female yellow robins stick pieces of bark onto their nests with spider web to produce a home that is a masterpiece of camouflage.

The male feeds the female while she broods the two to three eggs for two weeks. He then helps feed the young until they leave two weeks later.

Yellow Robins build a beautiful, cup-shaped nest which is generally placed in the shrub layer. It can also be found high in the canopy.

Eastern Whipbird

Psophodes olivaceus

The whipbird's call is one of the most distinctive sounds of the bush. Although it is heard quite frequently, its furtive owner uses camouflage colours and shy behaviour to avoid being seen.

Whipbirds are seldom seen in the open. Viewing a bird away from cover like this is a rare occurrence.

DIET

Insects, spiders and other small creatures.

FIELD NOTES

Most people have heard the whipbird's thin whistling note, followed by the explosive sound of a whip being cracked and then a few upwards or downwards whistles. Mostly, it's the male who performs the call up to and including the whipcrack and the female who does the answering whistles. Sometimes nearby males will be the ones to reply, although no-one knows quite what they're up to when they do it.

IN THE GARDEN

Habitat

Eastern Whipbirds need a very dense understorey for foraging and protection. They like to be near plenty of shrubs, generally under a canopy of larger trees. This means they are most common in and near the rainforests and dense eucalypt forests of eastern Australia. In such areas, their sombre colours match the dim surroundings so well that the birds just melt into the background.

Food

These birds need plenty of leaf litter which they turn over to reveal their insect prey. They move across the forest floor with surprising ease, even in overgrown gullies and other apparently impenetrable areas.

Nesting

Whipbirds build a camouflaged nest near the ground in very dense growth. The male feeds the female while she broods the two eggs, which take about two and a half weeks to hatch. Chicks leave the nest before they can fly, after only ten days. They spend their first week keeping very still in the undergrowth.

Adult whipbirds are very similar to each other, but immatures are easy to distinguish. They lack the white throats, which they only develop in their second year.

Golden Whistler

Pachycephala pectoralis

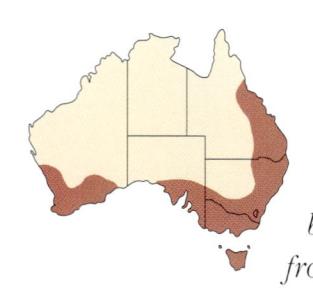

Golden Whistlers, one of our prettiest forest birds, don't venture far from their bushland homes. They only visit gardens that are close to natural forest areas and that have a dense canopy of local tree species.

DIET
Insects, spiders and other small creatures.

FIELD NOTES
Although Golden Whistlers' calls differ around the country, they nearly all end with an upwards whistling 'wshiit!' sound, which lets you know they are nearby. They will sometimes call in response to a loud noise such as a passing plane or even a rifle shot.

Of the eight whistlers found in Australia, the Golden Whistler is the one most likely to turn up in parks and gardens, especially those established near bushland.

The males and females are very different from one another. The male is one of Australia's most striking forest birds, while the females and juveniles have more drab colours and are more difficult to see.

IN THE GARDEN

HABITAT
Golden Whistlers live in the middle levels of the denser forests and like plenty of trees close together.

It's easy to tell who's who in the Golden Whistler world. Males are canary yellow with stylish black-and-white markings, females are greyish, while immatures are grey with brown wing feathers.

FOOD
These birds will find their own food in the branches and leaves of trees and taller shrubs in your garden. All you need do is make sure not to use pesticides and to keep cats at bay.

NESTING
Golden Whistlers build a fairly neat stick nest in the upper shrub layer, usually less than five metres from the ground. The two eggs hatch after about two weeks' brooding by both sexes. The young leave the nest in just under two weeks.

Restless Flycatcher

Myiagra inquieta

Also called the Scissors Grinder because of its call, this species is common in many inland areas. Its noisy habits and stylish black-and-white patterns make it easy to notice.

DIET

Flying insects, spiders, caterpillars and other little creatures.

Restless Flycatchers enjoy a varied diet of insects and spiders which they pick off the branches and from the ground, or they catch in the air.

As their name implies, these birds are very active as they hunt through the shrub and canopy layers for insects and spiders.

FIELD NOTES

Restless Flycatchers live up to their name by rarely keeping still. The fact that they are constantly on the move is one way to tell them from the similar Willie Wagtail. An alternative is to look for the white on the flycatcher's throat and the sides of the neck, which gives it a flashy 'racing stripe' appearance.

IN THE GARDEN

Habitat
These flycatchers like woodlands which have plenty of space between trees.

Food
Restless Flycatchers hawk for insects in the middle layers of the garden – generally higher than a few metres off the ground.

Nesting
These birds nest on a horizontal branch, often near water. Both sexes brood the eggs which hatch after about two weeks. The young leave the nest after a further two weeks.

Female Restless Flycatchers have grey lores (the area between the eye and the beak) while the males' are black. Immatures are very similar to adults except that their throats and sometimes their breasts have a beige tinge. Adults have short crests that they erect when excited.

DIRECTORY OF GARDEN BIRDS

Magpie-Lark
Grallina cyanoleuca

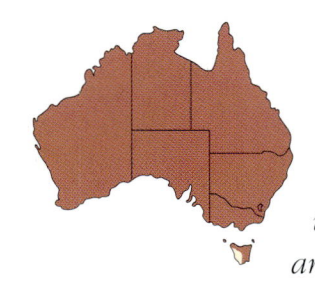

These birds are found across most of Australia wherever there are open areas dotted with trees.

Water is important to Magpie-larks, even though they are found both in the inland and on the coast. In the arid zones, they are restricted to creeks and waterholes.

DIET
Insects, spiders and other small creatures.

FIELD NOTES
Magpie-larks are common in many suburban parts of Australia where they nest in trees but spend most of their time on the ground. During the breeding season, males and females perform a delightful duet where each provides a part of the overall song, opening and closing their wings in time to the singing. The female has white feathers where the beak joins the face, while the male has black feathers.

Immature birds look like a cross between a female and a male – they have the females' white throats and the males' black foreheads.

IN THE GARDEN

HABITAT
These birds need open areas for feeding and nearby trees for shelter and nesting. They also require a good mud supply for nest building during winter and spring.

FOOD
They sometimes become quite tame, taking small pieces of cheese and natural food items that are flicked over to them as they stroll through the garden. Some birds will follow behind a gardener, picking up any worms or other morsels that are revealed.

NESTING
Magpie-larks build a mud nest on a horizontal branch in the upper layers of the tree, often over water. The nest is lined with fur, feathers or grass and has to be built slowly to let one layer set before the next one can be added. Both parents brood the three eggs which hatch in just over two weeks.

A male Magpie-lark follows a female as they hunt for insects and possibly nest-building mud in a shallow pond.

DIRECTORY OF GARDEN BIRDS

Grey Fantail

Rhipidura fuliginosa

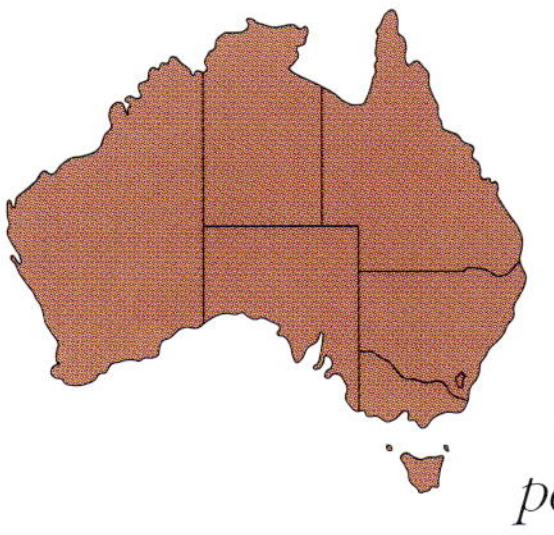

These fantails are restless characters, always flitting from one perch to another in the tree canopy and shrub layer. Their mottled grey patterns and long tails make them easy to identify.

DIET

Insects.

FIELD NOTES

Grey Fantails like to hang around people and other animals – probably to catch the insects they disturb. This means fantails are among the easiest bush birds to see.

Of Australia's five fantail species, only the Willie Wagtail is better known than the Grey Fantail. Their rapid, jerky movements give them their other name: 'Cranky Fan'.

They sing a very high-pitched, lilting song that drifts thinly through the forest, especially during winter and spring when the birds are flirting or fighting.

IN THE GARDEN

Habitat
Grey Fantails generally like forests and woodlands, where they spend most of their time in the mid- to upper levels. The best way to attract these birds is to re-create the local forest type in your garden.

Food
These birds will hunt on the wing for insects in gardens with shrubs and trees that emulate the local forest species. They use their long, elegant tails to twist and turn while flying through the tangled foliage.

Nesting
Grey Fantails build a beautiful cup-shaped nest of grasses, bound together with spider web, in the shrub layer of the forest. They lay two eggs which take just under two weeks to hatch.

These birds use their tails for rapid manoeuvres in the forest canopy and also spread the contrasting feathers as a display to each other when courting or setting up territories.

DIRECTORY OF GARDEN BIRDS

WILLIE WAGTAIL
Rhipidura leucophrys

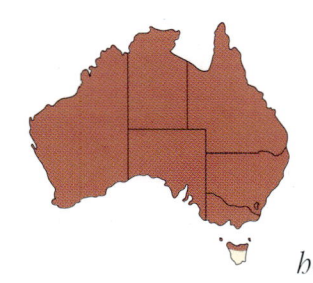

One of the most widely seen garden birds, Willy Wagtails are at home in most parts of Australia. They are also our most familiar fantail.

DIET
Insects.

Willie Wagtails generally hunt on the ground but they will also perch on passing livestock for a better view.

Wagtails build an elegant fantail-like nest on a low horizontal branch, or on a variety of artificial structures.

FIELD NOTES
This species is the only southern fantail to feed on or near the ground. It has adapted very successfully to the way Australia has changed since the arrival of Europeans and is a welcome addition to any garden.

You can tell when wagtails are being aggressive towards another bird: when aroused their flashing white eyebrows are much more visible.

IN THE GARDEN

HABITAT
Willie Wagtails enjoy cleared areas such as lawns or pastures with nearby trees providing low perches that they can use to spy out unwary insects.

FOOD
These birds hunt by watching for insects or by walking restlessly through the grass, turning their tails from left to right to disturb their prey.

NESTING
Wagtails like a low, horizontal branch, often over water, for their nest. They don't have to have a natural setting and have even nested on rotary clothes lines.

Both sexes brood the three eggs for about two weeks. When the brownish chicks hatch, they are fed by both parents for a further two weeks.

Spangled Drongo

Dicrurus bracteatus

No-one knows why this bird's name is used as an insult in Australia, but it may be their habit of bathing by plunging into water from a great height, or the fact that when other birds are migrating north for the winter, some drongos turn up as far south as Melbourne.

DIET
Insects caught on the wing or grabbed from foliage.

FIELD NOTES
Drongos are handsome birds with a distinctive forked tail which they use to twist and turn rapidly through their tangled forest homes in pursuit of insects. On each side of their beak is a clump of bristles that resembles cat's whiskers. These may act like a funnel to help direct insects into the mouth – or they may function like whiskers to help the birds feel any last-minute movements of their prey.

Immature Spangled Drongos are very similar to their glossy, metallic parents but they lack the brilliant sheen. Although they are superb aerial gymnasts, drongos are not very agile on their feet.

IN THE GARDEN

Habitat
In northern parts of Australia, drongos live on the edges of rainforest and other forested areas. In the south they can turn up almost anywhere, but generally they are spotted where there is a reasonable tree canopy with clearings in between.

Food
These birds will find their own food in a healthy garden with a good tree canopy, which provides the forest-edge environment they enjoy.

Nesting
Drongos build a small, shallow, cup-shaped nest out of vines, plant stems and other items. The nest is attached to a horizontal fork, often in the dense outer foliage and at a considerable height above the forest floor. The birds lay three to five eggs, each of which is washed with pink or purple and covered with fine streaks or spots. The eggs are incubated by both parents.

Drongos present a distinctive outline with their powerful bills, large flat-topped heads and long, elegant forked tails.

DIRECTORY OF GARDEN BIRDS

BLACK-FACED CUCKOO-SHRIKE
Coracina novaehollandiae

Although these birds are one of our most successful species, their quiet habits and virtually invisible nests mean that they're not noticed as often as more active birds.

FOOD
Cuckoo-shrikes scan the outer canopy leaves from a perch and then pounce on any insects unwary enough to be crawling about. A variety of large trees with open spaces between them is ideal for these birds.

NESTING
Both male and female birds help to build a tiny, camouflaged nest held together with spider webs. When the two chicks hatch after just over three weeks, they are so well camouflaged they are almost impossible to see – unless they are begging for food.

Adult Black-faced Cuckoo-shrikes generally have black faces and well-defined grey breasts. Immatures have more black, grading gradually to grey.

Cuckoo-shrikes enjoy lying on the ground in the sun. This removes feather parasites and probably feels great!

DIET
Insects and possibly fruits.

FIELD NOTES
This bird gets its unique grey appearance from the special powder produced by some of its feathers. As these 'powder down' feathers grow, the fine powder is spread through the plumage when the bird preens.

IN THE GARDEN

HABITAT
These cuckoo-shrikes live in the canopy of woodland areas and the more open types of forest. They enjoy gardens with a variety of indigenous trees, especially larger species such as eucalypts and she-oaks.

This nest is so wonderfully camouflaged it appears to be growing out of the branch. The eggs are often the most obvious feature.

OLIVE-BACKED ORIOLE
Oriolus sagittatus

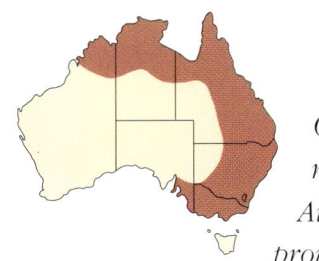

Orioles live across northern and eastern Australia where they prowl through the upper layers of forests and woodlands. They enjoy gardens with a good tree canopy.

DIET
Fruits and insects.

FIELD NOTES
Of the world's 27 species of oriole, three live in Australia, with the Olive-backed Oriole being the most widespread. In southern areas, orioles migrate north each year; their return to southern regions is announced by their warbling, one-second call.

Olive-backed Orioles mostly lay three eggs that soon hatch into hungry youngsters. Suspended by its rim, the nest is usually very well constructed so that it can support the weight of several large chicks.

Orioles hunt for insects and pick at bite-sized fruits in the forest canopy. Their warbling calls are often a feature of gardens in spring and early summer.

IN THE GARDEN

HABITAT

Orioles like forests or woodlands where they live in the canopies of trees. They are fairly well camouflaged and it's only when you hear the lovesick male's call that you notice their presence.

FOOD

The fact that Olive-backed Orioles live in the canopy makes them a difficult bird to feed, but they will readily inhabit a healthy garden that provides a reasonable tree canopy area.

They do best in gardens where local tree species such as eucalypts, she-oaks and wattles are grown and where pesticides and chainsaws are left in the shed.

NESTING

Like other orioles, these birds hang a nicely woven nest cup from a horizontal fork in the outer foliage, usually of a large, dense tree. The female broods the two to four eggs until they hatch in two and a half weeks. If conditions are good, she may lay more eggs, leaving the male to look after the chicks by himself.

FIGBIRD

Sphecotheres viridis

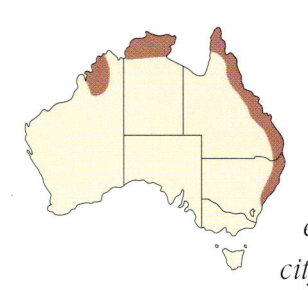

Figbirds are one of the few species that have enthusiastically taken to city parks. With their love of bite-sized fruits, these birds have prospered in the large fig trees that grace many city parks in eastern and northern Australia.

DIET
Fruit, berries and some insects.

FIELD NOTES
You can't visit a city park on the east coast in summer without hearing the downwards 'tsieww!' call of these birds. Watching them swallow Australian figs can be quite alarming. The bird juggles the over-large fruit for a while, then puts its head back and gulps awkwardly. Finally, you see a bulge rolling slowly down the bird's throat – surprisingly without ever choking it.

IN THE GARDEN

HABITAT
Figbirds need a forest canopy with large trees such as the native figs (*Ficus* sp.). They particularly like the fringes of such forested areas.

Juvenile and female Figbirds look very similar to orioles, but have a shorter beak and a generally rounder outline. The streaks on the breast are less clearly defined.

Male Figbirds are handsome creatures. In northern areas they are bright yellow with contrasting black caps. Southern birds are less gaudy, with grey-green breasts.

FOOD
These birds are likely to be attracted to a feeding table with chopped fruits – as long as it is about 10m up a tree! Otherwise, they can easily be attracted if you grow any of the indigenous berry trees such as Lilly Pillies mentioned in Chapter One.

NESTING
Figbirds build a neat, suspended cup nest hanging from a horizontal fork in the outer layers of a forest tree. Both sexes brood the three eggs.

DIRECTORY OF GARDEN BIRDS

Dusky Woodswallow
Artamus cyanopterus

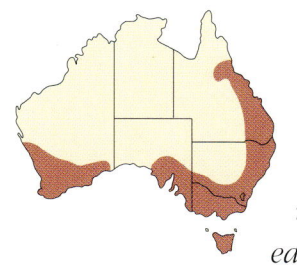

These aerial specialists are widespread over much of southern and eastern Australia, where their fluttering flight and swooping glides can be seen in many of the leafier suburbs.

DIET
Insects often taken in the air.

FIELD NOTES
Like all woodswallows, these birds catch their insect food on the wing, perching like Dollarbirds on high dead branches between feeding forays. They are gregarious birds and are seldom seen singly.

IN THE GARDEN

Habitat
Substantial tree canopies with clear spaces in between for feeding flights make the ideal habitat for Dusky Woodswallows.

Mottled colours and short feathers in their tails and wings make woodswallow fledglings easy to tell apart from their parents.

Dusky Woodswallows nest in a variety of places from shallow tree hollows to the ends of broken branches.

Food
A healthy pesticide-free neighbourhood will provide these birds with all the insects they need.

Nesting
Woodswallows build a grassy nest in a shallow tree hollow, a broken branch or similar setting. It can be high or low, depending on availability. Both parents brood the three eggs which hatch in about two weeks.

A very young chick peers over the rim of the nest. At this age, the bill is outlined in yellow.

DIRECTORY OF GARDEN BIRDS

Grey Butcherbird
Cracticus torquatus

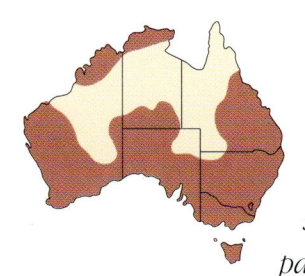

One of Australia's most melodious singers, this species enriches most parts of Australia with its complex songs. Accomplished hunters, butcherbirds pick off lizards, mice and even other birds.

This is a dangerous view of a butcherbird's nest. These aggressive birds defend their nests and if you're this close, the birds are probably lining up to bomb you.

DIET
Insects, lizards, mice and other small creatures.

Grey Butcherbirds live in many suburbs where their black, grey and white lines are appreciated by gardeners. The sexes are very similar and they sing long duets in spring.

FIELD NOTES
These butcherbirds will sometimes hunt with falcons by trying to catch birds driven under cover by the falcon's attack. If they catch an item too big too swallow, they will sometimes wedge it in a fork or on a broken twig. This ruthless practice has given rise to their common name.

IN THE GARDEN
Habitat
Grey Butcherbirds need an open forest environment where they can live in tree canopies.

Food
These birds can become quite tame, taking pieces of meat and pet food. Feeding them can sometimes curb their more aggressive tendencies around their nests.

Nesting
The nest is a neat cup of twigs built in a vertical fork from 3–10m above the ground. After nearly four weeks' brooding by the female, the eggs hatch into chicks that leave after a further four weeks.

Immatures are not as attractive as their parents – they have shades of brown where the parents are black and grey. The young birds learn their complex song gradually, starting with a call of only a few notes.

DIRECTORY OF GARDEN BIRDS

Pied Butcherbird
Cracticus nigrogularis

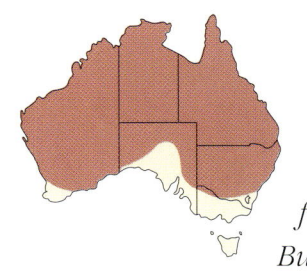

If there is any bird that can sing more beautifully than the Grey Butcherbird, it's the Pied. These birds sing a wonderful, clear song that is a memorable feature of frosty inland mornings.

DIET
Insects, lizards, mice and other small creatures.

FIELD NOTES
Pied Butcherbirds sit quietly in the branches waiting for unwary prey to reveal itself. Once they spot it, they glide silently into attack mode in much the same way that kookaburras hunt. They catch prey on the ground more often than Grey Butcherbirds do.

IN THE GARDEN

Habitat
Pied Butcherbirds live in the tree canopies, but compared with Grey Butcherbirds, choose more open forested areas.

Food
Like their grey cousins, these birds will take pieces of meat, cheese and pet food from a feeding tray. They become tame if fed regularly.

Pied Butcherbirds' elegant black-and-white lines and long, bluish bills show how close they are to magpies.

The sexes of this species are very similar – only other butcherbirds can tell who's who. Their prominent black bibs set them apart from Grey Butcherbirds.

Nesting
These butcherbirds nest in a neat cup of twigs built in a vertical fork more than 3m above the ground. They lay four or more eggs and the young may be cared for by older offspring, the last season's brood, as well as by the parents.

Juvenile Pied Butcherbirds have drab shades of brown that make them much more camouflaged than their parents.

DIRECTORY OF GARDEN BIRDS

Australian Magpie
Gymnorhina tibicen

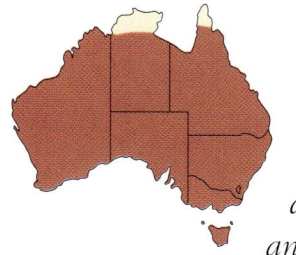

One of Australia's best known birds, magpies are named after a black-and-white English crow that doesn't have the impressive powers of flight that the Australian birds possess.

DIET
Insects, worms, spiders and other small creatures caught on the ground.

Male magpies can be very aggressive towards other birds and occasionally towards people, especially when they are breeding.

FIELD NOTES
Magpies' warbling carols grace many Australian suburbs each winter and spring when the birds engage in impressive aerial acrobatic battles over territory. The height of magpie society is to own a breeding territory. Lower status birds lead a nomadic life and are able to breed only if they can acquire a reasonable territory.

IN THE GARDEN

Habitat
Magpies need open, grassy feeding areas dotted with trees for nesting and roosting. The fact that much of Australia has been transformed into this sort of habitat since the arrival of Europeans has a lot to do with the success of these birds in the 20th century.

Food
Magpies will enjoy everything from pet food to cheese, and nice wriggly mealworms. If you use meat, it needs to be treated with calcium carbonate from the chemist (*see* page 32 for details).

Nesting
Female magpies build a large nest, sometimes with very little help from the male, who is too busy strutting around and chasing off intruders. The twig nest is built in an open spot in a high tree. Like currawongs, magpies don't have to hide their nests. The two to four eggs hatch after three weeks' incubation by the female and the young leave the nest after about four weeks.

Australian Magpies enjoy mealworms.

While sexual differences in many species are seen when facing the bird, magpies wear their gender badges on the back of their neck. Female magpies have a grey base to the nape of their neck; males' napes are pure white.

PIED CURRAWONG
Strepera graculina

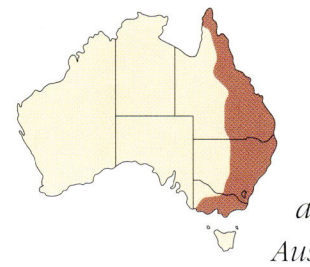

These vandals have done very well since the arrival of Europeans in Australia. They have been able to adapt to most of the new environments we have created and are now one of our most widespread species.

DIET
Insects, fruit, carrion and other items.

FIELD NOTES
Pied Currawongs (and Black Currawongs in Tasmania) are too smart for their own good. They've even worked out how to punch a hole in milk-bottle tops to get to the milk, and they can feed in almost any area from forest to heathland.

IN THE GARDEN

Habitat
Pied Currawongs are forest birds, but they are so adaptable that you will find them in most suburbs. They are also attracted by large trees, but do not necessarily need them.

Food
Putting food out for these characters might not be a good idea as the more currawongs you attract to your garden, the fewer small birds survive. If you really want to feed them, fruit pieces, pet food and mealworms are fine.

Nesting
An open spot high in a tall tree is the ideal place for currawongs to make their large twig nest. Since they are one of the meanest birds in the forest, they don't have to hide their nest. The three eggs hatch after three weeks' incubation by the female. The young leave the nest after about four weeks.

Currawongs will eat a wide range of foods, from insects to fruits and even dog biscuits.

It's easy to tell currawongs from magpies once you realise that currawongs have very little white on their body.

In spring, insects such as this juvenile grasshopper are popular with small chicks.

DIRECTORY OF GARDEN BIRDS

Australian Raven
Corvus coronoides

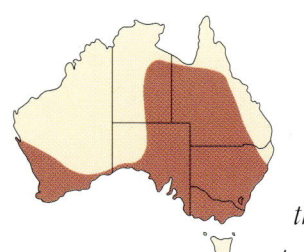

Although most people call these birds crows, they are one of our three species of raven. With more watering points in inland Australia and more carrion from dead sheep and cattle, there are probably more ravens now than in times past.

Ravens have done very well from the changes that agricultural development has brought to the inland.

DIET
Insects, mice, carrion and other items.

FIELD NOTES
There are five crow and raven species in Australia and identifying one from another is easier on windy days. When a crow's feathers are ruffled, you can see the white bases on its black body feathers; a raven has dark grey bases to its feathers. Beyond that, Little Ravens are the only ones to flip their wings when they call and Forest Ravens have the deepest throaty voice.

IN THE GARDEN

HABITAT
Ravens like tall trees with open areas in between so they can view their surroundings clearly. They live in the far inland where open country predominates and on the coast, where trees are plentiful.

FOOD
Ravens are usually too wary to come to a feeding table, but they can eventually be tamed. Suburbs where pesticides are avoided and the gardens are well planted with indigenous plants generally provide everything a pair of ravens needs.

NESTING
Both parents build a large untidy stick nest high in a tree, which gives them a good view of the surrounding area. The four eggs hatch after three weeks and the young leave after a further six weeks.

The nest is usually lined with fine plant fibres, together with a thick layer of animal fur and feathers. In sheep-growing areas chicks are often fed with lamb carcasses, but research has shown that only dead or dying sheep are taken.

With a taste for anything from insects to roadkill, Australian Ravens generally have little trouble in finding food. In winter and early spring they form noisy groups which congregate wherever there is food available.

DIRECTORY OF GARDEN BIRDS

Apostlebird
Struthidea cinerea

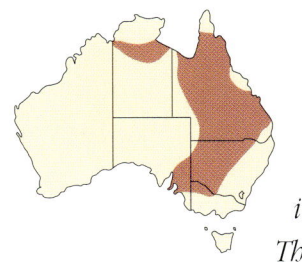

These noisy gregarious birds are widespread in inland eastern Australia. Their habit of hanging around in groups of about a dozen has led to their common name, Apostlebird.

Apostlebirds live in large happy groups where several females will lay eggs in one large mud nest. A noisy family of these birds is hard to miss.

Mutual preening is a vital part of an Apostlebird's daily routine. It rids the bird of feather lice and helps it to cement the group bond.

DIET
Insects, spiders, seeds and other vegetable matter.

FIELD NOTES
Apostlebirds do everything together, whether it is feeding, fighting, flirting or just loafing around. They are one of the most gregarious bird species – they even go as far as sharing the duty of sitting on the group's eggs.

IN THE GARDEN

Habitat
These birds feed mostly on the ground. They need a grassy woodland area with plenty of open space between the dotted trees which they use for shelter.

Food
Apostlebirds have a wide variety of food preferences and will take anything from chook pellets to fruit pieces. They will even eat pet food.

Nesting
Apostlebirds use mud and grass to build an amazing pudding basin of a nest on a fairly level branch more than 2m above the ground. The four or more eggs hatch after two and a half weeks' incubation by most members of the group. The young leave the nest after a further two and a half weeks.

The enormous nest is carefully lined with fine plant material such as grass and bark fibres.

SATIN BOWERBIRD
Ptilonorhynchus violaceus

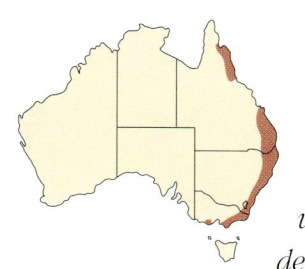

The Satin Bowerbird is renowned around the world for making and decorating a bower as well as building a nest. It sometimes paints the bower with charcoal, making it one of the few birds worldwide that can use tools.

Male bowerbirds don't turn black until they reach six or seven years of age. Younger males and females are difficult to distinguish, but their green colouration easily separates them from the mature males.

DIET
Fruits, insects, seeds and vegetable matter.

FIELD NOTES
Like Australia's other bowerbird species, the males build a bower to attract their female friends. Females then make the rounds of the various bowers on display in their area to see which one they like the look of. The males decorate their bowers with natural and artificial blue and sometimes yellow items. This increases their attractiveness by mirroring the colours in their own blue feathers and yellow beaks.

IN THE GARDEN

HABITAT
These bowerbirds like to shelter in a fairly dense understorey with a forest canopy overhead.

FOOD
Satin Bowerbirds will readily come to a feeding tray stocked with pieces of fruit, seeds or even pet food. Their natural food is berries, so start by growing any of the berry plants listed in Chapter One. They are also partial to green vegetables such as lettuce and can even become a pest in market gardens.

NESTING
Once the female has mated with her chosen male, she builds the nest in an upright fork or clump of mistletoe. She can nest anywhere from 2–20m above the ground, and raises the two chicks on her own.

The bowerbird's bower isn't a nest, it's a structure designed to enhance the males' courting display.

DIRECTORY OF GARDEN BIRDS

Great Bowerbird
Chlamydera nuchalis

These active birds never rest. Across many parts of northern Australia, this large fawn-coloured bowerbird is an obvious part of the wildlife community visiting gardens and bushland.

DIET
Fruit and occasionally insects.

FIELD NOTES
The Great Bowerbird decorates its bower with white shiny objects, including small bones and snail shells. This has led inexperienced anthropologists on a wild goose chase. Faced with long-abandoned bowers, some concluded they were looking at the remains of mysterious Aboriginal feasts where only snails and meat from tiny bones were eaten!

Great Bowerbirds are better builders than their southern cousins. They construct a very large, dense bower twice as large as the one built by the Satin Bowerbird.

IN THE GARDEN

Habitat
These birds need an area of shrubs as well as woodland trees in which to forage.

Food
Great Bowerbirds are partial to fruit pieces and other scraps of food. If the titbits are offered regularly, they can become quite tame.

Nesting
The female builds an obvious, bulky nest of twigs and grasses in a shrub or low bush, often a long way from the bower. She raises the single chick by herself.

What female bird could resist this handsome mottled male, standing proudly in front of his bower, his plumage complemented by a range of precious objects?

DIRECTORY OF GARDEN BIRDS

House Sparrow

Passer domesticus

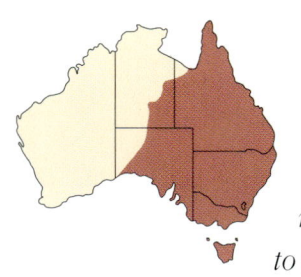

This is one species that many people wish had never been introduced to this country, as it has caused major problems for farmers and wildlife.

DIET
Seeds, insects and fruit.

FIELD NOTES
Nearly all the sparrows in south-east Australia are House Sparrows, although you can find the rarer Tree Sparrow in a band from Gilgandra to Melbourne. Tree Sparrows can be identified by their whiter cheeks and by the top of the male's head which is brown, not grey.

With his grey crown and black eye stripe, the male sparrow is more clearly marked than the female.

IN THE GARDEN

HABITAT

The more introduced plants you grow in your backyard, the more attractive it will be to sparrows. This is a great reason to fill your garden with indigenous plant species and encourage native Australian birds rather than these introduced rascals.

FOOD

If you really want to attract sparrows, it's easy. Just put out seeds or anything made from seeds, such as bread scraps or biscuits. The sparrows will love you – but the neighbours and the native birds might not.

NESTING

Sparrows build a huge untidy nest in a hollow space. Buildings are a favourite site with guttering and areas behind fascia boards being common choices. Their nests can be a source of lice as well as a fire hazard (yet another reason to discourage these birds). The five eggs hatch in about two weeks, after which the parents breed again and again and again!

House Sparrows have followed our ancestors around the world, and are considered to be pests. In farming areas they attack grain crops and in the suburbs they compete with native birds such as Fairy Martins.

DIRECTORY OF GARDEN BIRDS

Zebra Finch
Taeniopygia guttata

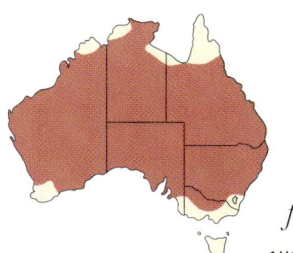

An ability to breed as long as conditions are favourable, together with truly impressive powers of flight, have made Zebra Finches successful in the drier parts of Australia, as well as in the cagebird industry.

Female Zebra Finches are grey-brown with orange beaks while males have orange cheek patches, flecked sides and handsome breast bars. Immatures have dark beaks.

DIET
Seeds and some insects, generally found on the ground.

FIELD NOTES
The thin, nasal voices of Zebra Finches can be heard over much of inland Australia. These birds are highly adaptable. They are often one of the very few small birds that greet travellers to isolated inland airstrips. In such areas they eke out a living in the few bushes that struggle to survive around the airport sheds.

IN THE GARDEN

Habitat
Zebra Finches need open areas for feeding on the ground, coupled with at least one or two bushes for shelter from the inland sun.

Food
A tray of mixed seeds can prove very popular with these finches, as can a birdbath in drier climates. During the breeding season, they relish insects and will happily make off with mealworms.

Most finches favour smaller, mixed seeds, especially if they're offered on the ground in cat-free areas.

Nesting
Like other finches, these birds build a large nest with a side entrance in a spiky shrub. The five eggs hatch after just under two weeks' brooding by both parents. The young leave after a further three weeks.

Providing welcoming areas of water in inland parts of Australia is a great way to attract a range of species, especially seed eaters such as these Zebra Finches.

DIRECTORY OF GARDEN BIRDS

Double-barred Finch
Taeniopygia bichenovii

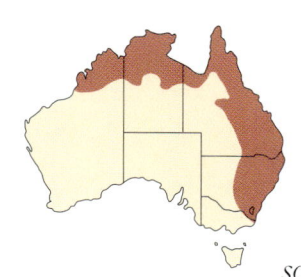

The distinctive jet-black ring around the pure white face of this handsome finch gives it a slightly owl-like appearance and leads to its other name, the Owl-faced Finch.

DIET
Seeds and occasionally insects.

While seeds are a finch's favourite food, some birds will also take insects and even nectar from grevilleas.

IN THE GARDEN

Habitat
These finches favour grassy woodland areas with open spaces for feeding and a generous scattering of trees or larger shrubs.

Food
They enjoy mixed seed scattered on the ground and just love indigenous seeding grasses, especially when the seeds are still green and juicy.

Nesting
Double-barred Finches build a typical, spherical finch nest with a side entrance in a bush, small tree or occasionally in a hollow tree. Both parents brood the eggs until they hatch in under two weeks.

FIELD NOTES
This is a typical finch, feeding on the ground and swooping off to perch in a nearby tree at the first sign of danger. Finches frequently feed as a flock, which has the advantage of many pairs of eyes to scan the surroundings for predators.

Double-barred Finches like to feed on the ground, so it's important to keep cats and pesticides away.

DIRECTORY OF GARDEN BIRDS

Red-browed Finch
Neochmia temporalis

These beautiful native finches live along the eastern rim of Australia, although small groups have been introduced into Western Australia. They live in tight-knit parties and pairs mate for life.

DIET
Seeds and a few insects.

FIELD NOTES
Red-browed Finches are one of the more common finches and the ones that are most likely to turn up in gardens. They were once trapped in large numbers for the bird trade, but are now protected.

IN THE GARDEN

HABITAT
These finches need open grassy areas for feeding with plenty of trees and larger shrubs scattered about for roosting, nesting and hiding from predators.

From a distance these birds appear dull, but up close, the subtle colours of the yellow bar on the upper back and the many shades of brown and grey contrast pleasingly with the crimson eye stripe and black tail.

FOOD
Red-browed Finches will readily visit a seed tray and will often take seeds offered to them on the ground. They are also partial to indigenous seeding grasses, which provide them with food and nesting material.

NESTING
In comparison to its size, this finch builds a substantial, messy nest in a large shrub, such as the particularly spiky Sweet Bursaria (*Bursaria spinosa*) or one of the prickly wattles. The nest is woven from grass.

The five eggs hatch in about two weeks and the young leave the nest after just over two weeks' care by both parents. After the nesting season, these birds will sometimes use the nest for shelter.

Red-browed Finches love the seeds of native grasses and are also partial to handouts of mixed grain, offered in open areas where they can keep a watch for approaching predators. Like other finches, they live in active groups.

DIRECTORY OF GARDEN BIRDS

GOLDFINCH
Carduelis carduelis

Goldfinches occur throughout south-east Australia with a few populations in the west. Although they are introduced, they don't seem to be causing any ecological problems.

Goldfinches generally nest in introduced trees – in this case, an apple tree. Although the adults feed mostly on seeds, they spend a lot of time during the breeding season foraging for insects to feed the chicks.

DIET
Seeds and insects taken from shrubs and trees.

FIELD NOTES
Unlike some other introduced birds, Goldfinches have not become much of a problem, either for wildlife or for farming. They mostly feed on the seeds of weeds and live in areas not colonised by indigenous species. They live in flocks which can number over 100 in areas where plentiful food is provided by grain crops.

IN THE GARDEN

HABITAT
Goldfinches enjoy open areas with thistles and other daisy-type flowers for feeding, coupled with a few trees for both roosting and nesting.

FOOD
These birds eat seeds on the ground, on shrubs or on a bird feeder. Gardeners can attract them by encouraging thistles and sunflowers or by offering a tray of seeds.

Sunflowers will attract Goldfinches to your garden.

NESTING
Goldfinches make a little camouflaged nest of grasses and other plant fibres, between 2–10m above the ground. The four eggs hatch after about two weeks' brooding by the female and the chicks leave the nest after a further two weeks.

Although Goldfinches are introduced, they haven't invaded natural bushland as weeds provide a ready supply of seeds.

DIRECTORY OF GARDEN BIRDS

Yellow-bellied Sunbird

Nectarinia jugularis

The Yellow-bellied Sunbird is the only representative of this tropical group that reaches Australia. It can become quite used to people in parks and backyards.

DIET
Nectar, insects and spiders.

FIELD NOTES
Sunbirds become quite tame around Queensland coastal settlements where the iridescent males and bright-yellow females are a feature of many gardens. They can roll their tongues into a long tube to get the nectar out of flowers efficiently.

Sunbirds use their tongues to sip nectar from grevilleas, bottlebrushes and other native plants.

IN THE GARDEN

Habitat
Found in the tropical parts of Australia, sunbirds are highly adaptable. They prefer rainforest margins and mangroves but will readily visit gardens with a good supply of nectar-producing flowers.

Food
A healthy garden will provide the insects and spiders these birds need for protein. Nectar is obtained from grevilleas, bottlebrushes and paperbarks.

Nesting
Female sunbirds build a long, dangly nest that looks like flood debris hanging in a tree. They use the same nest year after year and often build in gardens or under eaves. The two eggs are brooded by the female and the chicks are fed by both parents.

The female Yellow-bellied Sunbird builds a long, well-camouflaged nest using everything from plant fibres to spider web and lichen.

DIRECTORY OF GARDEN BIRDS

Mistletoebird
Dicaeum hirundinaceum

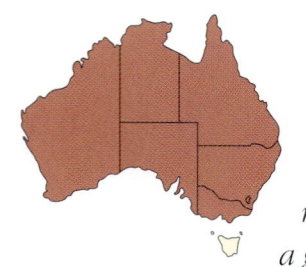

These beautiful birds are found wherever mistletoe grows. They are a great reason to tolerate some mistletoe in your garden, as long as it doesn't damage the host tree.

Male Mistletoebirds are beautiful creatures with a stunning crimson and black colour scheme. They perch on exposed branches to display to rivals and potential mates.

IN THE GARDEN

HABITAT
These birds prefer mistletoe growing on trees, but they will also visit the top of the shrub layer.

FOOD
Mistletoe is practically the only food these birds will eat, so providing for them is easy – just make sure you don't chop off any mistletoe growing in your garden.

Female Mistletoebirds are a soft grey which helps them to be less vulnerable to predation. Here the bird passes a sticky seed which may well start a new clump of mistletoe.

Sprouted mistletoe seeds tap into the host tree's nutrients.

NESTING
Female birds build a delicate, oval nest with a side entrance in the tree canopy. The three eggs hatch in just over two weeks and the chicks are then fed by both parents.

DIET
Mistletoe berries and insects caught in trees.

FIELD NOTES
Mistletoebirds live almost entirely on mistletoe berries. They gently squeeze the berry out of its skin and then swallow it – their digestive system is designed to pass the sticky seed within an hour. The seed generally sticks to the branch on which the bird is perching and so spreads the mistletoe to a new host tree.

DIRECTORY OF GARDEN BIRDS

Welcome Swallow
Hirundo neoxena

These birds are very common, and it's rare that you will walk across an Australian oval or playing field without seeing at least one of them. These gregarious swallows live in flocks.

DIET
Mainly small insects, such as flies and midges, taken on the wing.

FIELD NOTES
Like their European cousins whoare reputed to return each year to Capistrano in Italy, Welcome Swallows migrate north each winter. However, they don't go very far so the local swallows are simply replaced by more birds from further south. Local numbers drop in winter in Tasmania only.

Welcome Swallows like to perch in open places where they rely on their vision, speed and particularly agility to escape goshawks or falcons. It doesn't take predators long to realise that chasing swallows is a waste of time.

IN THE GARDEN

Habitat
Large lawns are perfect places for swallows to hawk insects – especially if there are exposed perches like dead branches or electricity wires for resting on between bouts of flying.

Food
Flying insects are the favoured food for swallows. The best way to provide them is to let nature take its course and to avoid pesticides.

Nesting
Swallows build a mud nest, lined with plant fibres and feathers, on cliff faces, under bridges or on buildings. They have also nested on boats, in fireplaces and even in a Cobb & Co coach! The four eggs hatch in two weeks and the young leave the nest after about three weeks' care by both parents.

There's nothing like a good mud hole as a place to pick up some tasty nesting material – at least if you're a swallow.

DIRECTORY OF GARDEN BIRDS

Fairy Martin
Hirundo ariel

These agile little birds look a lot like swallows, but instead of fluttering over level grassy areas, they swoop in and out of culverts, under bridges, and alongside cliffs and buildings.

DIET
Insects such as flies and mosquitoes taken in the air.

FIELD NOTES
These birds are the most social of our swallows. They feed together, migrate together and even build their extraordinary nests in groups. Many birds return to renovate the same nests each year. Fairy Martin nests provide habitat for a wide range of creatures. House Sparrows will sometimes usurp them and spiders, wasps and even snakes have been found in them.

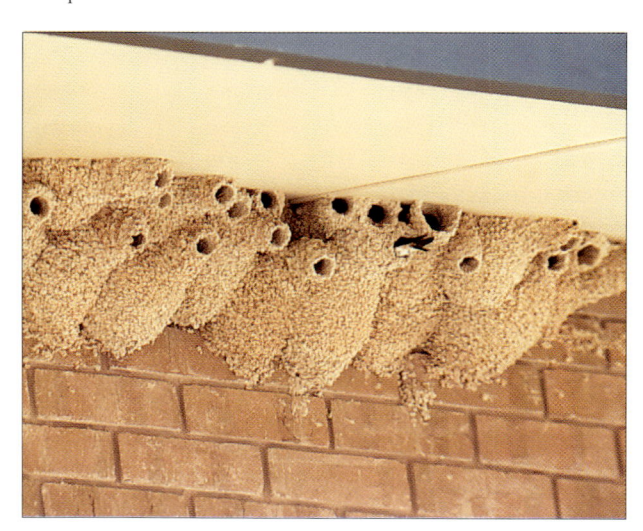

Fairy Martins build wonderful mud nests beneath overhanging eaves and on cliff ledges. A colony of these birds breeding in the area means that there will be fewer mozzies and other insect pests to bother us humans.

IN THE GARDEN

HABITAT
Fairy Martins love large ponds, swampy areas and other open water features. They like to swoop over wetlands to catch their insect prey. They gather the mud they need to build their nests from around the edges of these watery areas.

Martins resemble swallows but have short, square tails whereas swallows' tails are deeply forked.

FOOD
These birds catch insects on the wing and even drink as they fly low over water. Any open wetland will provide the food they need.

A group of these birds feeding their chicks in the neighbourhood spells disaster for flies.

NESTING
A colony of Fairy Martins will build bottle-shaped mud nests next to each other on the underside of a rocky overhang, concrete water tank or building. On the Hawkesbury River west of Sydney, several dozen birds have built nests under the eaves of a two-storey house – much to the delight of the owners.

Nests are lined with feathers. The four eggs hatch in two weeks after being brooded by both parents.

Red-whiskered Bulbul

Pycnonotus jocosus

Bulbuls come from India and south-east Asia. At one time, scientists thought they might be a serious threat to our indigenous birds, but thankfully, this has not happened.

Bulbuls are introduced, but have not been able to invade natural bushland. They are partial to both native and domestic fruits – especially bite-sized ones like mulberries.

DIET
Fruits, berries and insects taken in shrubs.

FIELD NOTES
These bulbuls seem to have been released in Sydney in about 1880, but did not become common until about 40 years later. Although they are a very effective competitor in the rainforests of India and Asia, bulbuls have not been able to invade Australian rainforests to the extent of other introduced birds as many ecologists feared they might. They have a pleasant range of calls which are heard in spring and summer.

IN THE GARDEN

Habitat
Dense shrubby areas are ideal for bulbuls who need the cover to hide from predators such as currawongs.

Food
Bulbuls need plants with bite-sized fruits or berries like grapes or mulberries. Suitable Australian plants include the Blueberry Ash (*Elaeocarpus reticulatus*), acronychia (*Achronychia oblongifolia*) and Lilly Pillies (*Acmena* and *Syzygium* spp.). If you have them on your block of land, the Bush Cherry (*Exocarpos cupressiformis*) and leucopogons are very useful berry plants – but not easy to establish.

Nesting
Dense shrubs or vine clumps are great nesting sites for bulbuls. The nest is a neat cup of grasses and bark with a lining of softer material. The three eggs are brooded by both parents.

Callistemons and other dense bushes provide good habitat for Red-whiskered Bulbuls.

SILVEREYE

Zosterops lateralis

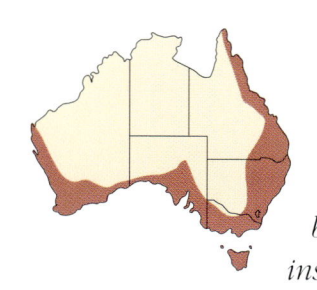

These birds skulk about the garden providing benefits in the form of insect control and the odd problem in the form of stolen fruit, but this is a small price to pay for such interesting visitors.

DIET
Insects, berries, nectar and some seeds.

FIELD NOTES
Each year, thousands of Silvereyes travel north for their winter holidays, with some birds from Tasmania reaching past northern New South Wales. During this time of year, it's easy to recognise the Tasmanian birds – they have cinnamon-coloured sides instead of the grey sides of mainland birds.

IN THE GARDEN

HABITAT
Silvereyes like a dense layer of small trees or larger shrubs in which to forage for food and avoid predators.

FOOD
They will take nectar mix and also help themselves to fruit pieces and the odd mealworm. But of course, having indigenous nectar and berry plants in your garden is the best way to provide for their needs.

NESTING
Both parents build the cup-shaped nest, which is constructed from grass, bark fibres and spider web, in the dense outer foliage of large shrubs or small trees. They brood the young who hatch in just under two weeks, leaving the nest after a further ten days or so.

These cinnamon-sided Silvereyes are from Tasmania, but can be seen as far north as southern Queensland in winter.

Silvereyes live in flocks except during the breeding season which can occur from mid-winter until mid-summer. During breeding they are more likely to be encountered in pairs, although non-breeding juveniles will still be flocking.

DIRECTORY OF GARDEN BIRDS

Common Blackbird
Turdus merula

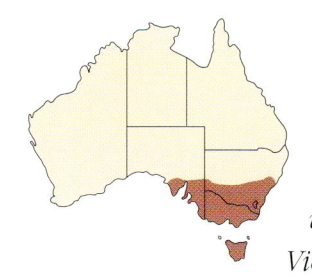

Blackbirds come from Europe and Asia. They were first released in Victoria in 1864, and thereafter in three other states – New South Wales, Tasmania and South Australia.

Male Blackbirds sing a melodious, complex song in late winter and spring, often emerging from the undergrowth so that they can display to repel rivals and attract the soft brown-coloured females.

DIET
Worms, insects, spiders and other small creatures, as well as fruits taken on the ground or from shrubs.

FIELD NOTES
Common Blackbirds sing very sweetly in spring, but they are one of the few introduced birds that have been able to invade natural bushland.

Besides gardens, Blackbirds live in the moist forests of southern Australia where they probably compete with native birds such as the Pilotbird and lyrebird.

Blackbirds love all the bramble fruits such as these loganberries. Growing them in the garden provides tasty treats for many birds as well as for the gardener!

IN THE GARDEN

Habitat
Common Blackbirds seek out a dense shrub layer within the first 2m of the ground, together with a deep mulch layer for foraging.

They will also help themselves to any berry bushes close to the ground, especially blackberries, raspberries and their relatives.

Food
A deep mulch layer is the best way to ensure food for Common Blackbirds, but they will also take pieces of cheese and other food scraps left on the ground.

Nesting
The female blackbird builds her nest in dense vegetation within a few metres of the ground. She broods the four greenish-blue eggs until they hatch after about two weeks. The males help feed the young who leave the nest after a further two weeks.

Common Starling

Sturnus vulgaris

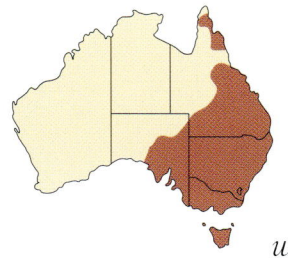

These birds vie with Common (Indian) Mynas as Australia's worst introduced bird. They have established themselves in many parts of the country to the great detriment of both agriculture and the environment.

DIET
Insects, seeds, fruits and other foods.

FIELD NOTES
Starlings are very tough nest competitors and are known to occupy nesting hollows to the exclusion of indigenous species such as rosellas and kingfishers. They tend to nest in groups which can make it doubly difficult for an indigenous bird to find a nesting hollow.

IN THE GARDEN

Habitat
Starlings like nice flat lawns and lots of introduced plants. The more your garden resembles natural bushland, the less the starlings will like it – a good reason to grow indigenous plants!

Although pesky, starlings are remarkably handsome. Early in the season, the feathers are tipped with a lighter colour.

Starlings can be quite accomplished vocalists. They include in their songs imitations of the calls of many other birds.

Food
These freeloaders are happy to eat anything we do, especially food scraps.

Nesting
If you want a large untidy grass and feather nest in your ceiling, these are the birds for you. But their nests are a source of itchy bird lice and can constitute a fire hazard, so they're well worth avoiding!

The five eggs hatch in under two weeks and the chicks leave in a further three weeks.

Starlings make a messy nest in almost any hollow. In houses, their nests are a fire hazard. In the bush, they are fierce nest competitors – often just stuffing their nest material on top of a native bird's nest or eggs.

Common (Indian) Myna

Acridotheres tristis

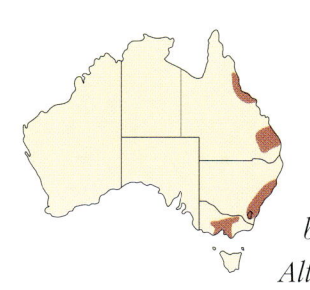

This species is arguably the worst bird ever brought to Australia. Although they have not spread as far into the country as starlings, they seem to be more effective at excluding native birds from their natural habitats.

Perhaps the most unpopular bird in the suburbs, Mynas are aggressive nest competitors for kingfishers, smaller parrots and other birds.

DIET
Insects, seeds, berries, carrion and other items.

FIELD NOTES
Common Mynas have spread through the more settled parts of eastern Australia but a concerted government program has succeeded in keeping them and other pests such as starlings out of Western Australia. Distinguishing these pests from the indigenous Noisy Miners is simple – just remember that the 'goodies' are grey and the 'baddies' are brown.

Mynas were released in Melbourne, Sydney and northeast Queensland in the second half of last century to control insects, but most insect populations are still thriving and the Mynas have only controlled the native birds.

IN THE GARDEN

HABITAT
Mynas like artificial surroundings, so the more indigenous plants you have in your garden, the less they will annoy you and your Australian bird visitors.

FOOD
Don't bother. These birds will eat virtually anything you will – and a lot more besides.

NESTING
Like their relatives, the starlings, these birds build a large, messy nest in ceilings or guttering. They are experts at stuffing nesting material into the downpipe, so it no longer carries water and rusts from being constantly wet. They surpass even starlings as vicious nest competitors. You really don't want these birds around and should discourage them.

Useful Contacts

Birds Tasmania,
GPO Box 68A,
Hobart, TAS 7001

Bird Observers Club of Australia,
PO Box 185,
Nunawading, VIC 3131
Tel: (03) 9877-5342

Canberra Ornithologists Group,
GPO Box 301,
Civic Square, ACT 2608
Tel: (06) 6247-4996

Cumberland Bird Observers Club,
c/- the Australian Museum,
PO Box A285,
Sydney South, NSW 2001
Tel: (02) 9320-6000

Landcare,
PO Box 5002,
West Chatswood, NSW 2057
Tel: 1800 15 1105

NSW Field Ornithologists Club,
PO Box Q277,
QVB Post Shop,
Sydney, NSW 1230

Northern Territory Field
Naturalists Club,
PO Box 39565,
Winnellie, NT 0821

Queensland Ornithological Society,
PO Box 97,
St Lucia, QLD 4067
Tel: (07) 3229-3554

Royal Australasian Ornithologists
Union, Head Office
21 Gladstone St,
Moonee Ponds, VIC 3039
Tel: (03) 9882-2622

Royal Australasian Ornithologists
Union, NSW Office
GPO Box 3943,
NSW 2001
Tel: (02) 9290-1810

Royal Australasian Ornithologists
Union, WA Office
71 Oceanic Drive,
Floreat, WA 6014
Tel: (08) 9383-7749

South Australian
Ornithological Association,
c/- South Australian
Museum,
North Terrace,
Adelaide, SA 5000
Tel: (08) 8207-7500

Western Australian Naturalists Club,
Naturalists Hall,
63-65 Meriwa St,
Nedlands, Western Australia 6009

Wildlife Information and
Rescue Service (WIRES),
PO Box 260,
Forestville, NSW 2087
Tel: (02) 9975-1643

Wombaroo Food Products,
c/- Native Trading,
PO Box 116,
Unley, SA 5061
Tel: (08) 8277-7788

The Society for Growing
Australian Plants (SGAP)

SGAP Canberra Region Inc,
11 Collingridge Street,
Weston, ACT 2611
Tel: (02) 6288-1430

SGAP NSW Ltd,
PO Box 744
Blacktown, NSW 2148
Tel: (02) 9621-3437

SGAP Queensland Region,
PO Box 586,
Fortitude Valley, QLD 4006
Tel: (07) 3844-4679

SGAP SA Region,
5 Marram Terrace,
Largs North, SA 5016
Tel: (08) 8248-1978

SGAP Tasmanian Region Inc,
GPO Box 1353P,
Hobart, TAS 7001
Tel: (03) 6227-9245

SGAP Victoria Inc,
11 Davies Street,
Bacchus Marsh, VIC 3340
Tel: (03) 9728-5891

SGAP Wildflower Society of WA Inc,
PO Box 64,
Nedlands, WA 6009
Tel: (08) 8383-7979

Further Reading

Australian Native Gardens,
D Snape, Lothian,
Melbourne (1992).

Bird Life,
I Rowley, Collins,
Sydney (1975).

Bird Wonders of Australia,
A H Chisholm, Angus and
Robertson, Sydney (1965).

*The Complete A-Z of Gardening
in Australia,*
W G Sheat and G Schofield,
New Holland, Sydney (1995).

*The Conservation of
Australian Wetlands,*
A J McComb and P S Lake (eds),
Surrey Beatty and Sons,
Sydney (1988).

Ecology of Birds,
H A Ford, Surrey Beatty and Sons,
Sydney (1989).

Encyclopedia of Australian Plants,
Volumes 1–6, W Elliot and D Jones,
Lothian, Melbourne (1980–1993).

*Gardening on the Wild Side:
The New Australian Bush Garden,*
Angus Stewart, ABC Books,
Sydney (1995).

Grow What Where,
Australian Plant Study Group,
Viking O'Neil, Melbourne (1990).

Growing Fruit in Australia,
P Baxter and G Tankard, Nelson,
Melbourne (1981).

*Growing Grevilleas in Australia
and New Zealand,*
Don Burke, Kangaroo Press,
Sydney (1983).

How to Propagate Plants,
J Plumridge, Lothian,
Melbourne (1975).

*An Introduction to
Australian Insects,*
P Hadlington and J A Johnston,
New South Wales University Press,
Sydney (1982).

*Native Gardens: How to Create
an Australian Landscape,*
B Molyneaux and R Macdonald,
Kangaroo Press, Sydney (1992).

*A Photographic Guide to Birds
of Australia,*
Peter Rowland, Australian Museum,
New Holland, Sydney (1995).

*The Reader's Digest Complete Book
of Australian Birds,*
R Schodde and S Tidemann,
Reader's Digest, Sydney (1986).

*The Robins and Flycatchers
of Australia,*
Walter E Boles, Angus and
Robertson, Sydney (1988).

The Seabirds of Australia,
T Lindsey, Angus and Robertson,
Sydney (1986).

*Tiny Game Hunting –
Environmentally Healthy Ways to
Trap and Rid Pests from your
House And Garden,*
H Klein, A Wenner and J Dengate,
Bantam Books, Sydney (1993).

Trees for the Back Paddock,
N Oates and B Clarke,
Goddard and Dobson,
Melbourne (1987).

The Waterbirds of Australia,
J Pringle, Angus and Robertson,
Sydney (1985).

*What Garden Pest or
Disease is That?,*
J McMaugh, Weldon Publishing,
Sydney (1985).

*The Wrens and Warblers
of Australia,*
V Serventy, A McGill, J Pringle and
T Lindsey, Angus and Robertson,
Sydney (1982).

Bird Field Guides

The Birds of Australia,
K Simpson and N Day, Viking
O'Neil, Melbourne (1986).

*A Field Guide to the Birds
of Australia,*
G Pizzey and R Doyle, Collins,
Melbourne (1980).

*The Slater Field Guide to
Australian Birds,*
P Slater, P Slater and R Slater,
Rigby, Sydney (1986).

Index

acacia 13, 68
Acacia baileyana 23
   A. longifolia 23
   A. melanoxylon 23
Acanthagenys rufogularis **154**
Acanthiza chrysorrhoa **150**
   A. nana **151**
   A. pusilla **149**
Acanthorhynchus tenuirostris **169**
Acridotheres tristis **203**
Acmena smithii 23, 92
Alectura lathami **96**
Alisterus scapularis **121**
Angophora costata 71
   A. floribunda 23
Anhinga melanogaster 91
Anthochaera carunculata **152**
   A. chrysoptera **153**
Apostlebird **187**
Artamus cyanopterus **181**
Ash, Blueberry 23
Atriplex sp. 17

Bacillus thuringiensis 79, 83
banksia 23, 68
   Giant Candles 66, 114
Banksia ashbyi 14
   B. serrata 16
Barnardius zonarius **126**
Bee-eater, Rainbow 21, 75, **137**
beetles, leaf-eating 81
Bidyanus bidyanus 91
birdbaths 26, 42
Black-cockatoo, Yellow-tailed 23, **114**
Blackbird, Common **201**
Boobook, Southern **132**
bottlebrush 17, 67
   Albany 13
   Captain Cook 15
Bowerbird, Great **189**
   Satin 15, **188**
Bridelia exaltata 23
Brush-turkey, Australian 16, **96**
Bulbul, Red-whiskered **199**
Bush Cherries 17, 71
Butcherbird, Grey **182**
   Pied **183**

Cacatua galerita **118**
   C. roseicapilla **116**
   C. sanguinea **117**
Cacomantis flabelliformis **129**
Callistemon 68
Callistemon phoenicius 13
Callocephalon fimbriatum **115**
Calyptorhynchus funereus **114**
Carassius auratus 46
Carduelis carduelis **194**
Casuarina sp. 13, 68
Caterpillar, Tent 83
cats 33
Cedar, White 23
Ceratopetalum gummiferum 68
Chenonetta jubata **97**
chicks, caring for 62
Chlamydera nuchalis **189**
Christmas Bush 68
Chthonicola sagittatus **145**
Cockatoo, Gang-gang **115**
   Sulphur-crested **118**
Columba leucomela **107**
   C. livia **106**

Conopophila rufogularis **168**
Coracina novaehollandiae **178**
Corella, Little 85, **117**
Cormorant, Little Pied **99**
Correas 17
Corvus coronoides **186**
Cracticus nigrogularis **183**
   C. torquatus **182**
Cuckoo, Channel-billed **131**
   Fan-tailed **129**
   Pallid **128**
Cuckoo-shrike, Black-faced **178**
Cuculus pallidus **128**
Cup Moth larvae 81
Currawong, Pied **185**
currawongs 21
cuttings, growing 72
Cyathodes 17

Dacelo novaeguineae **135**
dams 88–91
Darters 91
Dicaeum hirundinaceum **196**
Dichondra repens 15
Dicrurus bracteatus **177**
Dipel see *Bacillus thuringiensis*
Dollarbird **138**
Dove, Bar-shouldered **111**
   Laughing 52
   Peaceful **110**
   Rock **106**
dragonflies 49
Drongo, Spangled 24, **177**
Duck, Australian Wood **97**

ecological balance 43, 47
ecotones 14

Egretta novaehollandiae **100**
Elaeocarpus reticulatus 23
Elanus axillaris **102**
Entomyzon cyanotis **156**
Eopsaltria australis **170**
   E. griseogularis **170**
Epacris impressa 43
   E. longiflora 43
eucalpyts 23, 26
   bloodwood 23
   blackwood 23
   Gungurru 23
   Swamp Mahogany 23
   Yellow Box 23
Eucalyptus caesia 23
   E. camaldulensis 21
   E. gummifera 23
   E. meliodora 23
   E. robusta 23
Eudynamys scolopacea **130**
Eurystomus orientalis **138**
Exocarpos sp. 71
   E. cupressiformis 17

Faclo cenchroides **103**
Fairy-wren, Red-backed **142**
   Superb **140**
   Variegated **141**
Fantail, Grey **175**
farms 86
   bird-friendly 86
feeders 34
   commercial 34
   feeding platforms 34, 38–39
   mesh bags 34
   natural 35
feeding 30–39
   bottle 33
   table 33
   baby cereal 31

bird pudding mix 38
cheese 32
cuttlebone 32
grain 31
greens 31
insects 31
meat 31
nectar mix 31
pet food 32
pollen 31
seeds 30
ferns 42
fertilising 70
Ficus sp. 23
Figbird **180**
figs 23
    rainforest 23
Finch, Double-barred **192**
    Red-browed 48, **193**
    Zebra **191**
Firetail, Red-browed 14
fish 46, 90
    Empire 46
    goldfish 46
    Mosquito 46, 91
    rainbow 46
Flycatcher, Restless **173**
Friarbird, Noisy **155**
Frog, Striped Marsh 46
Frogmouth, Tawny **134**
Fuchsia, Native 43

Galah 15, **116**
Gambusia affinis 46, 91
Gania microstachya 25
garden
    habitats 13
    location, importance of 12
    planning 13
    bird-friendly 19
    bird-unfriendly 18

colour scheme 13
fruit and vegetable 35, 78
indigenous 66
managed 67–70
small 25
untamed 67
geebungs 17, 71
Geopelia humeralis **111**
    G. striata **110**
Gerygone mouki **147**
    G. olivacea **148**
Gerygone, Brown **147**
    White-throated **148**
Goldfinch **194**
goshawks 87
Grallina cyanoleuca **174**
grass, native 15
    Poa 15
Grebe, Australasian **98**
grevillea
    Bronze Rambler 15
    Honey Gem 15, 17
    Misty Pink 15
    Ned Kelly 67
    Robyn Gordon 9, 15, 17
    Royal Mantle 15
    Superb 17
Grevillea robusta 23, 26, 92
Gull, Silver **105**
Gum, River Red 21
    Sydney Red 71
Gymnorhina tibicen **184**

Hakea, needlebush 21
    pincushion 21, 54
Hakea gibbosa 21
Heron, White-faced **100**
Hirundo ariel **198**
    H. neoxena **197**
Honeyeater, Blue-faced **156**
    Brown 17, **165**

Lewin's 15, **159**
New Holland 15, 16, **166**
Rufous-throated **168**
Spiny-cheeked **154**
Varied **161**
White-cheeked **167**
White-eared **163**
White-plumed **164**
Yellow **162**
Yellow-faced 21, **160**
Hypseleotris compressa 46

Ibis, Sacred **101**

Kennedia prostrata 15
Kestrel, Nankeen 62, **103**
Kidney Weed 15
King Parrot, Australian **121**
Kingfisher, Sacred 48, **136**
Kite, Black-shouldered 51, 86, **102**
Koel, Common **130**
Kookaburra, Laughing **135**

Lapwing, Masked **104**
Larus novaehollandiae **105**
Leptospermum sp. 68
Leucosarcia melanoleuca **112**
Lichenostomus chrysops **160**
    L. flavus **162**
    L. leucotis **163**
    L. penicillatus **164**
    L. versicolor **161**
Lichmera indistincta **165**
Lilly Pilly 23, 92
Lopholaimus antarcticus **113**
Lorikeet, Rainbow 16, 25, 29, **119**
    Scaly-breasted **120**

Lymnodynastes peronii 46
Lyrebird, Superb **139**

Macquaria ambigua 90
Magpie, Australian **184**
Magpie-lark 14, **174**
Malurus cyaneus **140**
    M. lamberti **141**
    M. melanocephalus **142**
Manorina flavigula **158**
    M. melanocephala **157**
Marsilea sp. 25
Martin, Fairy 48, **198**
mealworms 32
Melaleuca quinquinervia 53, 90
Melanotaenia 46
Melia azedarach 23
Meliphaga lewinii **159**
Menura novaehollandiae **139**
Merops ornatus **137**
Miner, Noisy **157**
    Yellow-throated **158**
mint bush 68
mistletoe 23, 87
Mistletoebird 21, **196**
mulberries 17
Myiagra inquieta **173**
Myna, Common (Indian) **203**

Nardoo 25
nectar 17
Nectarinia jugularis **195**
Neochmia temporalis **193**
nest boxes, construction of 56–59
nest sites
    artificial 54–59
    natural 52–54
nesting 27, 51

nesting logs, construction of 55
nesting materials 61
nightwatching 39
Ninox novaeseelandiae **132**
Nymphaea caerula 43

Oak, Silky 23, 26, 92
Ocyphaps lophotes **109**
open areas 14
    on small farms 86
Oriole, Olive-backed **179**
Oriolus sagittatus **179**
Owl, Barn **133**

Pachycephala pectoralis **172**
paperbarks 89, 90
Pardalote, Spotted **143**
Pardalotus punctatus **143**
Parrot, Red-rumped 41, **127**
    Superb 91, **122**
Passer domesticus **190**
Perch, Golden 90
    Silver 90
Persoonia sp. 17, 71
pest control
    biological 76
    chemical 76
    elimination of 79–83
    integrated 77–78
    on small farms 92–93
Phalacrocorax melanoleucos **99**
Philemon corniculatus **155**
Phylidonyris nigra **167**
    P. novaehollandiae **166**
Pigeon, Crested **109**
    Topknot **113**
    White-headed **107**
    Wonga **112**
planting 70

plants
    buying 71
    choice of 26
    indigenous 9, 71
Platycercus elegans **123**
    P. eximius **124**
    P. icterotis **125**
Poa australis 15
Podargus strigoides **134**
Polytelis swainsonii **122**
ponds 43
    cleaning of 48
    concrete 45
    fibreglass 44
    inhabitants 46
    liners 44
predator perches 93
Prostanthera sp. 68
pruning 68
Psephotus haematonotus **127**
Psophodes olivaceus **171**
Ptilonorhynchus violaceus **188**
Pycnonotus jocosus **199**

rats 34
Raven, Australian **186**
reeds 25
rehabilitation, bird 63
Rhipidura fuliginosa **175**
    R. leucophrys **176**
Ringneck, Australian **126**
Robin, Eastern Yellow **170**
    Flame 9, 88
    Western Yellow **170**
    Yellow 62
rocks, as shelter 21
Rosella, Crimson **123**
    Eastern **124**
    Western **125**
Running Postman 15

saltbush 17
saw sedges 25
sawflies 81
Scrubwren, White-browed **144**
Scythrops novaehollandiae **131**
seedlings, harvesting 73
seeds, sprouting 71
Sericornis frontalis **144**
she-oaks 13, 68
shrike-thrush 12
shrub zones 15
    on small farms 86
shrubs 13
Silvereye 11, 23, **200**
slugs 82
Smicrornis brevirostris **146**
snails 82
soils
    bad drainage 70
    clay 69
    sandy 69
Sparrow, House **190**
Sphecotheres viridis **180**
Spinebill, Eastern 15, 65, **169**
Starling, Common **202**
strelitzia 8
Strepera graculina **185**
Streptopelia chinensis **108**
Struthidea cinerea **187**
Sturnus vulgaris **202**
Sunbird, Yellow-bellied **195**
Swallow, Welcome **197**

Tachybaptus novaehollandiae **98**
Taeniopygia bichenovii **192**
    T. guttata **191**
tea-trees 68
Telopea speciosissima 68

Thornbill, Brown **149**
    Yellow **151**
    Yellow-rumped 14, **150**
Threskiornis molucca **101**
Todiramphus sanctus **136**
tree canopies 21
    on small farms 88
Treecreeper, White-throated 12
Trichoglossus chlorolepidotus **120**
    T. haematodus **119**
Turdus merula **201**
Turtle-dove, Spotted 33, **108**
Tyto alba **133**

Vanellus miles **104**

Wagtail, Willie 14, 63, **176**
waratahs 68
Warbler, Speckled **145**
water features 26, 42–44
waterbirds 90
watering 69
waterlilies 24, 43
    Nymphoides 25
Wattle, Cootamundra 23
    prickly moses 21
    Sydney Golden 23
Wattlebird, Little **153**
    Red 14, **152**
Weebill **146**
wetlands 24, 47–48
    on small farms 89–91
    plant selection 49
Whipbird, Eastern **171**
Whistler, Golden **172**
windbreaks 91–92
Woodswallow, Dusky **181**

Zosterops lateralis **200**